Published by the Royal Ontario Museum
with the generous support of the
Louise Hawley Stone Charitable Trust

D1552787

THE ROM FIELD GUIDE TO

butterflies of
ONTARIO

PETER W. HALL
COLIN D. JONES
ANTONIA E. GUIDOTTI
BRAD HUBLEY

R•M ROYAL
ONTARIO
MUSEUM

Royal Ontario Museum
100 Queen's Park
Toronto, Ontario
M5S 2C6

www.rom.on.ca

A ROM Science Publication

Project Coordinator: Sheeza Sarfraz
Designer: Tara Winterhalt
Production Designers: Claire Louise Milne, Ingrid Paulson
Editor: James A. Burns
ROM Press Assistants: Alice Tallman, Sheida Azimi

Library and Archives Canada Cataloguing in Publication

Hall, Peter W.,
The ROM Field Guide to Butterflies of Ontario / Peter W. Hall, Colin D. Jones,
Antonia E. Guidotti, Brad Hubley.

ISBN 978-0-88854-497-1

1. Butterflies – Ontario – Identification. I. Hall, Peter W. II. Jones, Colin D. III.
Guidotti, Antonia E. IV. Hubley, Brad

The Royal Ontario Museum is an agency of the Ontario Ministry of Tourism,
Culture and Sport.

Printed and bound in Canada.

DEDICATION

Peter W. Hall
To my two loving and patient families who have encouraged me since my youth in my passion for butterflies and particularly to my wife Judy who has accompanied me around the world in search of rare butterflies and birds and also to my flying father-in-law Stan who passed away during the preparation of this book.

Colin D. Jones
In loving memory of my father, Bob and dedicated to him and my mother, Imelda, who have always supported my passion for natural history and my desire to have nature close at hand—even when, as a boy, it meant bringing home all sorts of living and dead things.

Antonia E. Guidotti
To my sons, Colin and Mason, whose love of field guides and all "life forms" inspired me to work on this butterfly guide. May it join the other much loved guides on our hikes and camping trips. To my husband Chris Walton, who has been very patient and understanding about slowing down our walks so that we can chase butterflies.

Brad Hubley
To my parents and my family who encouraged me throughout my life to pursue my passion for biology and have been there for me every step of the way; to my many colleagues over all of these years who have provided me with countless opportunities to follow this passion, and to my friends who, to this day, still don't understand why I am enthralled by anything with six or more legs.

CONTENTS

INTRODUCTION

Insects are the most diverse group of organisms on the planet, with more than one million species known to science. Many more await discovery—the total number of insect species may be between 5 and 30 million. There are more than 18,000 species of butterflies with diversity greatest in the tropics. In Ontario, 167 species of butterflies in five families have been observed and each is profiled in this field guide.

Butterflies are fascinating creatures and probably the most loved of all insects. Their colourful beauty and magical metamorphosis inspire poets, artists, children, scientists and many others.

Although there are some local butterfly guides for parks and some regions in Ontario, and *The Butterflies of Canada* (1998) covers all species across Canada, until now there has not been a comprehensive field guide to Ontario butterflies. This field guide will provide the butterfly enthusiast with a tool for learning more about these wonderful creatures, and encourage others to take up butterfly watching. Included are photos of the adults, upper- and undersides where appropriate, as well as images of caterpillars (larvae) for most breeding species in Ontario. Where there are differences in appearance between adult males and females, images of both have been provided. Selected images of eggs and chrysalides (pupae) have been included for each family.

To appreciate and ultimately protect butterflies, we must recognize them in their different life stages. By providing images of them in their different forms, readers should see the species as more than just beautiful flying visitors of flowers.

Each species account provides important information about similar species, behaviour, description of the caterpillar and its food-plants, flight season, habitat, distribution and abundance. Comparative plates, colour coding by family, further information sources, butterfly gardening and a checklist to track your sightings are also useful.

Two unique features of this guide are a detailed section on where to observe butterflies in Ontario and possibly the first-ever use of computer-modelled predictive distribution maps in a field guide.

Although the best times for observing adult butterflies are in the summer months, butterfly sightings in Ontario occur from March to November (with some rare February and December reports). Although many butterflies nectar on different species of flowers, to see some of the less common butterflies you must look for the foodplant of the caterpillars. Foodplants are listed for each species of butterfly and *The ROM Field Guide to Wildflowers of Ontario* (2004) is an excellent companion guide.

Whereas English common names are easy to remember, they may vary from region to region. Scientific names, while open to future revision, are more consistent globally; therefore, we have included both in this field guide.

We hope this guide will inspire you to look more closely at these delightful animals—the butterflies.

Ontario's 167 species of butterflies fall within five families: Papilionidae (Swallowtails), Pieridae (Whites and Sulphurs), Lycaenidae (Gossamer-wings), Nymphalidae (Brushfoots), and Hesperiidae (Skippers). For the reader who is not familiar with butterflies, we recommend that you start with the **BUTTERFLY LIFE HISTORY AND MORPHOLOGY** section (page 18) to familiarize yourself with the main physical features used in identification. You may also wish to review the **KEYS TO ONTARIO'S BUTTERFLY FAMILIES** (page 25). If you are observing butterflies and, have no opportunity to photograph or collect the specimen, you should carefully take into account the size, colour, pattern, posture, behaviour, habitat, location, date and any other relevant information. These can then be compared to the species-related information contained in the **SPECIES ACCOUNTS** section.

COMPARATIVE PLATES

The photos of butterflies in the species accounts were taken mostly from nature to show the species as they will be observed in the field. However, for similar-looking species it was felt that comparative plates would be useful for identification. A total of 16 comparative plates showing spread specimens from the Royal Ontario Museum (hereinafter ROM) collection and a few from the Canadian National Collection of Insects, Arachnids and Nematodes in Ottawa (hereinafter CNC) are included. Dorsal and ventral images of males, and females where appropriate, are used.

SPECIES ACCOUNTS

The bulk of this guide comprises the species accounts. Each family begins with an introductory page, along with a few representative photographs of eggs, caterpillars and chrysalides. An introduction to their subfamilies is included for the Skippers, Brushfoots and the Gossamer-wings. The species accounts themselves are laid out in a standardized format. They are mostly self-explanatory but here we outline their structure.

English Common Name

The common name is provided at the top of the species account in BLOCK CAPS. We generally follow the common names used in the *Checklist and English Names of North American Butterflies* (2005) prepared by the North American Butterfly Association.

Scientific Name

The scientific name is given in *italics* after the English common name. We generally follow the scientific names used in *The Butterflies of Canada* (1998) with some explained exceptions—see introduction to **CHECKLIST OF ONTARIO BUTTERFLIES** (page 468). For more information on scientific names see the **TAXONOMIC CLASSIFICATION** section (page 13).

Photographs

Two to five butterfly images are featured for each species with arrows pointing to key identification features. For a few species where upperside photos would be useful, but the species rarely rests with open wings, we have included photos of spread specimens. A photo of the caterpillar is included for most species where the caterpillars can be found in Ontario, usually of one of the later instars.

Size Bar

A size bar is featured beneath the photo on the left-hand page that provides both minimum and maximum wingspans based on Ontario specimens contained in the CNC.

Etymology

The origin of the scientific name of the butterfly is provided here.

Adult

A description of the adult including relative size as well as both the upperside and underside patterns. Abbreviations used include FW (forewing) and HW (hindwing).

Similar Species

How to distinguish the species from other, similar-looking species.

Behaviour

Information related to the behaviour of the adult, especially when it aids in identification.

Flight Season and Phenogram

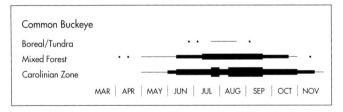

The number of generations in Ontario are presented along with a phenogram depicting the flight period within each of Ontario's major forest regions: Carolinian Zone, Mixed Forest, and Boreal/Tundra (which includes the boreal forest and maritime tundra found along the shoreline of Hudson Bay). Each phenogram spans March to November. The average flight period of the adults is indicated by shading along the line—the thicker the line the greater the proportion of adults likely to be flying at that time of year. Flight periods can vary by weeks in a given year and abundance can also vary dramatically in some years. The phenograms were prepared from data contained in the *Ontario Butterfly Atlas* database maintained by the Toronto Entomologists' Association.

Caterpillar and Foodplants

A description of the caterpillar (larva) is provided here along with a listing of known foodplants in Ontario. Plant species names, both common and scientific, follow the conventions of *VASCAN, the Database of Vascular Plants of Canada* (data.canadensys.net/vascan/search).

Overwintering Stage

The life stage in which the species overwinters.

Habitat

The type(s) of habitat where the species is most often encountered.

Distribution and Abundance

A brief statement about the general distribution of the species followed by a more specific statement about its status (e.g., common, rare, local, widespread) and distribution in Ontario.

Distribution Maps

Distribution maps for each species of butterfly have been created using all occurrences from a number of butterfly databases including *Ontario Butterfly Atlas*, *Species Access Canada*, and *eButterfly*. Each record is represented by a dot. In what we believe to be a first for a field guide, the computer modelled, predicted distribution of a species is also included on each map. Maps for extremely rare species or species with very scattered records have no predicted distribution since there are not enough records to create a model.

The averages from 1960–2010 for the following climate variables were used to generate the species distribution models: annual mean temperature, minimum temperature of coldest month, mean temperature of warmest quarter, mean temperature of coldest quarter, annual precipitation, and precipitation seasonality. Also used was the 2005 North American Land Cover classification. All Ontario records from 1960–2010 for each species were then superimposed to create a distribution model. In simple terms, based on the climate and land cover associated with each record used, the model then seeks other areas where the species has not been found but which have very similar climatic and land cover values.

After each distribution model was produced, it was reviewed and in some cases adjustments were made based upon expert opinion. The distribution maps appear in three standard formats—all province, northern province, southern province.

- represents a known occurrence of the species
- represents a historical record where the species is not believed to still exist
- represents the predicted distribution of resident species
- represents the predicted distribution of breeding migrant species

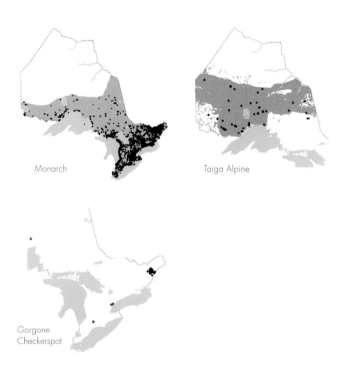

Monarch

Taiga Alpine

Gorgone
Checkerspot

TAXONOMIC CLASSIFICATION

All species are classified according to the internationally accepted classification system developed by the Swedish scientist, Carl Linnaeus. Linnaeus' classification system groups organisms in a hierarchical system; the order Lepidoptera contains many families of moths and butterflies, a family may contain many genera (singular = genus) and a genus may contain many species. The scientific name of a species consists of two parts—the genus and the specific epithet. In the case of the Monarch butterfly, *Danaus plexippus*, *Danaus* is the genus and *plexippus* is the specific epithet. The scientific name is always written in *italics*. Each scientific name is unique and is assigned to only one species—although these names could change over time due to taxonomic research.

THE HISTORY OF BUTTERFLY STUDY IN ONTARIO

The study of butterflies in Ontario appears to have started later than in most other jurisdictions in eastern North America. Whereas butterflies were collected and described from eastern Canada (today's Atlantic provinces and Quebec) and the United States from the eighteenth century onwards, it was not until almost the mid-nineteenth century that any butterfly study started in Ontario. This mostly involved young naturalists who emigrated to Ontario from the British Isles.

William Saunders

In 1861, **William Saunders** caught two butterflies near London that were sent for identification to the famous lepidopterist William H. Edwards in Philadelphia. The first was described as a new species by Edwards, which he named *Erora laeta* (Early Hairstreak) and is now one of the most sought-after butterflies in eastern North America. The second, originally described as *Lycaena scudderii*, was later renamed by the famous Russian-American novelist and lepidopterist, Vladimir Nabokov, *Lycaeides melissa samuelis*, which has recently been elevated to its own species, the Karner Blue, *Plebejus samuelis*.

Worth noting here is that Edwards, while never visiting Canada, described nineteen butterfly species recorded in Ontario. Four of these were first described as new species based on specimens sent to him from Ontario. These are: the Acadian Hairstreak (*Satyrium acadica*) from a London specimen sent by Saunders in 1861; the Early Hairstreak; Macoun's Arctic (*Oeneis macounii*) from a specimen taken at Nipigon in 1885; and the "Northern" subspecies of the Oak Hairstreak (*Satyrium favonius ontario*) collected at Port Stanley in 1868. Edwards initially described this subspecies as a separate species, *Thecla ontario*, in 1861. This is the only butterfly that has the name Ontario within its scientific name.

Only two other butterfly species were named from specimens caught in Ontario. These are Edwards' Hairstreak (*Satyrium edwardsii*) from a Queenstown specimen, named after William Edwards in 1867 by A.R. Grote and C.T. Robinson, and the Hickory Hairstreak (*Satyrium caryaevorus*) by James McDunnough from a specimen taken in 1942 at Merivale, now a part of the city of Ottawa.

In 1863, William Saunders co-founded the Entomological Society of Canada (ESC) with **Charles J. C. Bethune**. Bethune would go on to become Professor of Entomology and Zoology at the Ontario Agricultural College in Guelph. In the summer of 1882, Saunders accompanied friends to Point Pelee where he recorded a butterfly new to Canada—the Mexican Yellow (*Eurema mexicana*); this is still the only Canadian record for this species.

James Fletcher is another early Ontario lepidopterist who was self-taught in botany and entomology and co-founded the Ottawa

Field-Naturalists' Club in 1879. He was the first permanent Dominion Entomologist and Botanist. He described and named one of Canada's five endemic butterfly species, the Short-tailed Swallowtail (*Papilio brevicauda*). A subspecies of the Striped Hairstreak (*Satyrium liparops fletcheri*) is named after him.

James Fletcher

The late nineteenth-century scientist **John Macoun** was renowned for his botanical expertise. He was an all-round naturalist who spent much of his life exploring western Canada for the Geological Survey of Canada. He published mainly on plants and birds, but he also made large collections of insects, including butterflies that formed the basis for the Canadian Museum of Nature collections in Ottawa. Macoun's Arctic (*Oeneis macounii*), a butterfly with a mostly Canadian distribution, was named in his honour by William Edwards in 1885.

John Macoun

Prior to the founding of the ESC in 1863, there were several insect collectors in Ontario for whom butterflies were a major focus. In 1862, Bethune published a list of 36 entomologists that included the famous Canadian artist **Cornelius Kreighoff**. The society began publishing the journal *The Canadian Entomologist* in 1868 and continues to do so to this day. In 1870, the London branch of the ESC became the Entomological Society of Ontario (ESO). By 1871, entomologists were gaining a reputation in Ontario as indicated by a note from Bethune in *The Canadian Entomologist*:

"Time was when to be an entomologist was to render oneself a source of anxiety and care to one's friends, and an object of pity or derision to one's neighbours; but now, happily, people in general are becoming rather more enlightened, and do not think a man has a bee in his bonnet because he captures butterflies."

The ESO also published for many years its *Proceedings* that became the *Journal of the Entomological Society of Ontario* in 2002.

Entomology collections, including butterflies, of the ESC became part of the agricultural college at the University of Guelph; whereas the collections of William Saunders, along with those of James Fletcher, became the core for the CNC. The CNC is now part of Agriculture and Agri-Food Canada in Ottawa and contains the largest butterfly collection in Canada and one of the largest in the world. The third largest Ontario collection is maintained at the ROM in Toronto. Together, these three collections contain several million Lepidoptera, including a number of the type specimens mentioned earlier of butterflies found and described from Ontario. An additional public insect collection of note is located at the Great Lakes Forestry Centre of Natural Resources Canada in Sault Ste. Marie.

In 1919, **James McDunnough**, a noted lepidopterist, was made the first head of a new Division of Systematic Entomology at the CNC. McDunnough named four butterfly species and 26 subspecies from Canadian specimens. The Hickory Hairstreak was the only species named by McDunnough from an Ontario specimen. Two noteworthy research scientists at the CNC who have worked on Lepidoptera in Ontario, including butterflies, are **Eugene Munroe** and **J. Donald Lafontaine**.

James McDunnough   Eugene Munroe   J. Donald Lafontaine

The ROM has had a number of prominent butterfly specialists. **Fred Urquhart** occupied the position of Curator of Entomology, while maintaining a cross-appointment to the University of Toronto. Urquhart is best known for his research on Monarch butterflies; he and his wife Norah developed a tagging system that eventually led to the discovery

Norah and Fred Urquhart

of the Monarch overwintering sites in the highlands of central Mexico in 1975.

Father **J. C. E. Riotte** was a Research Associate at the ROM in the 1960s and 1970s. He specialized in Lepidoptera (particularly moths) and inspired many budding lepidopterists who regularly visited him at the museum. In 1967, he and other entomologists at the ROM founded a Toronto Branch of the Michigan Entomological Society; two years later it became the Toronto Entomologists' Association (TEA) and Father Riotte became its first president. The TEA has had many prominent lepidopterists as presidents and has also been the prime publisher of works related to Ontario butterflies. Special mention is made

Father J. C. E. Riotte

of *A Checklist of Ontario Skippers and Butterflies* by Father Riotte published in 1969 and *The Ontario Butterfly Atlas* by Anthony Holmes, Ronald Tasker, Quimby Hess and Alan Hanks published in 1991. Since 1969, the TEA has been publishing annual summaries of Lepidoptera sighted in Ontario entitled *Ontario Lepidoptera*. In 2012, TEA members Alan Macnaughton, Ross Layberry and Colin Jones updated *The Ontario Butterfly Atlas* by making it available online.

In the last 30 years, butterfly publications of interest to Ontario butterfly enthusiasts have proliferated. *The Butterflies of Canada* by Ross Layberry, Peter Hall and Donald Lafontaine was published in 1998, and contains a great deal of information on all the species in Ontario. Some regional butterfly publications have also been published. The same three authors wrote *Butterflies of the Ottawa District* in 1982 which was updated by Ross Layberry in 2007. Mike Gurr published *Butterflies of Presqu'ile and Southern Ontario* in 1999 and a similarly formatted *Butterflies of Point Pelee National Park Including Southern Ontario* was authored by Alan Wormington in 2001. Algonquin Provincial Park has been the subject of several butterfly publications, including *Butterflies of Algonquin Provincial Park* by Gard Otis (1994), updated by Gard Otis and Colin Jones in 2013, as well as *Checklist and Seasonal Status of the Butterflies of Algonquin Provincial Park* by Colin Jones (2003) which was also updated in 2013. In 2011, the City of Toronto in partnership with the ROM and others published *Butterflies of Toronto: A Guide to Their Remarkable World.*

There are now hundreds of butterfly enthusiasts in Ontario with dozens of regional and local checklists to support their activities. To mention all of them here would be impossible, but they ensure that butterfly studies will continue. Some are members of the international Lepidopterists' Society, which has published many articles pertaining to Ontario butterflies in its journal, and of the North American Butterfly Association, that has many annual butterfly counts in Ontario. They are also joining growing Internet-supported web groups, such as the *Ontario butterflies* web group and an Ottawa-based group that shares data and information on sightings in western Quebec and eastern Ontario. As well, in 2012, Maxim Larrivée started an online Canadian butterfly reporting system called *eButterfly* that contains records from observers across Canada and the United States with a large proportion being from Ontario.

BUTTERFLY LIFE HISTORY AND MORPHOLOGY

LIFE HISTORY

Butterflies and moths belong to the insect order, Lepidoptera, which in Ancient Greek means "scaly wings". Lepidoptera refers to the many individually coloured scales on the wings that separate this order from other insect orders. The scales form the stunning patterns that are characteristic of butterflies and moths.

Butterflies are "cold-blooded" organisms and their body temperature is influenced by the sun and the ambient temperature; when the temperature drops their body temperature drops and they slow down. To warm themselves on cooler days they may vibrate their wings to increase their thoracic muscle temperature. They may also bask in the sunshine by spreading their wings wide to maximize the surface area exposed to the warming sun or they may fold their wings above their body and thereby expose themselves to the sun's rays at an angle. Some arctic and high-alpine butterflies are adapted to life in cooler climates; their dark colour allows them to absorb radiant heat from the sun which is often at a lower angle at higher latitudes—they may also be covered in hairs which assist in thermoregulation.

During its life cycle, a butterfly will undergo dramatic changes in its physical appearance—this is known as complete metamorphosis and it involves four distinct stages: egg, larva (caterpillar), pupa (chrysalis) and adult. The length of time in each stage varies from one species to another and is dependent on a number of factors including food availability, temperature and the life history of individual species. In Ontario, depending on the species, a butterfly may have multiple generations per year, may take an entire year to complete its life cycle or even two years as is the case for some northern species. In tropical or sub-tropical areas of the world, generations may be continuous year-round. Each of the four stages is described in greater detail below.

Egg:

Monarch egg

Female butterflies lay anywhere from 100 to a few thousand eggs in their lifetime. The eggs are termed "upright eggs" since the male sperm enters the egg through a tiny pore found at the top of the egg. Some butterfly eggs are entirely smooth whereas others have vertical or horizontal ridges, some being elaborately sculptured. Eggs are glued to plants with an adhesive substance produced in the female's abdomen and are laid singly or in clusters depending on the species. In the majority of species, the plant upon which the egg is laid serves as the foodplant for the newly hatched caterpillar.

Caterpillar:

Monarch caterpillar

Caterpillars are soft-bodied, with 13 segments, a hardened head possessing small eyes, simplified antennae and chewing mouthparts. Six jointed "true" legs project from the three thoracic segments, and large fleshy prolegs project from the abdominal segments. Caterpillars eat ravenously (plants, except for the Harvester whose caterpillars feed on aphids) and every week or two they moult which allows their body to grow larger each time. Some species feed in the open but protect themselves from predators by camouflage, or by mimicking inedible things such as bird droppings. Others ingest toxins from their foodplant which then act as a deterrent to predators. Such caterpillars are often bright and colourful, alerting would-be predators to their toxicity. Some species also live in large colonies affording safety in numbers. After its last moult, the caterpillar exoskeleton peels away, exposing the chrysalis.

Chrysalis:

Monarch chrysalis

Unlike a moth cocoon, which encases the pupa in a silken web, a butterfly chrysalis has a chitinous shell protecting it from water loss. Despite this, many chrysalides are killed by adverse weather conditions, fungal growth, predators and parasites. The chrysalis relies on camouflage and inconspicuous placement for protection. Within the chrysalis, incredible transformations take place while the caterpillar is disassembled and the adult takes form. Close to emergence, the chrysalis darkens. Shortly thereafter, the shell of the chrysalis splits open and the butterfly emerges.

Adult:

Monarch

Adult butterflies are liquid feeders. They may feed on nectar, sap, mud, rotting fruit, carrion or dung. Although butterflies have been widely praised for their importance in pollination, their contribution may be incidental (except for some tropical species), since they don't sip nectar from only one type of flower.

BUTTERFLY MORTALITY

Monarch caught by an orb weaver

Braconid wasp larva emerging from a caterpillar

In all stages of a butterfly's life history it is prone to a number of mortality factors, including habitat loss, pesticide use, inclement weather, fires, fungi, disease pathogens, parasites and predators. The latter include a range of animals such as birds, spiders, dragonflies, wasps, ambush bugs and ants. While all these factors are difficult to quantify, estimates are that only about one percent of butterfly eggs laid will reach adulthood and many adults do not live to finally reproduce. For common and widespread species, these factors will average out and pose no threat to the species as a whole. However, for rare and local species, one or more of the mortality factors may result in losses sufficient to threaten or extirpate the species. Such species should be carefully monitored for possible long-term protection—see **CONSERVATION AND PROTECTION OF ONTARIO BUTTERFLIES** (page 38).

OVERWINTERING STRATEGIES

Ontario butterflies overwinter in different ways.

One method is to migrate. Monarchs, Painted Ladies, American Ladies, Red Admirals, Fiery Skippers, and Question Marks are examples of migrants that arrive during the warmer months in Ontario where they breed, sometimes producing multiple broods, but their offspring do not stay through the winter. Like their parents that migrated north in the spring, they migrate south to warmer climates when cold weather arrives.

Monarchs resting during fall migration

The rest of the species are residents and are found year-round in Ontario in one life stage or another. Such species pass the winter in a dormant, non-developing state called diapause.

Banded Hairstreak eggs

Some species overwinter in the egg stage including most hairstreaks, coppers and a few skippers. Examples include Banded Hairstreak, Edwards' Hairstreak, Acadian Hairstreak, Bronze Copper, European Skipper and Common Branded Skipper.

Silvery Blue caterpillar

Many species overwinter in the larval stage including most sulphurs, brushfoots and skippers, as well as many blues. Examples include Great Spangled Fritillary, Pearl Crescent, Silvery Blue, Northern Cloudywing, Dreamy Duskywing, Sleepy Duskywing, and Leonard's Skipper.

Cabbage White chrysalis

Still other species overwinter in the pupal stage. Silver-spotted Skipper, Spring Azure, all swallowtail species, Clouded Sulphur and Cabbage White are examples of species that overwinter in this stage.

Eastern Comma

Some species overwinter as adults. Compton Tortoiseshell, Mourning Cloak, Milbert's Tortoiseshell and all of the anglewings (*Polygonia* spp.), with the exception of the Question Mark, are species that spend the winter in Ontario as adults in a state of dormancy. During exceptionally warm winter days (+10°C) in February and March, some of these species can be seen flying, having awoken from their hibernation.

MORPHOLOGY

An adult butterfly has three main body parts: head, thorax and abdomen.

Head:

The head is the anterior portion of the body that contains the butterfly's brain, a coiled feeding tube known as a proboscis and the main sensory organs: labial palps, two antennae (singular = antenna) and two compound eyes. Butterflies have two labial palps—one on each side of its proboscis. Sensory hairs on the palps help the butterfly to determine if what it is examining is food. A butterfly's antennae are slender and club-shaped at the tip. At the base of the antennae (pedicel) is a sound- and motion-detecting organ called Johnston's organ. When searching for a mate, a butterfly will use Johnston's organ to detect the sounds and wing beats of another butterfly. A butterfly's compound eyes consist of thousands of small facets that provide the butterfly with the ability to see its environment. All butterflies see polarized light (light waves that move in only one direction); many species are capable of perceiving ultraviolet light (short light waves that humans cannot perceive) which assists them in detecting sources of floral nectar.

Thorax:

The thorax is the middle portion of the body and consists of three segments to which the two forewings, two hindwings and the three pairs of legs are attached. A butterfly's wings are transparent and are attached to the second and third segments of the thorax. Each wing is covered with thousands of tiny scales which give the butterfly's wings their colour. The colour of each scale is the result of either the reflection of light, as determined by the scale's chemical composition, or the refraction of light, which depends on the scale's physical structure, or both. Numerous fine sensory hairs known as setae are also found on the wings. Oxygen and nutrients are supplied to the wings' cells through veins. The six legs are both mobility and sensory organs. The tarsi (singular = tarsus) are the feet of a butterfly and they contain chemoreceptors which are capable of tasting potential sources of food. If the information relayed to the butterfly's brain indicates a substance is edible, then the butterfly's proboscis uncoils and it begins to suck up the nutrients. Females also use their feet to test leaves for appropriate larval foodplants on which to lay their eggs.

Abdomen:

The abdomen is the posterior portion of the body that consists of 10 segments and contains the butterfly's vital organs including its tube-like heart, most of its digestive system, breathing organs known as spiracles, Malpighian tubules (a type of excretory and osmoregulatory tube system) and reproductive organs. Male butterflies have claspers at the end of their abdomen that they use to grasp the female during mating; females have an egg-laying organ known as an ovipositor.

Wing shape and colour patterns are important features in distinguishing between butterfly species. The photographs below highlight morphological features that are referred to in the **SPECIES ACCOUNTS**.

Dorsal view of Harris's Checkerspot

1= Forewing (FW)	5= Basal Area	10=Fringe
2= Leading Edge (Costa)	6= Median Area	11=Hindwing (HW)
3= Cell (Forewing)	7= Postmedian Area	12=Cell (Hindwing)
4= Labial Palps	8= Submarginal Area	13=Trailing Edge (Forewing)
	9= Marginal Area	

Ventral view of Harris's Checkerspot

14=Forewing (FW)	19=Fringe	25=Proboscis
15=Median Band	20=Hindwing (HW)	26=Compound Eye
16=Postmedian Band	21=Anal Margin	27=Head
17=Submarginal Band	22=Abdomen	28=Labia
18=Marginal Band	23=Leg	29=Antenna
	24=Thorax	30=Antennal Club

23

Dorsal view of Tawny-edged Skipper

1= Subapical Spots
2= Leading Edge
3= Forewing
4= Hindwing
5= Fringe
6= Stigma (males only)

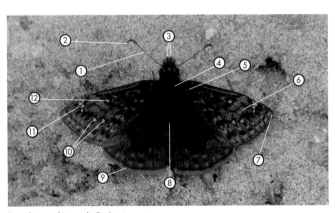

Dorsal view of Juvenal's Duskywing

1= Antenna
2= Antennal Club
3= Labial Palps
4= Thorax
5= Basal Area
6= Subapical Patch
7= Apex
8= Abdomen
9= Fringe
10= Postmedian Spots
11= Subapical Spots
12= Cell End Spot

KEYS TO ONTARIO'S BUTTERFLY FAMILIES

The first step to identifying a particular species of Ontario butterfly is to determine to which family it belongs: Papilionidae (Swallowtails), Pieridae (Whites and Sulphurs), Lycaenidae (Gossamer-wings), Nymphalidae (Brushfoots) or Hesperiidae (Skippers). Each family has physical characteristics that distinguish it from the others.

Close examination of the last segment of a butterfly's antennae, the size of its front legs compared to its middle and hind legs, the presence and size or absence of a tail on its hindwings, the size of the thorax, and the wing colour and patterns are all taken into consideration. Skippers have outwardly hooked antennal clubs, robust muscular thoraxes and short wings; swallowtails are large butterflies usually with hindwing tails; the hairy front legs of brushfoots are reduced and held closely to their heads; sulphurs and whites tend to have rounded hindwings, and are usually white, orange or yellow; gossamer-wings are small butterflies that are often brightly coloured with an iridescent gloss.

The steps outlined below, coupled with photographs, will assist the reader in distinguishing between the five families of Ontario butterflies. The steps are paired and act as a "yes or no"-type process. The diagram below will assist the reader in navigating the steps.

Begin at **1a**. If you answer "Yes" for **1a** then go to **2a**; if you answer "No" to **1a** then go to **1b**. Continue until you reach a family name.

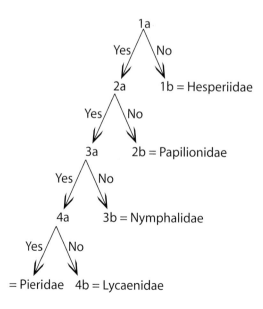

1a Thorax is not unusually large; antennal clubs are not distinctly hooked outwards; size and colour variable → **Go to 2a**

OR

1b Stout, heavily muscled thorax with short wings; antennal clubs are hook-shaped and curved outwards; small to medium-sized; usually brown, black, grey, orange or white → **Family = Hesperiidae (Skippers)**

2a Hindwing without a tail; wing and body sizes vary, or if thin tail present, then small butterflies (under 5 cm) → **Go to 3a**

OR

2b Hindwing with a prominent, thick tail; medium-sized to large butterflies → **Family = Papilionidae (Swallowtails)**

3a Fore-, middle and hindlegs of normal size, easily visible, forelegs not covered in long hairs; small to medium-sized → **Go to 4a**
OR
3b Forelegs covered in long hairs, reduced in size and may not be readily visible, giving the appearance that the butterfly has only four legs; medium-sized to large butterflies → **Family = Nymphalidae (Brushfoots)**

4a Small to medium-sized; hindwings lacking tails; white, orange or yellow rounded wings with black or orange markings; claws on feet are strongly forked → **Family = Pieridae (Whites and Sulphurs)**

OR

4b Small, often under 5 cm; hindwing may have small, thin tail and false eyespots at the base of the tail; brightly coloured wings often streaked with iridescent colour; males' forelegs lack claws on feet, females' claws are of normal size → **Family = Lycaenidae (Gossamer-wings)**

FACTORS INFLUENCING BUTTERFLY DISTRIBUTION IN ONTARIO

CLIMATE

All the present butterfly species in Ontario have existed here for at most about 10,000 years. For the 10,000 years preceding that, all of Ontario was covered with almost 2-km-thick glaciers that moved south during the last ice age and eliminated almost all life. Following the retreat of the glaciers and the draining of subsequent meltwaters, revegetation occurred and butterflies colonized those areas where temperature and precipitation allowed for the growth of their specific foodplants.

The range of climatic conditions, particularly variation in temperature from south to north, has influenced the development of widely differing vegetation regions in Ontario. In southern Ontario, within the Carolinian Zone, warmer temperatures, and relatively high precipitation, support the growth of forests composed of large deciduous trees with a lush understorey. This has encouraged many southerly butterfly species to become resident in this region. In Ontario's far north, the cold temperature of Hudson Bay is responsible for the persistence of a strip of maritime tundra along the Hudson Bay coastline, providing habitat for a number of arctic butterfly species. Between these extremes are found many widespread butterfly species, particularly in the more elevated Canadian Shield area.

For more southerly butterfly species, a major factor limiting the northern extent of their distribution is average winter temperature since many species cannot survive below a certain threshold. For arctic butterflies, the main factor preventing them from occurring farther south is the absence of their larval foodplants. These plants are cold-adapted and are dependent on cold, wet sub-arctic conditions that limit the growth of most trees and shrubs that would otherwise shade them out.

Historical climate changes in Ontario over the millennia helped to determine which butterfly species could survive in different regions of the province. Recently, increased production of greenhouse gases has caused shifts in global climates, with evidence now building that species are altering their distributions depending on local and regional changes in climate. Strong evidence in Europe is showing that the distribution of a large number of butterfly species is moving northwards, most likely due to climate change. While evidence of the expansion of butterfly ranges northward in Canada related to climate change has been largely anecdotal, some species are definitely appearing in regions where they had not been recorded previously. One study examined the range expansion of Giant Swallowtails in northeastern North America and suggested that the northern movement may be due to climatic effects on host plants, parasitoids and survival. In Ontario, butterflies have been intensively studied for more than a century. In eastern Ontario, several new, more southerly species have appeared for the first time in recent years and existing populations of normally rarer, more southerly species have increased. Changes in vegetation distribution due to a changing climate will directly affect butterfly distributions.

GEOLOGY AND ECOZONES

There are two major types of bedrock in Ontario. The first and oldest is the Canadian or Precambrian Shield, made up of igneous and metamorphic Precambrian rock (>540 million years old) stretching through the central part of the province. The soil here is relatively sparse and the area is covered with thousands of lakes. The regions to the north and south of the Canadian Shield are underlain by the second type of bedrock, younger sedimentary rocks (e.g., limestone, sandstone) that developed from sediments left by ancient seas. These rocks are easily weathered, non-acidic and relatively rich in calcium. These two bedrock types break the landscape in Ontario and beyond its borders into three distinctive zones (see map) which have been named according to the Canadian framework of ecozones. The **Hudson Bay Lowlands**, located on the sedimentary rocks in Northern Ontario, form a flat landscape with extensive, poorly drained, peat-forming wetlands (peatlands) interspersed with ancient beach ridges which extend in from the shores of Hudson and James bays. Immediately to the south and west, the **Ontario Shield** is the Ontario portion of the Canadian Shield. It extends in a band from the Kawartha Lakes to the Manitoba border and is characterized by areas of exposed bedrock, and mostly coarse, shallow, nutrient-poor soils. **The Mixedwood Plains** lie on the sedimentary rock south of the Shield. This flat rolling landscape, broken only by the Niagara Escarpment, has deep nutrient-rich soils. Each of these ecozones supports different vegetation which, in turn, supports mostly different wildlife, including butterflies.

Ecozones

① Hudson Bay Lowlands
② Ontario Shield
③ Mixedwood Plains

Vegetation Regions

■ Maritime Tundra
▨ Boreal Forest
░ Mixed Forest
(Great Lakes-St. Lawrence Forest)
■ Deciduous Forest
(Carolinian Zone)

Base map adapted from *Ecozones, Ecoregions and Ecodistricts of Ontario*, by W. J. Crins (2000; prepared for the Ecological Land Classification Working Group, Ontario Ministry of Natural Resources), and from maps of the forest regions of Ontario in *Forest Regions of Canada*, by J. S. Rowe (1972).

VEGETATION REGIONS

The factors above have determined the development of vegetation regions with their attendant wildlife, including butterflies, over the landscape of Ontario since the last ice age.

Tundra - Hudson Bay Lowlands

In Ontario's far north, the coastal area of Hudson Bay supports **Maritime Tundra** with few trees, and broad expanses of shrubs (grasses, sedges and rushes), lichens and mosses. Characteristic butterflies here include arctic species, such as Arctic Blue, Pelidne Sulphur and Melissa Arctic.

Boreal woodland - Hudson Bay Lowlands

The **Boreal Forest Region** (which makes up 60 percent of the land area of the province) is a fire-based ecosystem dominated by coniferous tree species, especially spruce, jack pine and tamarack. The weather alternates between long, cold winters and short, warm summers. Wetlands, including many lakes and bogs, are scattered throughout the region. Butterflies characteristic of the boreal forest include such species as Common Branded Skipper, Western Pine Elfin and Freija Fritillary.

Mixed Forest - Shaw Woods, Renfrew County

South of the Boreal Forest Region is the **Mixed Forest Region** which has a more temperate climate than the boreal forest due to the moderating influence of the Great Lakes. There are more deciduous trees, such as maples and birches, but there are also large stands of eastern white pine. This forest region is also called the Great Lakes-St. Lawrence Forest Region, as it extends from the Manitoba border, east to the Ottawa and the St. Lawrence river valleys and encompasses much of the area around the Great Lakes. Characteristic butterfly species of this region include Canadian Tiger Swallowtail and White Admiral.

Carolinian Forest - Point Pelee National Park

The most southerly vegetation region of Ontario is the **Carolinian Zone**, which is the northernmost edge of the eastern Deciduous Forest Region which extends across much of the northeastern United States, south to the Carolinas and Georgia. In Ontario, it is restricted to southwestern Ontario, from southern Lake Huron east to Toronto. Characterized by woody vines and southern tree species, including the tulip tree, common hackberry and several species of oak and hickory, the Carolinian Zone also has scattered tallgrass prairie and oak savanna remnants. In Ontario, several butterfly species are largely restricted to the Carolinian Zone including Dukes' Skipper and Spicebush Swallowtail.

HABITATS

A mosaic of habitats lie within the broader forest regions of Ontario, supporting a variety of butterfly communities. These are usually localized environments that vary in biotic or abiotic factors, including plant cover, soils, moisture, as well as exposure to sun, shade and wind.

Wetlands

Marsh - Carden

Bog - Thunder Bay

These are areas that have some shallow water during all or part of the year. There are several different types of wetlands, including **swamps** which are treed habitats—some only seasonally flooded—and **marshes** that have no trees but are characterized by emergent plants that are rooted in water and rise above it, such as cattails. Butterflies in these habitats usually stay along the water's edge, often where their larval foodplants, such as sedges and grasses, grow. Some butterflies of these open-water edge habitats are Least Skipper, Dion Skipper and Eyed Brown. **Wet meadows** often consist of a mix of native and introduced species. Although wet meadows can be dry for part of the year, seasonal flooding sustains plants such as willows and dogwoods. The variety of potential larval foodplants in these habitats is attractive to dozens of species. Some are localized, such as Baltimore Checkerspot and Acadian Hairstreak, but others are more widespread, like Meadow Fritillary and Viceroy.

Bogs and **fens** are two other wetland habitats collectively known as **peatlands**. A bog receives most of its water from rainfall and is therefore low in mineral nutrients and is characterized by acidic waters that limit the diversity of plants that can grow on or near them. Fens, in contrast, are fed by nutrient-rich ground water and are therefore less acidic than bogs—often neutral to alkaline—and support a richer community of plants. Bogs are characterized by large quantities of sphagnum moss and an abundance of heath plants, such as common Labrador tea and leatherleaf. Fens typically have less sphagnum, fewer heath plants, and more grasses and sedges as well as plants that prefer more alkaline conditions, such as shrubby cinquefoil. Older bogs and fens are treed with conifers, such as tamarack and black spruce. Some butterfly species in Ontario can be found only in, or proximal to, these habitats, including Bog Copper, Bog Fritillary and Jutta Arctic.

Drylands

Bur Oak-Red Cedar Savanna - Prince Edward County

Terrestrial or dryland habitats take on many forms, both wooded and open.

Wooded habitats are defined by the density of the tree cover. Generally **forests** are densely wooded habitats with >65% tree cover, whereas **woodlands** are less dense with 35-65% tree cover. **Savannas**, discussed below under grasslands, have only scattered trees. The composition of Ontario's forests follows the forest regions: predominantly conifers in the north of the province, deciduous trees in the south, and mixed forest in a band between them. The specific forest composition, i.e., the dominant tree species in a particular forest stand (e.g., maple, beech), is a function of the availability and richness of the soil and wintertime temperatures. Characteristic butterflies of the predominantly deciduous forests are Little Wood-Satyr and Northern Pearly-Eye. Typical coniferous forest butterflies are Satyr Comma and Common Branded Skipper.

Alvar - Bruce Peninsula

Dunes - Ipperwash

Open habitats have little or no tree or shrub cover and are often on a sandy or rocky substrate. **Alvars**, best represented in Ontario's Mixedwood Plains, are exposed and shallow-soiled limestone pavements. Alvars tend to flood in the spring and turn very hot and dry in the summer. Plants growing on them must be very tolerant of these conditions to survive. Sandy habitats include **sand barrens** and **dunes**. Butterflies found mainly in alvars and sandy open areas tend to be restricted to these locations, such as Mottled Duskywing, Sleepy Duskywing, Hoary Elfin, Garita Skipperling and, in interdunal meadows, Dusted Skipper. Unfortunately, three of Ontario's butterfly species associated with open sandy habitats are now extirpated: Eastern Persius Duskywing, Karner Blue and Frosted Elfin. **Rock barrens**, particularly common along the southern edge of the Canadian Shield, are areas of exposed bedrock interspersed with stunted trees and shrubs, with patches of mosses and lichens and attract often localized dryland species such as the Tawny Crescent and Olympia Marble. **Grasslands** are open habitats dominated by grasses and forbs (wildflowers). Among them are the **tallgrass prairie** and **oak savanna** remnants, in southern Ontario. These support a variety of grasses including the bluestems, yellow Indiangrass, prairie cordgrass, old switch panicgrass and characteristic herbs including the sunflowers, milkweeds—especially butterfly milkweed—tick-trefoils, ironweed, the blazing-stars, numerous asters and goldenrods. In Ontario, butterflies associated with prairies, such as Regal Fritillary, are among the rarest in the province. **Meadows** are grasslands inhabited by both native and introduced species. They may be naturally occurring or have developed in regions of cleared forest or farmland. A large number of more common butterfly species, such as Common Wood-Nymph and Great Spangled Fritillary, are usually found in flowery meadows.

Sandy-soiled Meadow with New Jersey Tea – Simcoe County

Old Field - Oxford Mills

Roadside Sedge Ditch – Larose Forest

Disturbed habitats predominate in southern Ontario and elsewhere where humans reside or travel. These are often abandoned areas that have started to revert to natural vegetation, and include **old fields, roadsides, railway corridors** and **ditches**. The vegetation is often mostly weedy annuals; many of them introduced species such as thistles and grasses. However, some native flowering plants important for butterflies, including the common milkweed, also occur in these habitats. Butterflies found in these areas are often some of the most common species, such as European Skipper, Cabbage White, Clouded Sulphur and migrants like Red Admiral.

LAND-USE HISTORY

Human history in Ontario, particularly since the arrival of Europeans, has greatly altered the landscape, especially in the southern part of the province. Agriculture, when it is present as large-scale monocultures, makes the terrain mostly inhospitable for butterflies. When this is combined with the use of pesticides that can destroy most caterpillars, the result is a very butterfly-depleted landscape, except for a few non-native species such as the European Skipper and Cabbage White. However, the practice of slash-and-burn-horticulture used by the First Peoples in

Ontario sometimes worked to the benefit of some species, as the burning sustained the tallgrass prairies and savannas by halting succession of shrubs and trees, exposing the natural seed bank and stimulating the growth of prairie plants. The Gorgone Checkerspot probably still exists in a few very localized grassy old fields in eastern Ontario as a result of former Aboriginal farming practices.

Forestry and land clearing for agriculture have also greatly changed the nature of the landscape. However, there were relatively few primary forest butterfly species, except in the Carolinian Zone. Today there are only scattered, small patches of Carolinian forest and, while many of these still maintain numbers of their characteristic butterflies, there are likely far fewer than before agriculture and forestry started in the region. An interesting fact in terms of butterfly numbers is that woodland edges and open meadows support a greater diversity and abundance of butterflies than completely forested areas. Land clearing for agriculture or for the forestry industry, with subsequent naturalization after the land was abandoned, therefore probably initially increased butterfly numbers in the province overall. The key to this increase may be the proliferation of caterpillar foodplants that thrive in direct sunlight and nectar-producing plants that attract adults.

Urbanization and industrialization have also taken their toll in terms of lost habitats and butterfly numbers, particularly in southern Ontario. In some cases, as in and around Toronto, Ottawa, Windsor, and other large cities, habitats like grasslands and woodlands are in increasingly short supply.

Transportation corridors and hydro rights-of-way are another factor affecting butterfly distributions in the province. Road and rail construction, while eliminating some native habitats, create verges and edges that grow back as sedge-filled ditches or fields with large numbers of flowering plants. These can be magnets for butterflies in areas that are mostly agricultural. In southern Ontario, some of these disturbed habitats along transportation corridors have allowed for range expansion of butterfly species, such as Wild Indigo Duskywing.

Finally, conservation management techniques, including those affecting butterflies, have varied widely over time and by region. In some areas, these techniques have supported populations of rarer species, but in other cases, they actually eliminated some species. An example is the Karner Blue whose caterpillar feeds exclusively on sundial lupine found in black oak savannas. Once abundant in black oak savanna, sundial lupine was greatly reduced by less frequent fires and the overplanting of pine trees that created too much shade for the sun-loving lupines. For more on this subject, see **CONSERVATION AND PROTECTION OF ONTARIO BUTTERFLIES** (page 38).

BIOLOGY

The biological opportunities for, and pressures on, butterflies have also influenced their distribution in the province. All Ontario butterflies, except the Harvester which feeds on aphids, require one or more specific larval foodplants. Those butterflies that exist on only one larval foodplant, particularly on rare or localized plants, tend to also be rare and localized. Those that exist on a wide variety of plants, or on common and widespread plants, are most often also widespread and common. Some butterflies have also been able to adapt to new larval foodplants. This is particularly true of some non-native plants, the introduction and spread of which have increased the population and range of some butterfly species.

Some butterfly species are better at dispersing than others (size being a factor); so, if their habitat is threatened, some are capable of moving to another area. Some butterfly species are also truly migratory, and for them new opportunities to colonize can present themselves, if only on a temporary basis.

INTRODUCED SPECIES

The introduction of plant species, either accidentally or deliberately, can have an impact on butterfly distributions. Some butterflies have increased their distributions by adopting non-native plants as larval food sources. The best example is the Wild Indigo Duskywing, formerly rare and localized in extreme southwestern Ontario, where it fed on the rare native herb, yellow wild indigo. Its distribution is becoming much broader as it moves eastwards in Ontario following its adopted foodplant, purple crown-vetch, which is planted to stabilize roadside embankments. However, other butterflies have been detrimentally affected by non-native invasive plants. The West Virginia White, a species of Special Concern in Ontario, faces a new threat. As a caterpillar, it feeds on toothworts, native members of the Mustard family. Throughout its northeastern North American range the caterpillars have, in recent years, been recorded on the non-native, incredibly invasive, garlic mustard. While females readily lay eggs on garlic mustard, the caterpillars fail to develop beyond the first instar. As garlic mustard continues to expand its range and density in Ontario, it could adversely affect numbers of this dainty white butterfly.

There are presently only two species of introduced butterflies in Ontario: the Cabbage White and the European Skipper; both were accidentally introduced in the late nineteenth and early twentieth centuries, respectively. They have now spread across Canada, in the process becoming two of the most abundant butterfly species in Ontario.

CONSERVATION AND PROTECTION OF ONTARIO BUTTERFLIES

Butterflies are charismatic insects and have a special place in our hearts. Due to the relative ease in the identification of many species, butterflies have been widely studied, resulting in a relatively high level of knowledge on their distribution and abundance. This makes them a useful group for monitoring and conservation efforts. Certain butterfly species in Ontario, particularly in southern Ontario, have benefitted from protective legislation, increased monitoring, protected areas and habitat restoration.

LEGISLATION

Legal mechanisms in the province to protect plant and animal species have historically focussed on the larger megafauna and especially game animals and fish. In recent years, more attention has been given to protecting habitats and smaller species, including insects.

At the federal level, the primary piece of legislation related to conservation is the *Species at Risk Act* (SARA) which was enacted in 2003 and aims to protect wildlife and their critical habitat on federal lands. The Committee on the Status of Endangered Wildlife in Canada (COSEWIC), made up of Canadian plant and animal specialists, assesses designated species to recommend a national list to the Minister of Environment for possible inclusion in SARA. As of 2014, there are four Ontario butterfly species listed for protection under SARA: Karner Blue—Extirpated; Frosted Elfin—Extirpated; Eastern Persius Duskywing—Endangered; and Monarch—Special Concern. In addition to these species, the Mottled Duskywing was designated Endangered by COSEWIC in November 2012 but at the time of publication of this book, this species had not been included in SARA.

The Ontario *Endangered Species Act* (ESA 2007) lists species as Extirpated, Endangered, Threatened, or Special Concern. Six butterflies are presently listed: Eastern Persius Duskywing—Extirpated; Mottled Duskywing—Endangered; West Virginia White—Special Concern; Frosted Elfin—Extirpated; Karner Blue—Extirpated; and Monarch—Special Concern. Endangered, Threatened and Extirpated species and their habitats automatically receive legal protection under ESA 2007. The ESA 2007 also calls for the creation of recovery strategies for Endangered and Threatened species, and management plans for Special Concern species. For more on butterfly legislation in the province, consult respective government websites—COSEWIC, SARA and the Ontario Ministry of Natural Resources (OMNR). Fourteen Ontario butterflies are also protected under Ontario's *Fish and Wildlife Conservation Act* (1997). This Act regulates the collection, possession, release, and trade of those species listed.

The federal and provincial governments have other legal tools to support habitat preservation and conservation. On crown lands, these tools can be used to restrict agriculture, forestry, mining, oil and gas operations, transportation, hydro-electric and municipal development where these activities might impact sensitive habitats and species.

To help ensure that legal mechanisms to protect butterflies and other species have accurate rankings of their conservation status in Canada, two other program areas generate conservation status ranks: the NatureServe Canada network of Conservation Data Centres (CDCs) and the National General Status of Species in Canada (NGS) program.

NatureServe Canada is a network of CDCs housed within provincial and territorial agencies or, in the case of the Atlantic Canada CDC, operating as a non-profit organization. The centres assess the status of species (including butterflies) in their corresponding jurisdictions; assigning conservation status ranks (i.e., subnational ranks or Sranks) for each species. Occurrence data are compiled for those species of conservation concern. These data and the resulting ranks are used to inform conservation actions as well as policy, program and operational decisions. Ontario's CDC is the Natural Heritage Information Centre (NHIC), Ontario Ministry of Natural Resources, located in Peterborough.

The NGS produces a report every five years on the status of species in Canada, compiled by the National General Status Working Group made up of representatives from each of the Canadian provinces and territories and the three federal agencies whose mandate includes wildlife (Canadian Wildlife Service, Fisheries and Oceans Canada, and Parks Canada). In 2008–2009, the NGS ranked all presently breeding butterfly species in Canada on a scale of one (at risk) to four (secure). "At risk" species are those that are formally listed as Endangered or Threatened under either of the federal or provincial acts. Other rare species (e.g., Bog Elfin, Gorgone Checkerspot) not currently listed have been identified as "may be at risk".

MONITORING

Many individuals and several nature organizations have been monitoring butterfly populations in Ontario. This is a critical activity for the protection of butterfly species as it is largely the knowledge based on these records of observations that allows the determination of which species in which parts of the province are changing distributions over time and may require protection.

Since the nineteenth century, most of what we know about butterflies in the province was built on specimens housed in major biological collections and on the reports and books based on these collections. In recent years, with the advent of new technologies, such as close-focus binoculars and digital cameras, butterfly watching and recording have become very popular pastimes with many people. The data resulting from these activities are being used to build large databases of butterfly records that are becoming critical for scientific evaluations of the health of species populations over time, particularly related to critical scientific questions around climate change. The Canadian Biodiversity Information Facility hosts about 300,000 butterfly records, many from Ontario, based on collections and observations, www.cbif.gc.ca/portal/digir-class.php?p_.

Among monitoring programs, three deserve special mention here:

1) Since 1969, the Toronto Entomologists' Association (TEA) has compiled records of butterflies observed in Ontario by amateur and professional entomologists and has published them in an annual report called *Ontario Lepidoptera*. The TEA has most recently launched the Ontario Butterfly Atlas Online in an attempt to map all known Ontario butterfly records including those published in the summaries (www.ontarioinsects.org/atlas_online.htm).

2) www.e-butterfly.org was established at the University of Ottawa and provides butterfly observers across North America with the opportunity to record their observations. Users can then prepare their own checklists, and build dynamic distribution maps and a virtual photo library. Scientists also have access to the data to help study the impacts of global climate change and other pressures on butterfly distributions and abundance.

3) The North American Butterfly Association (www.naba.org) has been running annual counts across North America, including many in Ontario. The combined results of these hundreds of counts across the continent are published and made available to scientists to track changes in butterfly distributions and populations.

In addition to these international, national and provincial programs, many naturalists' clubs across the province have butterfly-watching groups and networks that document observations of butterflies. They also maintain websites with regional butterfly sightings and checklists.

For more information on how to collect records for submission to monitoring initiatives, see **OBSERVING BUTTERFLIES AND DOCUMENTING RECORDS** (page 57).

PROTECTED AREAS

Protected areas for wildlife in Ontario range from large federal and provincial parks to very small pockets of land of a few hectares to protect particular localized habitats, such as bogs. Ontario provincial parks alone protect about 12 percent of the provincial land base. In addition, there are many regional Conservation Areas and Authorities, as well as privately owned nature reserves.

Almost all rare butterflies in Ontario are or were found in the south, close to the Canada/U.S. border, particularly in the Carolinian Zone. Only about 10 percent of the Carolinian Zone remains in a relatively natural state, in a discontinuous patchwork of locations; the rest has given way to agriculture and urban development. The tallgrass prairie and oak savanna habitats of the Carolinian Zone are perhaps the most highly endangered habitats in Ontario. This region contains the most rare butterfly species. There are 13 butterfly species characteristic of the Carolinian Zone that are considered at some level of risk. The two largest protected areas for these butterflies are Point Pelee National Park and Rondeau Provincial Park.

Some rare butterflies may be found in protected areas of the Mixed Forest Region. One example is the Bog Elfin, found in the Alfred Bog in eastern Ontario, administered by the Nature Conservancy of Canada (NCC) and partners. The NCC purchases and maintains a large number of sensitive habitats that protect a wide variety of species, including butterflies.

RESTORATION PROJECTS

While the protection of existing sensitive habitats is crucial to conserving wildlife species, the growing field of habitat restoration promises to create even more butterfly and wildlife habitat. Restoration projects range from planting newly constructed lands to rehabilitating cleared or degraded habitats, in particular by improving conditions and planting native species, with an aim to creating or restoring the natural landscape. Individuals and organizations in many towns and cities in the province are restoring natural areas and creating wildlife habitats to sustain native species, both local and migratory. Many of these projects have incorporated both adult butterfly nectaring plants and larval foodplants into the planting scheme so as to attract and sustain butterflies. Good examples of these are the Fletcher Wildlife Garden in Ottawa, the Gosling Wildlife Gardens in Guelph and the Humber Bay Butterfly Habitat in Toronto. See **BUTTERFLY GARDENING** (page 62) for more information.

Fletcher Wildlife Garden, Ottawa

WHERE TO OBSERVE BUTTERFLIES

To aid butterfly enthusiasts, the authors compiled a list of some of their favourite butterfly sites. The following 14 sites were also chosen to ensure that the various vegetation regions and habitats of this large province were represented and that most of the resident species are present at the combined sites. In addition, some of the southern sites regularly attract butterfly migrants. We also considered ease of access and ensured that all the sites were on public property, including parks and nature reserves. Many of these have restrictions on use of nets or any form of collecting. A few in the north are remote and would take some effort to reach, but we included them as they contain most of the northern species.

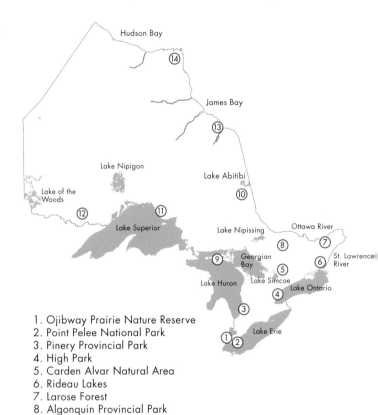

1. Ojibway Prairie Nature Reserve
2. Point Pelee National Park
3. Pinery Provincial Park
4. High Park
5. Carden Alvar Natural Area
6. Rideau Lakes
7. Larose Forest
8. Algonquin Provincial Park
9. Misery Bay Provincial Nature Reserve
10. Markle Lake
11. Pukaskwa National Park
12. Nym Lake Peatland
13. Moosonee
14. Polar Bear Provincial Park

OJIBWAY PRAIRIE

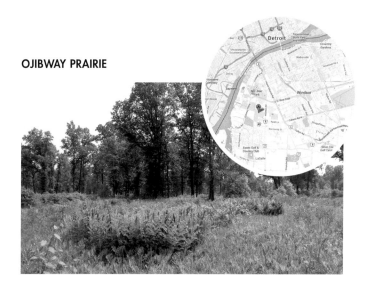

Description: The Ojibway Prairie complex is one of the last remaining tallgrass prairie sites in Ontario and is also one of the largest tallgrass prairie remnants in North America. The site is made up of more than 350 hectares divided into five distinct parts administered by a number of organizations, mainly the city of Windsor and the province. In addition to the prairie areas, it also has wetlands, woodlands and the rare oak savanna. For more information, see www.ojibway.ca/complex.htm.

 Location: The Ojibway Park and Nature Centre is located at 5200 Matchette Road in the southern part of Windsor, close to the Detroit River.

 Butterflies: The unique habitats of this site are home to a large variety of rare plants and animals. As a result of its location in extreme southwestern Ontario, this prairie complex often gets many southern butterfly migrants such as Pipevine and Zebra swallowtails, Cloudless Sulphur, Southern Dogface, Variegated Fritillary and even on several occasions, the Regal Fritillary. These could show up anywhere in the complex's natural areas and often appear on the flowering shrubs and wildflowers close to the Nature Centre.

 The Ojibway complex and surrounding area is best known for its resident skippers, many quite rare in other parts of Ontario. A few of the more noteworthy skippers are Hoary Edge, Southern Cloudywing, Sleepy Duskywing, Common Checkered Skipper, Common Sootywing, Black Dash and Dukes' Skipper. For a checklist of Lepidoptera of Ojibway, see www.ojibway.ca/lepidoptera_of_ojibway.pdf.

POINT PELEE NATIONAL PARK

Description: Point Pelee National Park, the most southerly mainland point in Canada, is a peninsula that extends into Lake Erie and has a worldwide reputation for natural diversity. It contains many vegetative and entomological characteristics of more southerly areas in the eastern United States. For a relatively small area (15 km²), the park contains a wide variety of habitats (Carolinian forest, marsh, meadow, beach) that have attracted almost 90 resident and migrant butterfly species. Of particular note are the many records of migrant butterfly species that stray north from the United States. For more information, see www.pc.gc.ca/pn-np/on/pelee/index.aspx.

Location: The park is southeast of Leamington in Essex County.

Butterflies: Resident species include Giant and Spicebush swallowtails, Red-spotted Purple, Juniper Hairstreak, and Hackberry and Tawny emperors; they can be found along trails in and around the park's forested areas. Several local and uncommon skippers are also residents—two of the most noteworthy are Dukes' and Dion skippers.

Regular migrants arriving in the park include Fiery Skipper, Gray Hairstreak, American Snout, Question Mark, Painted Lady, Common Buckeye and Variegated Fritillary. These usually establish temporary residence with several subsequent generations. One of the most spectacular sights is the annual massing of Monarchs each September before they launch across Lake Erie on their southward migration to Mexico.

The regular arrival of rare migrants attracts many butterfly watchers to the park. In good migratory years, but even in less noteworthy years, some interesting rarities arrive. Recorded migrants have included Brazilian Skipper, Ocola Skipper, Funereal Duskywing, Zebra Swallowtail, Great Southern White, Southern Dogface, Cloudless Sulphur, White-M Hairstreak and Marine Blue. These species are more likely to arrive later in the summer or early autumn.

PINERY PROVINCIAL PARK

Description: This is a large park for southwestern Ontario, occupying over 25 km² of sand dunes along the south shore of Lake Huron. The dunes are open and sandy along the lake shore, and become progressively more vegetated away from the lake, grading into open oak-pine-juniper savanna, then oak and oak-pine woodland, and finally oak and pine forest. The Old Ausable River channel flows through the length of the park. The southern section of the river meanders, allowing marshes to develop and grow. Elsewhere, low flat areas in the Burley Campground support provincially rare wet meadows. Provincially rare plants occur throughout the park, many of which are host plants for equally rare arthropod species including some butterflies. For more information, see www.pinerypark.on.ca/friends.html.

Location: Pinery Provincial Park is located 8 km south of the village of Grand Bend on Hwy 21; it is about 50 km northeast of Sarnia.

Butterflies: About 60 species of butterflies have been reported in the park. Seven species of duskywing skippers occur at Pinery, including the southern specialties: Sleepy, Wild Indigo and Horace's duskywings. The Mottled Duskywing was a resident here until recently when its decline across the province appears to have started. The park also has one of the few resident Ontario populations of the Dusted Skipper in Canada and the rare Black Dash can be found in wetter meadows. Leonard's Skipper flies later in the summer.

Several large, showy swallowtails fly through the park including the Giant, Spicebush and Eastern Tiger. The Dorcas Copper reaches its southernmost point in the province at Pinery. Migratory butterflies such as Little Yellow, Common Buckeye and American Snout reach the park in most years. For a checklist of the butterflies of Pinery, see www.pinerypark.on.ca/pdf%20files/bucheck.pdf.

HIGH PARK

Description: Established in 1873, High Park is one of Toronto's oldest and most popular parks. While it has many recreational facilities, it is also one of the city's most natural parks with a large area of the provincially rare black oak savanna, as well as wetlands surrounding Grenadier Pond. A portion of the park has been designated a provincial Area of Natural and Scientific Interest. Administered by Toronto Parks, Forestry and Recreation, there is a large volunteer group which has been actively maintaining and restoring natural habitats. For more information, see www.highparknature.org/wiki/wiki.php.

Location: High Park is easily accessible by a large number of footpaths, with main vehicle entrances off Bloor Street and The Queensway.

Butterflies: Considering it is in the middle of a large city, an astounding 90 species of butterflies have been recorded in High Park. Sixteen species were recorded historically that are no longer present, but new species are observed every year including Ocola and Long-tailed skippers which appeared in the amazing migratory butterfly year of 2012.

There are five species of swallowtails, including breeding populations of the Giant, Eastern Tiger and Spicebush. Other resident species include Compton Tortoiseshell (most likely to be seen in early spring), and Red-spotted Purple. High Park is known as an exciting butterfly migrant trap, usually in the autumn, when species such as Little Yellow, Gray Hairstreak and Variegated Fritillary often arrive, and rarities such as Marine Blue and Funereal Duskywing sometimes appear.

The Karner Blue was extirpated from the park by 1926. Regular, controlled burns maintain the savanna habitat so that other savanna plants once abundant here are restored from the seed bank. If sundial lupine, its larval foodplant, becomes abundant, the Karner Blue may be successfully re-introduced. For further information, see www.highparknature.org/wiki/wiki.php?n=Insects.ButterfliesAndMoths.

CARDEN ALVAR NATURAL AREA

Description: Among the globally endangered alvar habits, the Carden Alvar of the Great Lakes region is one of the largest and best protected. The alvar was formed when the glaciers of the last ice age retreated northward and cleared the soil from the limestone bedrock. The sparse soils existing today support mainly grassland with some important wetlands. The grassy vegetation with scattered small shrubs contains some unusual western prairie wildflowers such as prairie smoke and scarlet paintbrush. Several endangered and/or local bird species, such as the Loggerhead Shrike and Upland Sandpiper, breed in the alvar. The 25 km² of protected areas are administered by a variety of organizations, including Nature Conservancy Canada and Ontario Parks. For more information, see www.natureconservancy.ca/en/where-we-work/ontario/our-work/carden_alvar_natural_area.html.

    Location: Situated to the north of Lake Ontario and east of Lake Simcoe, the alvar is north of the town of Kirkfield. Good butterfly-viewing sites accessible to the public include Cameron Ranch, Windmill Ranch, Prairie Smoke Nature Preserve and along Wylie and Alvar roads.

    Butterflies: The Carden Alvar supports a number of localized, uncommon butterflies that fly in the spring. These include Olympia Marble and Columbine Duskywing. The Tawny Crescent has been disappearing from much of its eastern North American range but it may be seen in the open, drier areas of the Carden Alvar in June. During the same period, Indian Skippers visit the abundant wildflowers. Several difficult-to-find skippers that prefer wet sedge meadows can be found in July in the wetter parts of the alvar, including the Mulberry Wing and Dion Skipper.

RIDEAU LAKES

Description: An extension of the Precambrian Shield called the Frontenac Axis extends south from Algonquin Provincial Park to the shores of the St. Lawrence River. In the southern part of the arch, between Kingston and Smiths Falls, this rugged, granite-outcrop region has many small to mid-sized lakes and wetlands and is referred to as the Rideau Lakes Region through which the Rideau Waterway flows. Largely forested, it is dominated by maple, beech and pine with some Carolinian elements mixed in, such as shagbark hickory and chinquapin oak. For more information, see www.rideaufriends.com/paddling/fauna.html.

Location: The Rideau Trail, a part of the Trans-Canada Trail, traverses northeast to southwest across the region. The area north of Lake Opinicon affords access to some of the best butterfly sites. The Opinicon Road runs west from Hwy 15 north of Elgin through Chaffey's Locks. Access to the Rideau Trail is obtained at marked locations. Three provincial parks in the Rideau Lakes area provide good butterfly-viewing opportunities: Frontenac, Murphys Point and Charleston Lake.

Butterflies: Along the Rideau Trail may be found a number of more southern butterflies that are associated with woodlands including the West Virginia White and Little Glassywing. Several scarcer Great Lakes-associated species can also be found here, including Hickory Hairstreak and Columbine Duskywing. In recent years, the Giant Swallowtail has moved into the region as the caterpillars feed on the abundant prickly-ash. This area is also a hybridization zone for the Canadian and Eastern Tiger swallowtails.

Some more northerly species, like the White Admiral and Compton Tortoiseshell, are regularly seen here. Worth noting are two rarer hairstreak species—Early and Juniper—that have been recorded a few times in the Chaffey's Locks and Mallorytown Landing areas in the vicinity of their foodplant trees.

LAROSE FOREST

Description: This is one of the largest forests in southern Ontario (more than 100 km²) with a variety of habitats, a wide diversity of butterflies and easy access. Tree cover is a mixture of planted conifers and native deciduous and mixed-wood forests. There are also wetlands—mainly marshes—and large areas of riparian thickets. A number of dirt roads and trails criss-cross the forest, which is managed by the United Counties of Prescott and Russell. For more information, see www.ofnc.ca/conservation/larose/laroseforest.php.

Location: North of Hwy 416, about 60 km east of Ottawa. The closest town is Limoges. Most of the best butterfly sites can be accessed from Clarence-Cambridge Boundary Road that cuts the forest in two, running east to west.

Butterflies: Among the almost 70 species of butterflies recorded in the forest are three highly localized sedge skippers: Mulberry Wing, Dion and Broad-winged skippers. These are best seen in mid-summer in the roadside ditches. The regionally rare Pepper and Salt Skipper occurs occasionally in the spring. Larose Forest is also one of the best locations in eastern Ontario to see the Harvester.

The brushfoots are well represented in the forest. Some of the species that are most often associated with more northern parts of the province are regulars here. The anglewings and tortoiseshells are particularly numerous, with eight species recorded including the Compton Tortoiseshell, Green Comma and the often difficult-to-find Satyr Comma. Several checkerspots can also be seen regularly, including Harris's and Baltimore.

For more information on the butterflies of Larose Forest, see www.ofnc.ca/conservation/larose/butterflies.php.

ALGONQUIN PROVINCIAL PARK

Description: Established in 1893, Algonquin Provincial Park is Ontario's oldest, and one of its largest parks. The park lies on a broad dome of Precambrian Shield bedrock and is situated in the Mixed Forest Region. Visitors can explore the campgrounds, lakes, trails, museums and other sites along Hwy 60 or venture into the interior on multi-day canoe trips. For more information, see www.algonquinpark.on.ca.

Location: The park is situated in south-central Ontario between Georgian Bay and the Ottawa River. Hwy 60 runs through the southern portion of the park. The park's east side is accessible from the vicinity of Pembroke via the Barron Canyon Road. Many access points are located around the park's periphery. For detailed directions, see www.algonquinpark.on.ca/visit/general_park_info/directions-to-algonquin-park.php.

Butterflies: Algonquin's butterfly diversity is relatively well known and documented. A total of 87 species of butterflies have been recorded here, representing a mixture of southern and northern species. Some of the northern species that are at, or near, the southern edge of their range include Common Branded Skipper, Western Pine Elfin, Bog Fritillary and Jutta Arctic. Others that are relatively easy to see here but are otherwise uncommon or very local in southern Ontario include Pepper and Salt Skipper, Pink-edged Sulphur, Bog Copper and Green and Gray commas. Early Hairstreaks are occasionally seen around mature beech trees. On Algonquin's east side is an isolated population of Macoun's Arctic; in Algonquin, this species flies only in even-numbered years and can be found in jack pine forests in the month of June.

More information on the biology and ecology of Algonquin's butterflies can be found in the book, *Butterflies of Algonquin Provincial Park*, fully updated and reprinted in 2013; it now includes the "Checklist and Seasonal Status of the Butterflies of Algonquin Provincial Park".

MISERY BAY PROVINCIAL NATURE RESERVE

Description: Covering an area of 2,766 km², Manitoulin Island is the largest freshwater island in the world. The island is a continuation of the Bruce Peninsula and the Niagara Escarpment and is therefore composed mostly of dolomite bedrock. Some of the most significant features of the island are the many alvars dotting the landscape. Although there are many interesting areas to explore on the island, one site of particular interest is the Misery Bay Provincial Nature Reserve. This area has a variety of habitats including forest, a large fen complex, and a beautiful alvar on the west side of the bay. For more information on Manitoulin Island, see www.manitoulintourism.com and additional details on Misery Bay can be found at www.miserybay.org.

Location: Manitoulin Island is located in the northern portion of Lake Huron and divides the main portion of the lake from Georgian Bay to the east and from the North Channel to the north. Manitoulin is accessible from the mainland in either of two ways: from Tobermory in the south via the Chi-Cheemaun ferry or from the north via Hwy 6 from Espanola. Misery Bay Provincial Nature Reserve is located on the south side of the island in the western half, approximately 35 km west of Gore Bay.

Butterflies: Butterfly diversity is much more similar to areas farther south than it is to the mainland directly to the north. Butterflies such as Columbine Duskywing, Crossline Skipper, Black Swallowtail and Red-spotted Purple can be observed on the island. There are also western species present such as Large Marble, Garita Skipperling (very local and rare) and Purplish Copper. Dorcas Copper is very common in open areas supporting the foodplant, shrubby cinquefoil. Two-spotted Skippers can be found in wet sedge habitats. The alvar supports local species such as Olympia Marble, Purplish Copper, Hoary Elfin and Tawny Crescent.

MARKLE LAKE

Description: The Markle Lake area does not have any formal designation—it is neither a park nor a conservation area, nor is it identified with any kind of boundaries on a map. This relatively small area is, however, an easily accessible location with a variety of habitats including jack pine forests, alder-lined streams, ponds, lakes and peatlands.

Location: The Markle Lake area is located approximately 10 km east of the town of Matachewan in Timiskaming District. From Hwy 11 between New Liskeard and Matheson, journey west on Hwy 66 toward Matachewan. At the junction with Hwy 65 (4 km east of Matachewan), turn south and travel 3 km to a prominent logging road on the east side of the highway. This road leads first through jack pine flats (that have been actively logged) before crossing an alder-lined stream about 2 km ahead. About 500 m past the stream, the road turns south. Drive another 1 km or so until you reach Markle Lake (on the east side of the road) and a number of peatlands shortly thereafter. There are several roads that one can explore on foot; if you choose to drive, a 4-wheel-drive vehicle with high clearance is recommended. Caution is necessary when travelling northern backroads as wash-outs are common and fast-moving logging trucks may be encountered.

Butterflies: Due to the diversity of habitats in this area, a trip here at the right time of year will likely yield some excellent butterfly viewing. Late May to early June is the best time of year for Brown, Hoary, Eastern and Western Pine elfin. This is also one of the southernmost areas where Red-disked Alpine can be found, either in logged areas or along the edge of peatlands. Check the dry jack pine flat areas for Grizzled Skipper, Gray Hairstreak, Freija Fritillary and, in late June, for Chryxus Arctic. The alder-lined stream is a worthwhile spot to look for Harvester. In June and July, the peatlands may yield Bog and Dorcas coppers, Bog, Frigga and Arctic fritillaries, as well as Jutta Arctic.

PUKASKWA NATIONAL PARK

Description: Pukaskwa National Park covers an area of 1,878 km^2 and is the only wilderness national park in Ontario. Since 1978, Pukaskwa has been set aside to protect a representative sample of the central boreal upland forest and the Great Lakes coastal habitats. The vast majority of the park is backcountry or wilderness that is accessible only on foot or by canoe or kayak. There are several relatively short walking trails in the vicinity of the Hattie Cove Campground and Visitor Centre, and a longer day hike to the White River where you can enjoy crossing a suspension bridge 23 metres above the gushing Chigamiwinigum Falls.

Location: Pukaskwa National Park is located near the town of Marathon on the north shore of Lake Superior, halfway between Sault Ste. Marie and Thunder Bay. The only road access to the park is at the north end, near Hattie Cove. Along the northwest side of the Pic River, in and around the Ojibways of the Pic River First Nation traditional community gathering area, is an area also worth exploring. This location is outside the park and is accessible by turning west on the gravel road on the north side of the Pic River bridge.

Butterflies: By exploring the various day-use trails around Hattie Cove, as well as the dune areas on the northwest side of the Pic River, many northern and western species can be found including Western White, Large Marble, Western Tailed Blue, Northern Blue, Greenish Blue, Satyr and Hoary commas, Freija and Arctic fritillaries, Taiga Alpine, Macoun's and Jutta arctics. For more information, see www.pc.gc.ca/eng/pn-np/on/pukaskwa/index.aspx.

NYM LAKE PEATLAND

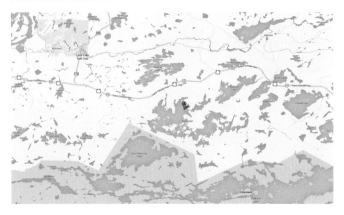

Description: The Nym Lake Peatland does not have any formal designation—it is neither a park nor a conservation area, nor is it identified with any kind of boundaries on a map. While the primary target may be the peatlands, there are other habitats along Nym Lake Road, including boreal forest and wetlands.

Location: The Nym Lake Peatland is located approximately 15 km east of the town of Atikokan, just north of Quetico Provincial Park in Rainy River District. The peatlands are easily accessible by driving south on Nym Lake Road (located approximately 10 km east of the junction of Hwys 11 and 11B). A few hundred metres south on Nym Lake Road, the route crosses a hydro right-of-way within the middle of open peatlands that is very good for a variety of butterfly species. From here, continue to drive south on Nym Lake Road through boreal forest and explore other habitats along some of the side roads.

Butterflies: Within the peatlands, several western and northern butterflies can be found, including Purplish Copper, Freija, Frigga, Arctic and Bog fritillaries, Taiga and Red-disked alpines and Jutta Arctic. Elsewhere along Nym Lake Road you may see a diversity of other butterflies including Pink-edged Sulphur, Silvery Blue, Brown Elfin and Compton Tortoiseshell.

MOOSONEE

Description: Moosonee lies within the Hudson Bay Lowlands, the largest wetland complex on Earth. Although there are no roads leading to Moosonee from the south, there are roads within the town, some of which lead through interesting habitats beyond the town limits. The main road south of town leads past sewage ponds, a waste disposal site and passes through boreal forest and muskeg. For visitors to Moosonee, there are several options for accommodation, and travel is either on foot or by hiring a local "water taxi" to take you to other locations up or down the Moose River. Knowledgeable guides can also arrange for excursions farther afield to more remote camps located at points along the shores of James Bay. For more information, see www.moosonee.ca.

    Location: Moosonee is located along the Moose River, approximately 20 km south of James Bay, and can be accessed only by rail or air.

    Butterflies: Moosonee is the only relatively easily accessible location in the Hudson Bay Lowlands and as such, a trip there can yield some species otherwise very difficult to see in Ontario, including "Boreal" Persius Duskywing, Old World Swallowtail, and both Pelidne and Palaeno sulphurs. Greenish Blue and Jutta Arctic can be quite common in the area. Other species of note include Western White, Northern Blue, Hoary and Satyr commas, and all six of Ontario's lesser fritillaries—Bog, Silver-bordered, Meadow, Frigga, Freija and Arctic.

POLAR BEAR PROVINCIAL PARK

Description: Polar Bear Provincial Park is Ontario's largest (23,552 km²) and most northerly provincial park. Lying within the Hudson Bay Lowlands, the park features vast areas of low-lying maritime tundra. Subarctic in nature, this vast wilderness supports Woodland Caribou, Arctic Fox, Wolverine, Gray Wolf and Polar Bear as well as many subarctic nesting birds including large colonies of Snow Geese and many species of shorebirds. In early summer, the tundra becomes blanketed in a bloom of arctic flowers including Lapland rosebay, black crowberry, northern hedysarum and eastern mountain avens.

 Location: Polar Bear Provincial Park is located along the shorelines of Hudson Bay and northern James Bay. The park is accessible only by air, and landing and camping permits must be obtained in advance from the park office located in Cochrane. There are no visitors' facilities within the park. Ontario Parks recommends that visitors should be prepared for any eventuality; that they bring along at least one week's extra supplies as bad weather may delay their departure, and that they use low-profile tents as strong winds occur throughout the area. Hiring a local guide is strongly recommended, several of whom are based out of the small northern Cree community of Peawanuk.

 Butterflies: Although most people will likely not entertain a trip to Polar Bear Provincial Park, it is featured here as the near coastal areas of the Hudson Bay Lowlands are the only locations in Ontario to see several arctic/subarctic butterflies. Among these are Giant and Pelidne sulphurs, Melissa Arctic, and Arctic Blue. Other species that are rarely found farther south, but are relatively common here, include Grizzled Skipper, Palaeno Sulphur and Frigga Fritillary. In addition, there are several species, like the Cranberry Blue and White-veined Arctic, which have been recorded from other areas of Hudson Bay adjacent to Ontario that could occur in this remote area.

OBSERVING BUTTERFLIES AND DOCUMENTING RECORDS

This section focusses on how you can get the most out of observing butterflies by documenting your observations for your own enjoyment and benefit, or for sharing with larger monitoring programs and initiatives.

WHEN TO OBSERVE BUTTERFLIES

In most of Ontario, butterfly activity occurs between late April and mid-September with peak butterfly diversity occurring in late June or early July. Butterflies that overwinter as adults (e.g., Mourning Cloak) may be seen as early as March, or even February in some years, and some of our hardier species (e.g., Clouded Sulphur) may continue to fly throughout October and into November in the extreme south. Depending on the species, flight periods vary—some species have a single generation with adults on the wing in one season (e.g., spring, early summer or late summer)—whereas other species have multiple generations and occur in more than one season. To see as many species as possible, field outings should be planned throughout the full flight season. In order to target a particular species, refer to the **Phenogram** provided on each species account page and time your outing to coincide with the peak flight period.

A well planned outing also takes into account, time of day and weather conditions. Most people are fully aware that butterflies are largely inactive on rainy days. Likewise, butterflies, at least in our part of the world, are not active at night. Generally speaking, the best time period for butterfly activity in Ontario is from mid-morning to late afternoon. On very hot, humid summer days, this period is often earlier, (from 9 a.m. or earlier until about noon), after which butterfly activity often diminishes as the heat of the day becomes too much for them and they seek shelter and shade to prevent overheating and dehydration.

WHERE TO FIND BUTTERFLIES

As has already been mentioned in **FACTORS INFLUENCING BUTTERFLY DISTRIBUTION IN ONTARIO** (page 29), some butterfly species occur over a large range (e.g., all of Ontario); whereas others have a limited range (e.g., restricted to the Carolinian Zone). In addition, some species are generalists and can be found in a wide variety of habitat types; whereas others are specific to a certain habitat (e.g., bog, fen, wet sedge meadow, dry field). Those species that are common and widespread usually require no special effort to find. For those species that are more habitat-specific and locally distributed, field outings must be planned so that observers visit sites containing target habitats. By referring to the **Habitat** and **Distribution and Abundance** sections within **SPECIES ACCOUNTS**, one can plan field outings accordingly. In addition, online resources such as *The Ontario Butterfly Atlas* (www.ontarioinsects.org) and *eButterfly* (www.e-butterfly.org) provide locations of past records.

HOW TO OBSERVE BUTTERFLIES

Butterflies are naturally quite skittish and can be difficult to approach. To observe them closely enough to make a positive identification, most butterfly enthusiasts use a variety of tools and techniques.

Stalking: Because butterflies are wary, especially skippers and some species of satyrs (e.g., arctics and alpines), very slow movements often allow for close approach. Watch the behaviour of the butterfly and adjust your movements accordingly. You may need to remain motionless from time-to-time waiting for the butterfly to resume normal activity before continuing with your approach. One useful hint is to approach the butterfly with its head pointing away from you. Also, waiting for them to become engrossed in their activity (e.g., flower-nectaring or sap-sipping) often avoids alarming them.

Binoculars: Most butterfly enthusiasts use a pair of close-focussing binoculars in order to bring the subject "closer", thus enabling identification without scaring off the butterfly. Binoculars that can focus down to about 1.5 metres are best, although with reasonable success many people use those that focus down to only 2 or 2.5 metres.

Net: Whereas in the past a net was a critical part of a butterfly enthusiast's equipment, this is no longer considered essential. A net can certainly be handy, however, in order to capture a small or extremely skittish butterfly that is otherwise difficult to observe and identify in the field. After capturing such a butterfly, it can be transferred to a transparent container for closer examination. However, such butterflies (especially skippers) may thrash around in containers knocking scales off their wings, potentially damaging themselves in the process. Often in these situations, putting the container into a dark place (even cupping it between your hands) for a few moments will calm down the butterfly. Alternatively, you can place the container into a cooler place for a while which helps to lower the butterfly's body temperature, thus reducing its activity. After examining the butterfly and making a positive identification, it can then be released unharmed.

Camera: With the advent of relatively inexpensive, high-quality digital cameras, the popularity of field photography has increased dramatically. The number of people taking excellent photographs of butterflies and other organisms is readily apparent by taking a few minutes to search on the internet for photos of any given species. Most naturalists and field biologists carry a camera which allows them not only to document their observations in a digital format but also to study their subjects more closely at a later time to confirm identification. Good results can be achieved by many compact digital cameras, especially those with zoom and macro features. The use of a tripod or monopod will greatly enhance your ability to take clear images.

In order to obtain a good "record shot", one needs to be sure they are photographing all of the important field marks that distinguish one species from another, especially if there are similar species in the area.

In some instances, this means photographing the dorsal surface of the wings, or the ventral surface, or both. Multiple photographs at various angles may provide additional information. Begin by photographing your subject at a distance where you are not disturbing its behaviour. A zoom or telephoto lens helps with this but even when lacking, you can still make out important features in a high-resolution digital image by using computer software to later zoom in on the subject and crop your photo. Gradually and slowly, move closer to your subject taking more images as you approach. At any time, the butterfly may fly off and disappear out of sight—but at least you'll have a few shots that might provide the details needed to verify your sighting. With patience, you may be able to approach closely enough to get not only a great record shot but also a fantastic photo that you'd be happy to publish or frame.

DOCUMENTING RECORDS

Keeping detailed notes on butterflies that are observed serves several purposes: 1) this aids in learning important identification features and behavioural traits of a species; and 2) records are made of important distributional information and seasonal patterns, especially if the information is contributed to an organized survey or monitoring program. Most people who take field notes use a small notebook (look for the kind that contains waterproof paper). At a minimum, the following information should be recorded:

  Location (as specific as possible)
  Date
  Observer(s)
  Species name(s)
Additional useful information includes:
  Number of individuals
  Behaviour noted (including identity, and use, of nectar plants and,
    in the case of caterpillars, foodplants)
  Habitat description
  Time of day
  Weather conditions

Hand-held global positioning system (GPS) receivers have become more accessible to the general public and with online mapping resources, observers are also able to easily include precise latitude and longitude co-ordinates with their records. Many butterfly observation websites, such as *eButterfly*, allow for recording precise co-ordinates of all sightings on a zoomable map of North America.

In addition to the above information, many people document their butterfly records with a digital photograph. With the exception of the most difficult-to-identify species, a photograph that illustrates important identification features (even if it is not an award-winning photo) can serve as an important "voucher" of the observation, precluding the need to collect a specimen. Such "proof" is often very valuable to support records of rare species, species outside their known range, or even of early or late records of common species.

SUBMITTING YOUR RECORDS

You can contribute in a meaningful way to the understanding of butterfly distribution, flight seasons and behaviour, and also aid in conservation efforts by submitting records or reporting your observations to an organized survey. In Ontario, butterfly enthusiasts are encouraged to contribute their records to one of the two largest initiatives:

1) The Toronto Entomologists' Association annual Lepidoptera summary and the *Ontario Butterfly Atlas* project (see www.ontarioinsects. org to learn more, including detailed information on how to contribute).

2) *eButterfly* allows you to add your observations and photos using an intuitive data-input system, with drop-down lists of sites, species and dates (see www.e-butterfly.org for more information).

Both initiatives share their data; so there is no need to send your records to both surveys. The data from these initiatives are also shared with Ontario Ministry of Natural Resources' Natural Heritage Information Centre where it is used for a variety of conservation and land-use planning initiatives (see **CONSERVATION AND PROTECTION OF ONTARIO BUTTERFLIES**, page 38). The detailed data are also available to scientists to aid them in building distribution maps and flight charts, and to assess butterfly responses to changes in their habitats over time, including climate changes.

In addition to these two initiatives, the North American Butterfly Association (NABA) co-ordinates annual butterfly counts across Canada and the United States. These single-day events, modelled after the better known Christmas Bird Counts, involve teams of individuals recording and counting individual butterflies of each species encountered within a count circle of approximately 24 km diameter. There are well over 400 such counts across North America with approximately 20 occurring in Ontario. NABA publishes an annual report on the results, providing information about the geographical distribution and relative population sizes of the species counted. Comparisons of the results across years can be used to monitor changes in butterfly populations and study the effects of weather and habitat change on North American butterflies. More information on NABA and its annual butterfly counts, including counts in your area, can be found at www.naba.org.

COLLECTING

In the past, the definition of a butterfly enthusiast was that of an individual wandering around with a net, capturing, collecting and pinning the butterflies that were encountered. As has been mentioned in **THE HISTORY OF BUTTERFLY STUDY IN ONTARIO** (page 14), much of what we know about the taxonomy and distribution of butterflies can be attributed to collecting efforts of the past.

Today, fewer individuals collect butterflies, and in many instances this is no longer necessary, although some collecting still occurs. However, collecting within national parks or Ontario's provincial parks as well as protected areas such as conservation areas and privately owned nature reserves is strictly prohibited without first obtaining a scientific collector's permit from the relevant park or agency office. The collecting of species at risk, no matter where they are found, is strictly prohibited without a permit from the provincial and/or federal government.

There are legitimate reasons to collect live specimens for preservation and study. Some species are extremely difficult to distinguish and in some instances require dissection of their genitalia in order to confirm identification (e.g., some species of duskywings). In other cases, regional variation exists among species and such variation is studied by taxonomists. In the event that our understanding and definition of a particular species changes, scientists can re-examine voucher specimens and determine the identity and ranges of what may once have been considered a single species that has been split into two or more species. Another relatively recent purpose for collecting is the extraction and analysis of DNA. This is an incredibly powerful tool that allows scientists to check identifications, establish species relationships and study genetic changes in populations through time; DNA can even be extracted from very old specimens. DNA barcoding is a method that uses a piece of an organism's DNA to identify it as belonging to a particular species.

Great Spangled Fritillary (*Speyeria cybele*) barcode image courtesy of The Barcode of Life Data Systems (www.boldsystems.org).

Butterfly gardens on private or public property are useful not only as a means of attracting butterflies for observation and enjoyment, but also as vegetated corridors for butterflies and other wildlife between separated natural areas. They are particularly successful in this regard when native plants are included. Especially for caterpillars, native plants with which they have co-evolved provide the best and sometimes the only food source. Native plants also serve to increase overall biodiversity by attracting other insects and birds, and by helping to exclude invasive species.

Wherever you live in Ontario, whether in the midst of a major urban centre, in the depths of Ontario's boreal forest, near a wetland or close to an agricultural area, you can develop a butterfly garden. There are four main elements to a successful butterfly garden: 1) foodplants for caterpillars; 2) food sources, particularly flowers rich in nectar, for adults; 3) shelter; and 4) plenty of sunshine.

The precise selection of plants for your garden should be based on the requirements of the butterflies found in your area of the province. This can be done by referring to the distribution maps included in the **SPECIES ACCOUNTS**. Make a note of the larval foodplants, as adult females will not lay their eggs in your garden if the foodplants are not available for the ravenous caterpillars that will emerge. For some species, preferred nectar sources are also given. Many species or families of butterflies use entire genera or families of plants, increasing your options for planting. A **PARTIAL LIST OF PLANTS FOR USE IN BUTTERFLY GARDENS** (page 455) will provide you with other species to consider.

The inclusion of native plants in gardens is beneficial to butterflies and many other species of wildlife. Native plants should never be dug up in the wild; rather, they should be purchased as seed or plants from a reputable grower. Some species that are sold by large commercial growers as native plants are in fact native to other parts of North America but not to Ontario. The Ontario Chapter of the Society for Ecological Restoration publishes a Native Plant Resource Guide that is helpful in locating reliable suppliers throughout the province (see chapter.ser.org/ontario).

When planting cultivated species, gardeners should avoid planting any species that can be invasive. Invasive plants are introduced species that survive without human assistance and negatively impact native biodiversity by reproducing aggressively and taking over, to the exclusion of other plants. The Ontario Invasive Plant Council publishes useful information on actual and potentially invasive species, and native alternatives for gardens (see www.ontarioinvasiveplants.ca/index.php/publications).

The optimum flowering plants to attract adult butterflies have high nectar content and a structure that allows the butterfly to get the nectar. Flowers with a landing platform—for instance the ray petals of a black-eyed Susan or eastern purple coneflower, or the flat-topped flower cluster of milkweeds or pearly everlasting—allow the butterfly to settle before it feeds. Tubular flowers are well suited to a butterfly's long proboscis which it uses to obtain the nectar. Some flowers have petals with markings or hairs that serve as nectar guides. If you include cultivated ornamental plants in your garden, choose pure species and avoid highly bred varieties—especially those with double petals, e.g., hybrid roses or phlox. Flowers with multiple petals or other specialized features present two problems for butterflies: the dense petals obscure the path to the nectar if any is present and these plants often have little or no nectar. Plan your garden so that it blooms throughout your area's growing season. A garden that has a continual bloom of high-nectar flowers has a good chance of attracting a higher diversity of butterfly species than a garden that blooms all at once. Finally, include trees and shrubs in your garden as some species of butterflies prefer to feed on the nutrient-rich sap that drips from trees and others feed as larvae only on the leaves or buds of certain trees.

In addition to nectar, many adults require water, salts and other nutrients. If squirrels and raccoons are not a concern, consider putting out pieces of decaying fruits such as oranges and grapefruits. The inclusion of a small mud puddle, or a very shallow pool of water, will provide adults with the opportunity to "puddle" around them and acquire needed moisture.

Shelter is essential for all butterfly life-stages. Eggs are often laid under leaves to avoid detection from predators; caterpillars will often feed out of sight; chrysalides are often attached in areas sheltered from extremes in the elements; and adults will be attracted to gardens that provide shelter from strong winds. Include a wall of shrubs, bushes or trees as protection from the wind.

Adults tend to be most active in large, open sunny areas. Here you can plant ground cover that is high in nectar. Include some perches, such as flat rocks oriented towards the midday sun, so the adults can rest and bask. When planning your open area, design it so it receives as much of the day's sun as possible, as different species nectar at different times of the day. However, if you are adjacent to a wooded area, keep a wooded edge for some woodland species like the Northern Pearly-Eye.

By following the suggestions above, as your garden develops and blooms, you should enjoy Mother Nature's finest flying jewels as they flit about in the sunshine.

COMPARATIVE PLATES

Photos of spread specimens. The left-hand half is the upperside and the right-hand half is the underside of the same specimen.

PLATE 1 – Pipevine Swallowtail Mimicry Complex

(0.4x magnification)

♀ Black Swallowtail   ♀ Spicebush Swallowtail

♂ Pipevine Swallowtail

♂ Red-spotted Purple

♀ Eastern Tiger Swallowtail (black form)

PLATE 2 – *Colias* Sulphurs

(0.75x magnification)

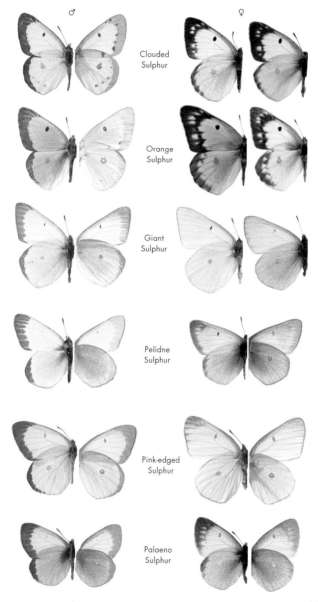

♂ ♀

Clouded
Sulphur

Orange
Sulphur

Giant
Sulphur

Pelidne
Sulphur

Pink-edged
Sulphur

Palaeno
Sulphur

PLATE 3 – Whites

(0.75x magnification; females similar in appearance)

♂ Large Marble

♂ Olympia Marble

♂ Mustard White
(spring form)

♂ Mustard White
(summer form)

(0.75x magnification)

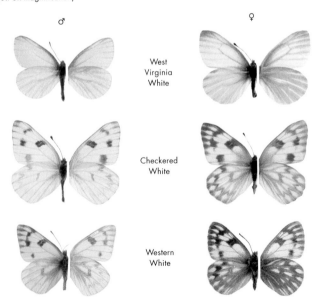

♂

♀

West
Virginia
White

Checkered
White

Western
White

PLATE 4 – Coppers and Blues

(1x magnification)

♂   ♀

Bog Copper

Dorcas Copper

Purplish Copper

Eastern Tailed Blue

Western Tailed Blue

Northern Blue

Karner Blue

PLATE 5 – Blues

(1x magnification)

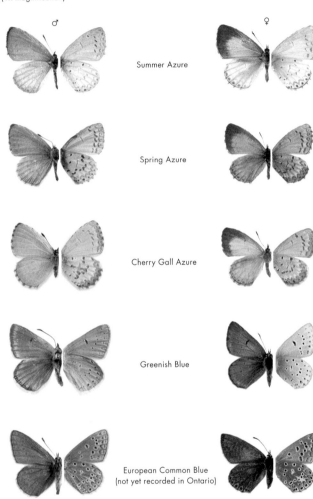

♂   ♀

Summer Azure

Spring Azure

Cherry Gall Azure

Greenish Blue

European Common Blue
(not yet recorded in Ontario)

Silvery Blue

PLATE 6 – Hairstreaks and Elfins

(males at 1x magnification; females similar in appearance)

Acadian Hairstreak

Coral Hairstreak

Edwards' Hairstreak

Banded Hairstreak

Hickory Hairstreak

Striped Hairstreak

Brown Elfin

Hoary Elfin

Frosted Elfin

Henry's Elfin

Bog Elfin

Western Pine Elfin

♂   Eastern Pine Elfin   ♀

PLATE 7 – Greater Fritillaries

(0.75x magnification)

Great Spangled Fritillary

Aphrodite Fritillary

Atlantis Fritillary

PLATE 8 – Lesser Fritillaries

(males at 1x magnification; females similar in appearance)

Silver-bordered Fritillary

Bog Fritillary

Meadow Fritillary

Frigga Fritillary

Freija Fritillary

Arctic Fritillary

PLATE 9 – Anglewings

(males at 0.75x magnification; females similar in appearance)

Question Mark
(summer form)

Question Mark
(overwintering form)

Eastern Comma
(summer form)

Eastern Comma
(overwintering form)

Satyr Comma

Gray Comma

Green Comma

Hoary Comma

PLATE 10 – Checkerspots and Crescents

(male Checkerspots at 0.75x magnification; females similar in appearance)

Silvery
Checkerspot

Gorgone
Checkerspot

Harris's
Checkerspot

(0.75x magnification)

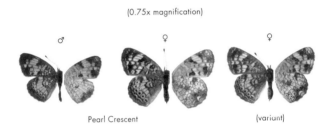

♂

♀

♀

Pearl Crescent

(variant)

Northern Crescent

(variant)

Tawny Crescent

PLATE 11 – Browns and Arctics

(males at 0.75x magnification; females similar in appearance)

Appalachian Brown

Eyed Brown

Northern Pearly-eye

Jutta Arctic

Melissa Arctic

Chryxus Arctic

Polixenes Arctic
(not yet confirmed in Ontario)

Macoun's Arctic

PLATE 12 – Duskywings

(1x magnification)

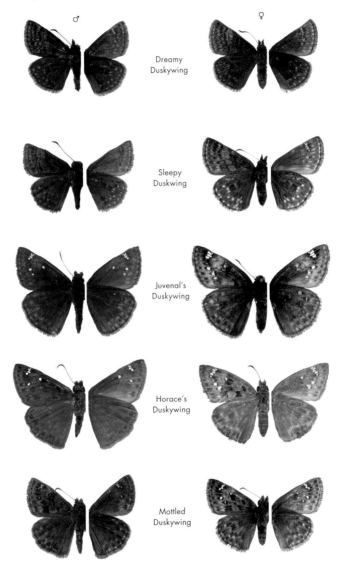

♂ ♀

Dreamy
Duskywing

Sleepy
Duskwing

Juvenal's
Duskywing

Horace's
Duskywing

Mottled
Duskywing

PLATE 13 – Duskywings

(1x magnification)

♂   ♀

Zarucco
Duskywing

Funereal
Duskywing

Wild Indigo
Duskywing

Columbine
Duskywing

Boreal
Persius
Duskywing

Eastern
Persius
Duskywing

PLATE 14 – Branded Skippers

(0.75x magnification)

♂ Common Branded Skipper ♀

Leonard's Skipper

Indian Skipper

Long Dash Skipper

Peck's Skipper

Hobomok Skipper   ♀   (pocahontas form)

Zabulon Skipper

Mulberry Wing

PLATE 15 – Branded Skippers

(0.75x magnification)

♂   ♀

Black Dash

Broad-Winged Skipper

Dion Skipper

Dukes' Skipper

Two-Spotted Skipper

Dun Skipper

Northern Broken-Dash

Little Glassywing

PLATE 16 – Branded Skippers

(0.75x magnification)

♂   ♀

Fiery Skipper

Whirlabout

Sachem

Tawny-Edged Skipper

Crossline Skipper

Delaware Skipper

European Skipper

Least Skipper

Eastern Tiger Swallowtails

THE SWALLOWTAILS
Family Papilionidae

In Ontario, there are eight species of this diverse, mainly tropical, family of butterflies. Our species are medium-to large-sized and all have tails on the HW. These tails help to make the wings more aerodynamic when the butterflies glide. From an evolutionary point of view, the swallowtails are the oldest of the extant butterfly families. As shown in recent taxonomic work, the swallowtails diverged early on from all the other butterflies. Most species are not considered migratory, but because they are strong flyers some may stray beyond their normal range during their flight season.

The adults are active flower visitors, often seen in gardens. Most keep their wings vibrating to help support their bodies as they perch on flower heads. As they are large butterflies, they prefer large or composite flowers for nectaring, including lilacs (*Syringa* spp.), phlox (*Phlox* spp.), thistles (*Cirsium* spp. and *Carduus* spp.) and milkweeds (*Asclepias* spp.). The males of some species are hilltoppers. When they emerge, they immediately head for the highest point of land around and then circle there steadily waiting for the females. These emerge later, and also head for these same elevated points of land. This behaviour aids the butterflies to find a mate quickly. Many swallowtail species are also mudpuddlers, settling on wet spots on roads and open patches of ground, sipping the moisture with their proboscis. These are mostly males and it is believed that the moisture contains salts and nutrients, particularly sodium and nitrogen, which aid in their sexual maturation and in their ability to pass on nutrients to a female during mating.

Eggs

Swallowtail eggs are plain and spherical. They are usually laid one at a time on the foodplants.

Pipevine Swallowtail

Eastern Tiger Swallowtail

Spicebush Swallowtail

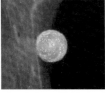

Giant Swallowtail

Black Swallowtail

Caterpillars

Most immature caterpillars of the first few instars are dark with light patches (the middle one resembling a saddle shape) that gives them the appearance of a bird dropping, thus giving them some camouflage protection.

All swallowtail caterpillars also have a fleshy Y-shaped organ that can be extended from the head when alarmed. This osmeterium gives off a strong, putrid odour that is thought to deter predators, including parasitic wasps and birds.

Black Swallowtail with
extended osmeterium

Black Swallowtail,
second instar

Canadian Tiger Swallowtail

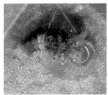

Giant Swallowtail,
second instar

Pipevine Swallowtail,
second instar caterpillars

Eastern Tiger Swallowtail

Chrysalides

The chrysalides are mostly mottled green or brown and are attached to a surface by a pad of silk at the posterior end with a silken girdle to hold it in an upright position.

Pipevine Swallowtail

Eastern Tiger Swallowtail

Black Swallowtail

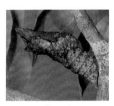

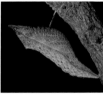

Giant Swallowtail

Spicebush Swallowtail

Spicebush Swallowtail

PIPEVINE SWALLOWTAIL *Battus philenor*

♂

58–83 mm

ETYMOLOGY: *Battus* was a Greek mythological figure who was turned into stone by the God Hermes. In Greek, *philenor* means "loving one's husband" or "fond of man/men".

ADULT: Medium-sized to large. Individuals that emerge in summer tend to be larger than spring-emerging individuals. **Upperside:** Black with green-to-blue iridescence (most prominent on the HW especially on the male) with small submarginal white spots. **Underside:** HW with a row of large postmedial round orange spots encircled by iridescent blue. FW blackish with some submarginal white spots.

SIMILAR SPECIES: The Pipevine Swallowtail is part of a mimicry ring with four other species: the Black, Eastern Tiger, and Spicebush swallowtails, and the Red-spotted Purple. Wings of female Black Swallowtails and black form female Eastern Tiger Swallowtails lack the overall greenish iridescence and have yellowish/greenish submarginal spots on the upperside. Spicebush Swallowtails have two rows of orange spots on the underside HW. Red-spotted Purples lack tails and have extra red-to-orange spots close to the body on the undersides. See Plate 1.

BEHAVIOUR: Has a very rapid flight.

FLIGHT SEASON: Two, possibly three, overlapping generations.

Boreal/Tundra								
Mixed Forest								
Carolinian Zone								
	MAR	APR	MAY	JUN	JUL	AUG	SEP	OCT	NOV

Fourth instar caterpillar

CATERPILLAR: Purplish to black body with long, fleshy tubercles behind the head and shorter orange tubercles along the body. **Foodplants:** In Ontario, the caterpillars feed on dutchman's-pipe (*Isotrema macrophyllum* and possibly *Aristolochia tomentosa*).

OVERWINTERING STAGE: Chrysalis.

HABITAT: Gardens, particularly where dutchman's-pipe has been planted, and nearby open fields. May occur anywhere as a vagrant.

DISTRIBUTION AND ABUNDANCE: Widespread in Mexico and the United States. In Ontario, a rare-to-uncommon breeding migrant largely confined to the province's Carolinian Zone. In some years, there are many migrants, such as in 2012, when large numbers were reported as far east as Port Hope. There is an unusual record of an almost dead individual that washed up on the shores of Caribou Island in the middle of Lake Superior.

COMMENTS: Dutchman's-pipe leaves contain toxic chemicals that are absorbed by the caterpillars and are passed on to the adults, making both stages unpalatable to potential predators such as birds.

ZEBRA SWALLOWTAIL *Eurytides marcellus*

52–70 mm

ETYMOLOGY: In Greek mythology, *Eurytides* (or Hippasus) was the son of Eurytus and a hero of the Calydonian Boar hunt. *Marcellus* was the nephew and son-in-law of the Roman Emperor Augustus.

ADULT: Medium-sized. The spring form is smaller and appears lighter than the summer form. **Upperside:** This species has the longest tails of any North American butterfly giving it a stretched appearance with greenish-white and blackish stripes running lengthwise along the wings. **Underside:** A bright red stripe runs between the two central dark stripes on the underside HW.

SIMILAR SPECIES: None in Ontario.

BEHAVIOUR: Often flies near the ground with a very rapid, direct flight pattern. This butterfly can sometimes be seen perching with rapidly vibrating wings on flowers of milkweeds, particularly butterfly milkweed (*Asclepias tuberosa*).

FLIGHT SEASON: Two generations when present in Ontario.

Boreal/Tundra								
Mixed Forest								
Carolinian Zone			———————					
	MAR	APR	MAY	JUN	JUL	AUG	SEP	OCT	NOV

CATERPILLAR: Usually green (sometimes black) with multiple light-coloured bands (orange to white). Thickest at the thorax where there is a prominent black band. **Foodplants:** Pawpaw (*Asimina triloba*), a rare Carolinian tree in Ontario.

OVERWINTERING STAGE: Chrysalis.

HABITAT: Carolinian Zone grasslands and savannas near swamps and rivers.

DISTRIBUTION AND ABUNDANCE: A widespread resident of the eastern United States. In Ontario, the Zebra Swallowtail is now generally considered a rare and sporadic, occasionally breeding migrant. Earlier in the twentieth century, prior to major habitat fragmentation in SW Ontario, this butterfly was likely a regular resident breeder. This species is restricted to the Carolinian Zone of the province; its easternmost records are from the Toronto area, but it is most often seen along the north shore of Lake Erie.

COMMENTS: The wing shape has given this species and other members of its mainly tropical group, the name of "kite" swallowtails.

OLD WORLD SWALLOWTAIL *Papilio machaon*

50–95 mm

ETYMOLOGY: The genus name *Papilio* is Latin meaning "butterfly or moth". In Greek mythology, *Machaon* was a highly valued physician in the Trojan War.

ADULT: Medium-sized to large. **Upperside:** Bright yellow with black areas sprinkled with a light dusting of yellow scales and black along the wing veins. There is a distinct submarginal row of blue spots on the upperside of the HW and next to the short tails is an orange eye-spot in which the black pupil touches the inner wing margin. **Underside:** Similar to the upperside but duller yellow.

SIMILAR SPECIES: The superficially similar Canadian Tiger Swallowtail has much more yellow and lacks the prominent eye-spot on the HW of Old World Swallowtail. Black Swallowtails have much more black on the wing and the dark pupil on the HW eye-spot is more central rather than positioned toward the HW margin as in Old World.

BEHAVIOUR: Regularly basks on rocks in the sun.

FLIGHT SEASON: One generation per year.

	MAR	APR	MAY	JUN	JUL	AUG	SEP	OCT	NOV
Boreal/Tundra									
Mixed Forest									
Carolinian Zone									

Ventral view

Early instar larva

CATERPILLAR: The mature caterpillar is generally black with green bands and orange spots. The early stages of the subspecies *P. machaon hudsonianus,* the Ontario subspecies, are not well known. **Foodplants:** Along the coast of James Bay, Scotch lovage (*Ligusticum scoticum*) appears to be the primary foodplant. Farther south, however, where Scotch lovage does not occur, coltsfoots (*Petasites* spp.) or wormwoods (*Artemisia* spp.) may be used.

OVERWINTERING STAGE: Chrysalis.

HABITAT: Open meadows and along roadsides within the boreal forest. On the lower James Bay coast (Albany River south) adults never seem to wander far from stands of Scotch lovage, which typically occur above the supratidal zone along the banks of drainage creeks, old storm beaches and the back sides of sand dunes.

DISTRIBUTION AND ABUNDANCE: A holarctic species with populations of a variety of subspecies stretching across northern North America and northern Eurasia, hence its common name of Old World Swallowtail. In Ontario, an uncommon-to-rare resident of northern Ontario only, with the most southerly records running in a line from Thunder Bay to the southern part of James Bay. Its seeming scarcity may be attributed to the little butterfly observation that has taken place in its remote northern Ontario habitat.

COMMENTS: This butterfly and the Black Swallowtail are not yet known to hybridize where they overlap in Ontario, but they have in southern Manitoba (see Black Swallowtail).

BLACK SWALLOWTAIL *Papilio polyxenes*

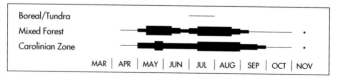

52–94 mm

...

ETYMOLOGY: *Polyxena* was the youngest daughter of Greek mythological figures King Priam of Troy and Queen Hecuba; she was the beloved of Achilles.

ADULT: Medium-sized to large. **Upperside:** Mostly black with two rows of yellow spots (the inner row reduced or, rarely, absent in the female) with a frosty blue row on each HW. A distinct orange eye-spot with a black centre is present close to each tail. **Underside:** Similar to the upperside but with two rows of orange spots on the HW.

SIMILAR SPECIES: A member of the Pipevine Swallowtail mimicry group (see Plate 1). In southern Ontario, the most similar species is the Spicebush Swallowtail which looks like a female Black Swallowtail but with spoon-shaped tails, a single row of yellow spots on the upper wings, and no black central spot in the orange spot near the tails.

BEHAVIOUR: A regular mudpuddler, but usually not in large numbers like the Canadian Tiger Swallowtail. The most noted hilltopper among Ontario swallowtails, with males gathering and patrolling around the highest point of land awaiting females who usually ascend the nearest hill upon emerging.

FLIGHT SEASON: Two generations per year.

	MAR	APR	MAY	JUN	JUL	AUG	SEP	OCT	NOV
Boreal/Tundra									
Mixed Forest									
Carolinian Zone									

CATERPILLAR: Young caterpillars are black with branched hairy knobs and a white saddle in the middle of the back (see page 82). Mature caterpillars are green with black bands and yellow or orange spots circling the body. Commonly found in gardens. **Foodplants**: Species in the Carrot family (Apiaceae) including cultivated carrot (*Daucus carota* ssp. *sativus*), garden parsley (*Petroselinum crispum*), dill (*Anethum graveolens*), celery (*Apium graveolens*), as well as wild carrot (Queen Anne's lace; *Daucus carota*).

OVERWINTERING STAGE: Chrysalis.

HABITAT: Meadows, roadsides, and gardens.

DISTRIBUTION AND ABUNDANCE: Found from South America to central and eastern North America. In Ontario, a common resident south of the Canadian Shield; it is also found in the Rainy River area. Uncommon to rare in central Ontario.

COMMENTS: In southern Manitoba, the Black and Old World swallowtails sometimes hybridize; such hybrids should also be looked for in northwestern Ontario. Like the closely related Old World Swallowtail, the chrysalis comes in two colour forms, mottled brown/grey and green.

GIANT SWALLOWTAIL *Papilio cresphontes*

83–113 mm

...

ETYMOLOGY: In Greek mythology, *Cresphontes* was the great-great-grandson of Heracles; he became the king of Messene, the southernmost region of mainland Greece.

ADULT: Ontario's largest butterfly. **Upperside:** Blackish-brown with rows of yellow spots. The tail has a broad, rounded end with a yellow spot in the middle. **Underside:** Mainly yellow with black outlines and on the HW a median row of blue spots, dusted with some orange scaling.

SIMILAR SPECIES: In flight at a distance, because the underside is largely yellow, Giant Swallowtails could be mistaken for the almost-as-large yellow form of the Eastern Tiger Swallowtail. With closer views, however, Giant Swallowtails have much less yellow in the upperside than Eastern Tiger Swallowtails.

BEHAVIOUR: The wings often vibrate rapidly while nectaring.

FLIGHT SEASON: Two to three generations per year in Ontario.

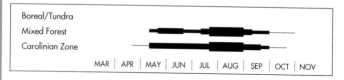

Boreal/Tundra								
Mixed Forest								
Carolinian Zone								
MAR	APR	MAY	JUN	JUL	AUG	SEP	OCT	NOV

CATERPILLAR: Brown with a broad white saddle on the back and white markings towards the head and rear giving it the appearance of a bird dropping to confuse possible predators. These caterpillars have the ability to detoxify the noxious chemicals present in the leaves of their foodplants. **Foodplants:** In the United States and Mexico, feeds mainly on wild and cultivated members of the Citrus family (Rutaceae) and has been a pest on citrus crops, which is why the caterpillar is often called "Orange Dog". In Ontario, the caterpillars feed on the provincially rare common hop tree (*Ptelea trifoliata*) and common prickly-ash (*Zanthoxylum americanum*), both members of the Citrus family. Adults may oviposit (and larvae have been observed) on common rue (*Ruta graveolens*) and gas plant (*Dictamnus albus*).

OVERWINTERING STAGE: Chrysalis.

HABITAT: Open areas in forests and woodlands, as well as fields and gardens.

DISTRIBUTION AND ABUNDANCE: Mainly a butterfly of Central America, Mexico and the eastern United States. In Ontario, an uncommon resident, until recently, confined to the Carolinian Zone, but expanding its range north and east. This swallowtail is now well established as a breeding species north and east through Peterborough and Hastings counties to the Ottawa region. In all likelihood this species will become a breeding butterfly in most of eastern Ontario where common prickly-ash is widespread. There is also a 2008 record of a stray from Sault Ste. Marie.

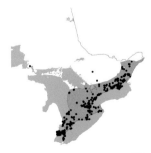

CANADIAN TIGER SWALLOWTAIL *Papilio canadensis*

53–90 mm

ETYMOLOGY: *Canadensis* refers to the mainly Canadian range of this butterfly.

ADULT: Medium-sized to large. This species does not have a black female form. **Upperside:** A predominantly yellow butterfly with black stripes. There is a wide, black stripe down the inner margin of the HW. **Underside:** Similar to upper but paler. The submarginal band on the FW is continuous yellow.

SIMILAR SPECIES: In most of the province (north of the southern edge of the Canadian Shield) the Canadian Tiger Swallowtail is the only tiger swallowtail to be found. In the Carolinian part of southern Ontario, the Eastern Tiger Swallowtail predominates. In the intervening areas, the Eastern can usually be identified by its generally larger size—however, there is overlap—and by the narrower black band along the inner HW margin. The Canadian Tiger also tends to have a continuous submarginal yellow band along the underside FW; the Eastern has a row of separate spots. However, this is complicated by hybridization between the two species.

BEHAVIOUR: Sometimes an ardent mudpuddler, it may be found in large numbers sipping at wet areas on roads.

FLIGHT SEASON: One generation per year.

	MAR	APR	MAY	JUN	JUL	AUG	SEP	OCT	NOV
Boreal/Tundra									
Mixed Forest									
Carolinian Zone									

Hybrid Canadian and Eastern Tiger Swallowtail

Early instar caterpillar

Mature caterpillar

CATERPILLAR: Similar to that of the Eastern Tiger Swallowtail.
Foodplants: Leaves of a wide variety of tree species, including ashes (*Fraxinus* spp.), willows (*Salix* spp.), poplars (*Populus* spp.) and cherries (*Prunus* spp.).

OVERWINTERING STAGE: Chrysalis.

HABITAT: Openings in forests and other open habitats in the Boreal and Mixed Forest regions; also observed at treeline and occasionally out onto the tundra and the supratidal zone.

DISTRIBUTION AND ABUNDANCE: Ranges from Alaska through much of Canada and into parts of the United States. In Ontario, a common resident throughout most of the province. It is not found in the southwest south of a line from Hamilton to the southern edge of the Bruce Peninsula.

COMMENTS: There is an area of hybridization running from Ottawa to Lake Huron between the main populations of the Canadian and Eastern Tiger swallowtails. Where there is a second generation in this zone, they are generally considered Eastern Tigers, but DNA work has shown that they are a mix of genes. Until the early 1990s, the two species were considered subspecies of the same species— *P. glaucus*.

PAPILIONIDAE / The Swallowtails

EASTERN TIGER SWALLOWTAIL *Papilio glaucus*

58–83 mm

ETYMOLOGY: *Glauco* in Greek and Latin is a silvery colour or bluish-green. There are numerous characters in Greek mythology named *Glaucus* but since Linnaeus named many butterflies after mythological Greek heroes, it is likely this species was named for a hero of the Trojan War or the sea-god.

ADULT: Medium-sized to large. **Upperside:** Creamy-yellow ground colour. There are black, bold stripes running the length of the wings giving this species its common name. There is also a narrow black band along the inner margin of the HW. Some females in the most southerly parts of the province are blackish overall with faint tiger stripes. **Underside:** A paler version of the upperside.

SIMILAR SPECIES: The Canadian Tiger Swallowtail is smaller but similar to this species. The submarginal yellow band along the underside FW is usually comprised of elongated spots (see COMMENTS for that species for hybrid discussion). Black females of the Eastern Tiger Swallowtail are part of the Pipevine Swallowtail mimicry complex (see Plate 1).

BEHAVIOUR: They are avid mudpuddlers and can be viewed up close, sometimes in large numbers when they are actively sipping moisture from sand along dirt roads and lake edges.

FLIGHT SEASON: Two overlapping generations per year.

	Boreal/Tundra								
Mixed Forest								
Carolinian Zone								
	MAR	APR	MAY	JUN	JUL	AUG	SEP	OCT	NOV

Dark form

CATERPILLAR: Immature caterpillars are brown with white splashes; this camouflage gives them the appearance of a bird dropping. Mature caterpillars are green with two spots on the thorax that resemble eyes. **Foodplants:** Many different tree species, including tulip tree (*Liriodendron tulipifera*) and common hop tree (*Ptelea trifoliata*), as well as cherries (*Prunus* spp.) and ashes (*Fraxinus* spp.).

OVERWINTERING STAGE: Chrysalis.

HABITAT: Forest and woodland clearings and edges as well as nearby open fields and gardens.

DISTRIBUTION AND ABUNDANCE:
This is a mainly Carolinian butterfly of the eastern United States. In Ontario, a common resident largely confined to areas south of the Canadian Shield but does occasionally stray farther north.

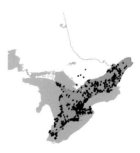

SPICEBUSH SWALLOWTAIL *Papilio troilus*

70–90 mm

ETYMOLOGY: In Greek mythology, *Troilus* was a son of King Priam of Troy and Hecuba; he was killed by Achilles.

ADULT: Medium-sized to large. Broad, rounded tail on HW. **Upperside:** Blackish-brown with green submarginal crescent-shaped markings on the HW and a single row of yellowish submarginal spots on the FW. The male has a greenish and the female a bluish wash inside the submarginal markings of the HW. **Underside:** Two rows of bright orange spots on the HW with a bluish wash between the rows.

SIMILAR SPECIES: The Spicebush Swallowtail is a member of a mimicry complex made up of five species in Ontario but is the only member of the complex that has broad, rounded tails (see Plate 1).

BEHAVIOUR: This swallowtail is a rapid-flying species with wings that vibrate while nectaring. Sometimes mixes with other butterflies in mudpuddling clubs.

FLIGHT SEASON: Two overlapping generations per year.

Boreal/Tundra									
Mixed Forest									
Carolinian Zone									
	MAR	APR	MAY	JUN	JUL	AUG	SEP	OCT	NOV

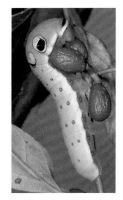

CATERPILLAR: Green with a humpbacked appearance and large eyespots on the humped area. When alarmed, the caterpillar arches the hump which gives it the appearance of a small snake. **Foodplants:** Many different trees and shrubs, including northern spicebush (*Lindera benzoin*), sassafras (*Sassafras albidum*) and tulip tree (*Liriodendron tulipifera*).

OVERWINTERING STAGE: Chrysalis.

HABITAT: Forest clearings and edges in the Carolinian Zone, but also strays into gardens.

DISTRIBUTION AND ABUNDANCE: A widespread butterfly of the eastern United States. In Ontario, an uncommon and local resident largely confined to the Carolinian Zone. There is a single observational record from Constance Bay, west of Ottawa—perhaps this individual strayed from New York State where it is found as far north as the eastern end of Lake Ontario.

Cabbage Whites

THE SULPHURS AND WHITES
Family Pieridae

These mainly white, yellow or orange butterflies are found worldwide, but only 21 species of two subfamilies (Pierinae and Coliadinae) have been recorded in Ontario. They are generally small to medium-sized butterflies but some of the migrants into southern Ontario can be larger. Most of the Ontario members of this family have little patterning other than black borders and spots, except a few members of the whites that have some green on the HW undersides.

They are strong-flying, avid flower visitors and many are commonly seen in gardens. Except for a few of the northern *Colias* sulphurs which overwinter as caterpillars, the resident members of this family overwinter as chrysalides. The adults all have equal-length legs. The sulphurs almost always perch with their wings closed.

Some species are among our most common and widespread butterflies. However, the tropical migrant species are not often seen in Ontario, usually only in the southwest part of the province and migration numbers vary widely from year to year. A few species have arctic or western distributions and reside only in the most northerly and westerly parts of Ontario. Special scales on the wings of some males—particularly the sulphurs—contain pigments called pterins, which reflect ultraviolet radiation. These are used to attract mates, but are also visible, in a few species, to the human eye. Many species also present differences in the patterns of the sexes and some sulphurs have two different female forms (yellow/orange, similar to the male, and white).

Most species are known to "mudpuddle" during which they sip moisture, containing salts and nutrients from the ground, that aid in sexual maturation and in male sperm production. Only one species, the West Virginia White, is protected by legislation in Ontario.

Eggs

The eggs are tall and ribbed.

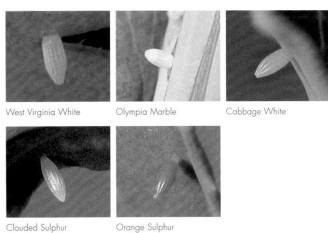

West Virginia White

Olympia Marble

Cabbage White

Clouded Sulphur

Orange Sulphur

Caterpillars

Caterpillars are shaped like cylinders and some feed on many garden and crop plants, such as members of the Mustard and Legume families (Brassicaceae and Fabaceae). The caterpillars are usually greenish with yellow or white stripes and well camouflaged on their foodplants.

Cabbage White

Little Yellow

Clouded Sulphur

Pink-edged Sulphur

Olympia Marble

Mustard White

Chrysalides

Sulphurs and whites pupate in an upright position and, like the swallowtails, have a silken girdle around the middle.

Clouded Sulphur

Orange Sulphur

Palaeno Sulphur

Olympia Marble

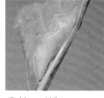
Cabbage White

Cabbage White

DAINTY SULPHUR *Nathalis iole*

22–30 mm

ETYMOLOGY: *Natha* is Sanskrit for "lord protector, refuge". In Greek mythology, *Iole,* which means "violet-coloured dawn", was the beautiful daughter of the king of the city of Oechalia, and was promised in marriage to the hero Heracles (Hercules).

ADULT: The smallest of Ontario's sulphurs with a distinctive elongated FW. **Upperside:** Yellow with the apex of the FW black. Black bars extend along the trailing edge of the FW and the leading edge of the HW. Males have an orange oval scent patch (called an androconial spot) in each HW bar. **Underside:** HW yellowish-grey in the summer form that migrates into Ontario. FW similar colour but with a black bar and spots along the trailing edge and yellow-orange in the medial area.

SIMILAR SPECIES: The Little Yellow lacks the black bar and spots and is pale yellow on the underside.

BEHAVIOUR: This species has a slow flight close to the ground. A strong migrant that occasionally appears in southern Canada.

FLIGHT SEASON: Migrants usually seen in late summer but may arrive as early as May.

Boreal/Tundra									
Mixed Forest			•						
Carolinian Zone		—	—	—	—	—	—		•
	MAR	APR	MAY	JUN	JUL	AUG	SEP	OCT	NOV

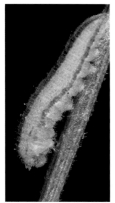

♂

Dorsal view

CATERPILLAR: Green with a broad dorsal purple stripe and a lateral yellow and black stripe. **Foodplants:** Some members of the Sunflower family (Asteraceae), such as marigolds (*Tagetes* spp.), and of the Pink family (Caryophyllaceae), such as chickweeds (*Cerastium* spp.).

OVERWINTERING STAGE: Not known to overwinter in Ontario.

HABITAT: Mostly disturbed habitats, including fields and roadsides.

DISTRIBUTION AND ABUNDANCE:
Primarily a butterfly of Mexico, Florida and the American Midwest, but migrants are recorded from as far north as southern Manitoba and Saskatchewan. In Ontario, a rare migrant that occasionally breeds here. In 2012, large numbers were reported from across southwestern Ontario with several broods.

MEXICAN YELLOW *Eurema mexicana*

33–44 mm

Summer form

ETYMOLOGY: *Eurema* was the Greek goddess of invention; the word means "invention or something found unexpectedly". *Mexicana* refers to this species' main area of distribution.

ADULT: A small sulphur and the only one in Ontario where the HW ends in a point. **Upperside:** Pale yellow with an irregular black border (somewhat in the shape of a dog's head on the FW and limited black on the HW). The male has some orange colouring along the front edge of the HW. **Underside:** Pale yellow with scattered reddish or black markings in "summer" brood individuals (the form most likely to occur in Ontario) and yellow with more pronounced rust-coloured markings in "winter" brood individuals.

SIMILAR SPECIES: Best differentiated from other yellow sulphurs by the unusual, pointed HW. The Southern Dogface is larger and has a more sharply defined dog's-head pattern with a black eye-spot on the FW.

BEHAVIOUR: In most of its range, males will often be found mudpuddling alone, or on occasion with one or two other males.

FLIGHT SEASON: While not to be expected in Ontario, non-breeding migrants may appear from June into September.

Boreal/Tundra									
Mixed Forest									
Carolinian Zone				•					
	MAR	APR	MAY	JUN	JUL	AUG	SEP	OCT	NOV

Winter form

♂

Dorsal view

CATERPILLAR: Has not been recorded in Ontario. Smooth green with several yellow stripes. **Foodplants:** Legumes (Fabaceae), including acacias (*Acacia* spp.) and the locust (*Robinia neomexicana*), but none of the known larval foodplants occur in Ontario.

OVERWINTERING STAGE: Does not overwinter in Ontario.

HABITAT: Disturbed areas.

DISTRIBUTION AND ABUNDANCE: A mainly Central American species, it strays north through the central and eastern United States and has appeared as far north as southern Manitoba. In Ontario, a very rare, non-breeding migrant; it is known from a single individual collected at Point Pelee in June 1882 by the famous naturalist William Saunders. The specimen is in the CNC.

LITTLE YELLOW *Pyrisitia lisa*

♀

31–36 mm

ETYMOLOGY: *Pyrisitia* is Latin for "pertaining to fire". *Lisa* is a female name, short for Elizabeth.

ADULT: Small. **Upperside:** Bright yellow with a black border on all wings (reduced in the female). There is a white female form. **Underside:** Pale yellow with black to brownish spots and usually with a largish red spot at the leading edge of the HW that is often reduced and sometimes absent, especially in males.

SIMILAR SPECIES: The Little Yellow looks like a smaller version of the Clouded and Pink-edged sulphurs but note the central silvery spot on the HW of those two larger species. The Dainty Sulphur is smaller than the Little Yellow with more black on the upperside of the wings and a very different pattern on the underside.

BEHAVIOUR: An avid mudpuddler at wet spots on dirt roads. It generally flies close to the ground.

FLIGHT SEASON: Migrants typically appear by June or July but have occurred as early as May. Two (possibly three) generations have been recorded in Ontario.

Boreal/Tundra			•						
Mixed Forest						•	•		
Carolinian Zone									
	MAR	APR	MAY	JUN	JUL	AUG	SEP	OCT	NOV

White form female

Dorsal view

CATERPILLAR: Smooth and green with several white lateral stripes.
Foodplants: Several species of legumes (Fabaceae), mainly showy partridge pea (*Chamaecrista fasciculata*) in the eastern United States.

OVERWINTERING STAGE: Does not overwinter in Ontario.

HABITAT: Open areas, such as fields, roadsides and gardens.

DISTRIBUTION AND ABUNDANCE: Mainly a tropical and subtropical species that migrates northward each season, breeding well north into the United States and southern Canada. In Ontario, usually a rare migrant that occasionally breeds and that is largely restricted to the southwest where, in some years, it can be common. For a small butterfly, it can fly long distances and has been recorded as far north as Nakina and Cochrane.

SLEEPY ORANGE *Abaeis nicippe*

30–48 mm

Summer form

ETYMOLOGY: *Abae* is a town in Phocis, Greece, named after *Abas*, the twelfth king of Argos and grandson of Danaus. *Nicippe* is the name of several women in Greek mythology.

ADULT: Small to medium-sized. **Upperside:** Bright orange wings with a wide black border (narrower on the female HW). There is a small crescent-shaped black marking in the FW cell that reminded its author of a closed eye—hence the name 'sleepy'. Males do not reflect ultraviolet light as do some other sulphurs. **Underside:** Varying orange-yellowish with irregular diagonal brown markings.

SIMILAR SPECIES: The Orange Sulphur is appreciably larger and has a more regular edge to the black border on the uppersides. The Orange Sulphur also has a silver spot in the centre of the underside HW which is absent in the Sleepy Orange.

BEHAVIOUR: Fast-flyer; males regularly patrol for females.

FLIGHT SEASON: Migrants have been recorded from May to September.

Boreal/Tundra								
Mixed Forest				•		•		
Carolinian Zone		•	•	•	•			
	MAR	APR	MAY	JUN	JUL	AUG	SEP	OCT	NOV

Winter form

Captured by ambush bug

CATERPILLAR: Has not been recorded in Ontario. Green with short fine hairs and a lateral white and yellow stripe on each side. **Foodplants:** Legumes (*Cassia* spp. and *Chamaecrista* spp.).

OVERWINTERING STAGE: Does not overwinter in Ontario.

HABITAT: Open areas, such as fields and gardens.

DISTRIBUTION AND ABUNDANCE: Widespread in Central America, Mexico and across the southern United States, migrating northward where it breeds only as far north as Washington, D.C. In Ontario, a very rare, non-breeding migrant that before 2012 had only been recorded a few times: once in Toronto in May; once at Quetico Provincial Park in June; twice at Point Pelee in June and July; and, once in Kitchener in September. Many individuals appeared at Point Pelee in May 2012.

CLOUDED SULPHUR *Colias philodice*

♀

32–54 mm

ETYMOLOGY: The genus name *Colias* is derived from *Kolias*, the name of a temple for the Greek goddess Aphrodite. In Greek mythology, *Philodice* was a Naiad nymph and daughter of the river god Inachus.

ADULT: Medium-sized, with a pink fringe on wings. **Upperside:** Bright yellow with a relatively broad back border; the female has yellow spots in the border. The upper HW of both sexes has an orange spot in the centre. The FW has an elongate medial black dot. There is a white to whitish-blue female form (see Plate 2). **Underside:** Yellow with a double silvery spot surrounded by pink in the centre of the HW. There is also a submarginal row of small black spots.

SIMILAR SPECIES: All the other yellow *Colias* sulphurs in Ontario are similar, but the Clouded Sulphur can be distinguished from them by the presence of a submarginal row of small black or brown spots on all the undersides (these are sometimes reduced or even absent).

BEHAVIOUR: Frequently seen nectaring at flowers. An avid mudpuddler, sometimes with dozens sipping the salts and nutrients from wet spots along roads.

FLIGHT SEASON: Two or more overlapping generations each year.

	MAR	APR	MAY	JUN	JUL	AUG	SEP	OCT	NOV
Boreal/Tundra									
Mixed Forest									
Carolinian Zone									

White form female

Male left, female right

CATERPILLAR: The cylindrical, smooth, green caterpillars are covered in fine hairs and have lateral white stripes. **Foodplants:** Many different legumes (Fabaceae), particularly cultivated crops.

OVERWINTERING STAGE: Chrysalis.

HABITAT: Open fields, along roadsides and in woodland clearings; in late summer, often abundant in fields of clover (*Trifolium* spp.) and alfalfa (*Medicago sativa*).

DISTRIBUTION AND ABUNDANCE:
Widespread throughout most of its North American range, the Clouded Sulphur can even be found in northern Alaska. In Ontario, a common resident, often becoming abundant late in the summer, ranging as far north as southern James Bay. Numbers can vary from year to year.

ORANGE SULPHUR *Colias eurytheme*

34–55 mm

ETYMOLOGY: *Eurytheme* from the literal Latin translation *eury* = broad and *theme* = composition.

ADULT: Medium-sized. **Upperside:** An orange ground colour. Some individuals have less orange in the form of a central blush to the FW. FW with a broad black border in both sexes, but the female has some yellow spots in the border. There is also a white form of the female that often appears bluish-white (see Plate 2). **Underside:** Some orange on the lower FW and there is a submarginal row of small dark spots on all undersides.

SIMILAR SPECIES: Best separated from other *Colias* sulphurs in Ontario by the orange on the uppersides. The white form of the Orange Sulphur female cannot be distinguished in the field from the white form of the Clouded Sulphur female. The extremely rare migrant Sleepy Orange is considerably smaller.

BEHAVIOUR: The Orange Sulphur is somewhat migratory. Early season individuals seen along the northern edge of its range (including much or all of Ontario) are probably migrants of the first brood from farther south: this may be due to its lack of winter hardiness, unlike the Clouded Sulphur.

FLIGHT SEASON: Two generations per year.

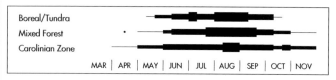

	MAR	APR	MAY	JUN	JUL	AUG	SEP	OCT	NOV
Boreal/Tundra									
Mixed Forest									
Carolinian Zone									

Captured by ambush bug

White form female

CATERPILLAR: Green with a lateral white stripe on the sides. **Foodplants:** Many different legumes (Fabaceae). Often associated with cultivated clovers (*Trifolium* spp.) and alfalfas (*Medicago* spp.).

OVERWINTERING STAGE: Chrysalis but may not overwinter in Ontario.

HABITAT: Agricultural areas, roadsides and gardens.

DISTRIBUTION AND ABUNDANCE:
Found from Central America north into central Canada. In Ontario, a common breeding migrant throughout much of southern Ontario, becoming less common farther north. One of the most widespread of Ontario's butterflies, it has been recorded as far north as the western coast of James Bay and Favourable Lake near the Manitoba border.

GIANT SULPHUR *Colias gigantea*

37–55 mm

ETYMOLOGY: *Gigantea* refers to the large size of this species.

ADULT: One of the largest *Colias* sulphurs in North America with a bright pink fringe. **Upperside:** Rarely seen but bright yellow with a narrow black border in the male and a small amount of black in the apex of the FW in the female. Some females may show a white ground colour (see Plate 2). A pale orange spot is present in the centre of the HW. **Underside:** Yellow, with very little dark scaling and a small white spot surrounded by brown or pink in the middle of the HW.

SIMILAR SPECIES: This butterfly is like most other *Colias* sulphurs, except it is generally the largest. In its very northern range in Ontario, the Giant Sulphur might be mistaken for the Pink-edged Sulphur that is smaller with more rounded wings, or the Pelidne Sulphur that has darker scaling on the underside HW.

BEHAVIOUR: A very active, fast-flying species that often stops at flowers, including asters (Asteraceae), to nectar.

FLIGHT SEASON: One generation per year.

Boreal/Tundra	———							
Mixed Forest								
Carolinian Zone								
	MAR	APR	MAY	JUN	JUL	AUG	SEP	OCT	NOV

Dorsal view

Caterpillar of *Colias
gigantea inupiat*

CATERPILLAR: Green with white and yellow lateral stripes. The caterpillar of the Alaskan subspecies *inupiat* has been described and is shown here. **Foodplants:** Many species of willows (*Salix* spp.).

OVERWINTERING STAGE: Half-grown caterpillar.

HABITAT: Wet habitats, including wet tundra, fens and moist woods.

DISTRIBUTION AND ABUNDANCE: Mainly a western boreal Canadian species but also ranges far north into Alaska. In Ontario, at the eastern edge of its range, it is an uncommon resident, restricted to areas along the coasts of Hudson Bay and northern James Bay and at least 80 km inland.

PELIDNE SULPHUR *Colias pelidne*

34–44 mm

ETYMOLOGY: The specific epithet may be based on *Pelides*, the son of Peleus (Achilles), or on the ancient Greek word *pelidnos*, meaning "livid or dark coloured".

ADULT: Medium-sized, with pink wing fringes. **Upperside:** Rarely seen but pale yellow with a narrow black border on both wings in the males and pale yellow or white in the females with some black towards the FW tips (see Plate 2). In both sexes, there is some basal black scaling. FW has a submedial black spot. **Underside:** The HW appears olive-coloured due to extensive black scaling, and has a medial, pink-rimmed, white spot.

SIMILAR SPECIES: In northern Ontario, the most similar species is the Pink-edged Sulphur, but it lacks basal black scaling on the wings and its distribution is more southerly. The Palaeno Sulphur shares a similar distribution in Ontario but lacks the pink around the lower HW white spot.

BEHAVIOUR: Males patrol close to the ground seeking females.

FLIGHT SEASON: One generation per year.

	MAR	APR	MAY	JUN	JUL	AUG	SEP	OCT	NOV
Boreal/Tundra				——— ·					
Mixed Forest									
Carolinian Zone									

Dorsal view

CATERPILLAR: The early stages of this species are still undescribed (no photo available). **Foodplants:** Blueberries (*Vaccinium* spp.).

OVERWINTERING STAGE: Caterpillar.

HABITAT: Tundra and bogs with blueberries.

DISTRIBUTION AND ABUNDANCE: This species has three widely separated populations in Canada (the Rocky Mountains, northwestern tundra regions, and northern Ontario east to Newfoundland). In Ontario, an uncommon resident recorded only along the coasts of Hudson and James bays and up to 40 km inland. The most southerly record is near Moosonee. As the range map predicts, it is expected to occur further inland, throughout much of the Hudson Bay Lowlands.

PINK-EDGED SULPHUR *Colias interior*

♀

35–47 mm

ETYMOLOGY: The name *interior* refers to this species' distribution in the interior of North America.

ADULT: Medium-sized. The wing margins are fringed in bright pink. **Upperside:** Rarely seen but a bright yellow with very little basal black scaling on the wings. Males have an even, narrow black border and a bright orange spot in the centre of the HW. Females have only a small amount of black in the FW apex; there is a rare white form. **Underside:** Yellow with little black scaling. The single silver spot on the HW is pink-rimmed. There is no row of submarginal black spots.

SIMILAR SPECIES: The three most similar species in the far north of Ontario are the Pelidne, Palaeno and Giant sulphurs. The Pink-edged Sulphur differs from the first by having a yellower HW underside and rarely has pink suffusion over the white underside spot. The Palaeno Sulphur lacks the pink rim around the underside HW spot; whereas the Giant Sulphur is larger and lacks the bright orange spot on the HW upper surface. The Clouded Sulphur has a submarginal row of black spots on the HW underside that is lacking in the Pink-edged Sulphur. See Plate 2.

BEHAVIOUR: Adults nectar at flowers and also sip mud in moist areas.

FLIGHT SEASON: One generation per year.

| | MAR | APR | MAY | JUN | JUL | AUG | SEP | OCT | NOV |

Boreal/Tundra
Mixed Forest
Carolinian Zone

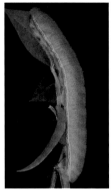

CATERPILLAR: Yellowish-green with white stripes. The lateral stripe has a red line through it. **Foodplants:** Blueberries (*Vaccinium* spp.).

OVERWINTERING STAGE: Caterpillar.

HABITAT: Mostly boreal, restricted to areas where blueberries (*Vaccinium* spp.) grow but also found in open rocky areas, particularly where there has been recent wood-cutting or burns. In the more southerly parts of the province, tends to be found in bogs and woodland clearings.

DISTRIBUTION AND ABUNDANCE: This species is widespread in Canada from British Columbia to Labrador, and south through the Rocky Mountains to Idaho. In Ontario, an uncommon and local resident throughout the north, and even more uncommon and highly localized in southern Ontario.

COMMENTS: In the CNC in Ottawa, there is a very unusual gynandromorph specimen of this species taken in the Ottawa Valley with yellow male wings on the left and white female wings on the right.

121

PALAENO SULPHUR *Colias palaeno*

32–45 mm

ETYMOLOGY: *Palaeno* may be a form of *Palaemon*, a Greek sea god of sailors and harbours. *Palae-* in Greek is "ancient or old".

ADULT: Medium-sized. **Upperside:** Rarely seen but the male Palaeno Sulphur is bright yellow with wide black borders (narrower on the HW). Unlike most other sulphurs, there is no, or a very faint, black spot in the middle of the FW. Females are mostly white. **Underside:** Yellowish-green; HW is heavily dusted with dark scales and the central white spot has no rim.

SIMILAR SPECIES: Pelidne Sulphur shares a similar distribution but has a pink ring around the central HW spot. Pink-edged Sulphur has a yellower underside and also has a pink rim around the central HW spot. Its distribution is more southern. See Plate 2.

BEHAVIOUR: Adults nectar on low-lying flowers.

FLIGHT SEASON: One generation a year.

Boreal/Tundra			———————	•	
Mixed Forest					
Carolinian Zone					
	MAR	APR	MAY	JUN	JUL	AUG	SEP	OCT	NOV

Dorsal view

CATERPILLAR: Green with a yellow stripe along the sides. **Foodplants:** Blueberries (*Vaccinium* spp.), especially alpine bilberry (*Vaccinium uliginosum*).

OVERWINTERING STAGE: Half-grown caterpillar.

HABITAT: Tundra and muskeg, sometimes in sparse woodlands farther south.

DISTRIBUTION AND ABUNDANCE: Holarctic, in North America ranging from Alaska across northern Canada to Labrador. In Ontario, an uncommon resident occurring along the coasts of Hudson and James bays, especially along stream valleys, with a few records farther south in boreal forest clearings with blueberries (*Vaccinium* spp.).

SOUTHERN DOGFACE *Zerene cesonia*

50–57 mm

ETYMOLOGY: The name *zerene* may be a variation of the word "serene" meaning calm, peaceful and untroubled. *Milonia Caesonia* was a Roman empress and the fourth and last wife of the Roman Emperor Caligula.

ADULT: Medium-sized. **Upperside:** Bright yellow with black markings on the pointed FW that leave the image of a yellow "dogface", including large black eye-spots. Leading edge of FW has dark dusting. The upper HW has a limited black border. **Underside:** Paler yellow with the dogface showing slightly through on the FW. On fresh individuals, there is often a bright pink lining to the inner veins, wing edges and around the two white spots on the HW.

SIMILAR SPECIES: Superficially, this butterfly looks like most of the yellow-winged *Colias* sulphurs. However, except for the Mexican Yellow, the dogface pattern is unique to Ontario butterflies.

BEHAVIOUR: A strongly migratory species with a very rapid flight, and often seen avidly feeding at flowers in gardens or fields.

FLIGHT SEASON: Migrants have been recorded between late June and September.

Boreal/Tundra									
Mixed Forest									
Carolinian Zone				• • • •		•	•		
	MAR	APR	MAY	JUN	JUL	AUG	SEP	OCT	NOV

Variant

CATERPILLAR: Has not been recorded in Canada. Green or yellow with small black bumps. The number and pattern of the yellow and black lines varies with the individual. **Foodplants:** Legumes (Fabaceae).

OVERWINTERING STAGE: Does not overwinter in Canada.

HABITAT: Migrants could occur anywhere but usually found in open areas, particularly gardens.

DISTRIBUTION AND ABUNDANCE: Mainly a tropical species ranging from Argentina north into the southern United States that occasionally strays northward as far as southern Canada. In Ontario, a very rare, non-breeding migrant that has been found as far north as the Toronto area.

125

CLOUDLESS SULPHUR *Phoebis sennae*

♀

63–78 mm

ETYMOLOGY: The generic name is likely from the Greek *phoibos* meaning "bright or radiant". *Sennae* refers to the larval foodplant.

ADULT: Large. **Upperside:** Rarely seen but bright lemon yellow with a very narrow to non-existent black edge on the pointed FW and with a large black spot in the centre of these wings. Females are duller, yellowish-orange with some black trimming on the margins of the wings. **Underside:** Yellow with an orangish cast and two HW silver spots with a pink margin. The mid-FW has a large, reddish spot corresponding to the black spot on the upper surface.

SIMILAR SPECIES: The Cloudless Sulphur is appreciably larger than most of the other yellow sulphurs in Ontario and lacks the broader black borders of most of these. Some yellow-form females of other sulphurs have little or no black border, but they are found much farther north in the province. The Orange-barred Sulphur is similar in size, but has some bright orange banding on the upperside; the females are very similarly coloured, but the Orange-barred Sulphur is usually brighter.

BEHAVIOUR: A very rapid, deliberate flight and is often seen fluttering its wings rapidly while nectaring at large flowers. An avid mudpuddler.

FLIGHT SEASON: Migrants have been recorded from May to October.

	MAR	APR	MAY	JUN	JUL	AUG	SEP	OCT	NOV
Boreal/Tundra									
Mixed Forest						•			
Carolinian Zone			———	—	———————				

♂
Dorsal view

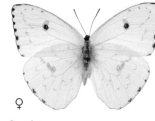

♀
Dorsal view

CATERPILLAR: Has not been recorded in Canada. Two forms: one is green with a yellow lateral stripe, blue lateral dashes and many small black dots; the other is yellow with black stripes across the back. **Foodplants:** Sennas (*Cassia* spp., *Chamaecrista* spp., *Senna* spp.).

OVERWINTERING STAGE: Does not overwinter in Ontario.

HABITAT: Migrants could occur in any open habitat.

DISTRIBUTION AND ABUNDANCE: Mainly a tropical species ranging from Argentina north into the southern United States. Migrates north of permanent range each summer and establishes temporary breeding colonies as far north as Maine, occasionally straying farther north. In Ontario, a very rare, non-breeding migrant that has occurred as far north as Orillia.

COMMENTS: During strong butterfly migrations into Ontario from the southern United States, up to 20 individuals of this butterfly have been seen in a day at favoured locations such as Point Pelee. These migratory appearances often follow storms, such as hurricanes in the southern United States, which push individuals farther north.

127

ORANGE-BARRED SULPHUR *Phoebis philea*

♀

68–80 mm

ETYMOLOGY: *Philea* is Greek for "love or affection".

ADULT: Largest Ontario sulphur. **Upperside:** Rarely seen but the male has bright yellow uppersides crossed by two orange bars with ultraviolet highlights; one bar across the FW and the other at the base of the HW. The female is yellow to orange-yellow with irregular black trimming; off-white females also occur. **Underside:** Male orangey-yellow with irregular dark markings and two circular silver spots on both the FW and HW. Female similar to male, but with more dark markings.

SIMILAR SPECIES: Only the Cloudless Sulphur comes close to this sulphur in size but it lacks the bright orange bars of the Orange-barred Sulphur.

BEHAVIOUR: A very fast-flying species, it is usually seen around flowers, particularly in gardens. An avid mudpuddler.

FLIGHT SEASON: Migrants to Ontario have been recorded from June to October.

Boreal/Tundra									
Mixed Forest									
Carolinian Zone				•			•	•	
	MAR	APR	MAY	JUN	JUL	AUG	SEP	OCT	NOV

CATERPILLAR: Has not been recorded in Canada. Yellow and green with black markings that interrupt the yellow lateral stripe giving it the appearance of yellow triangles. **Foodplants:** Sennas (*Cassia* spp., *Chamaecrista* spp., *Senna* spp.).

OVERWINTERING STAGE: Does not overwinter in Canada.

HABITAT: Migrants could occur in any open habitat, including gardens.

DISTRIBUTION AND ABUNDANCE: Widespread in the tropical Americas from Brazil north to the extreme southern United States. Migrates north of permanent range each summer and establishes temporary breeding colonies as far north as South Carolina, occasionally straying farther north. In Ontario, a very rare non-breeding migrant with a few records extending from Windsor to Toronto.

LARGE MARBLE *Euchloe ausonides*

30–48 mm

ETYMOLOGY: *Euchloe* is made up of the Greek *eu* for "good" and *chloe*, meaning "first shoots of young grass". *Ausonides* refers to its resemblance to the Eastern Dappled White of Italy, *Euchloe ausonia*.

ADULT: Small to medium-sized. On average, this is the largest of the marble species. **Upperside:** Chalky white with blackish FW tips and a narrow black bar at end of cell. **Underside:** A very complex pattern of green markings with extensive yellow scaling along the veins on the HW.

SIMILAR SPECIES: The Olympia Marble looks very similar, except it has a less complex marbling that forms three irregular bars across the underside HW. See Plate 3.

BEHAVIOUR: Flies about in a marked zigzag pattern.

FLIGHT SEASON: One generation per year.

Boreal/Tundra								
Mixed Forest								
Carolinian Zone								
	MAR	APR	MAY	JUN	JUL	AUG	SEP	OCT	NOV

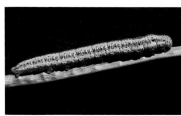

CATERPILLAR: Green with many lateral grey and yellow stripes and covered with many black spots. **Foodplants:** Species in the Mustard family (Brassicaceae), including tower mustard (*Turritis glabra* formerly *Arabis glabra*).

OVERWINTERING STAGE: Chrysalis.

HABITAT: Prefers sandy areas, especially open pine forests.

DISTRIBUTION AND ABUNDANCE: Mainly western North America, ranging from the Alaskan tundra east to Ontario and south to California and New Mexico. In Ontario, an uncommon and local resident whose numbers fluctuate annually. It is primarily restricted to northern Ontario, from the Manitoba border to Lake Superior, with a single disjunct record from Fraserdale in Cochrane District. Several colonies also occur farther south on Manitoulin Island and the adjacent mainland.

131

OLYMPIA MARBLE *Euchloe olympia*

30–40 mm

ETYMOLOGY: *Olympia* is a site in Greece where the Greek Gods were said to dwell.

ADULT: Small to medium-sized. **Upperside:** Chalky white, the FW with a dark brown mark at the end of the cell (this shows through on the underside) and dark wing tips. **Underside:** HW with green and yellow marbling in the form of three irregular bands. Fresh individuals have a bright rosy flush towards the base of the wings.

SIMILAR SPECIES: Similar to Large Marble, except Olympia Marble has a less complex marbling that forms three irregular bars across the underside HW. See Plate 3.

BEHAVIOUR: Slow and low-flying except when males are searching for females.

FLIGHT SEASON: One generation per year.

		MAR	APR	MAY	JUN	JUL	AUG	SEP	OCT	NOV
Boreal/Tundra										
Mixed Forest										
Carolinian Zone										

CATERPILLAR: Green with yellow and grey stripes along its length and covered with black spots. **Foodplants:** Flowers and buds of rockcresses including tower mustard (*Turritis glabra,* formerly *Arabis glabra*), spreading-pod rockcress (*Boechera divaricarpa,* formerly *Arabis divaricarpa*) in most of its Ontario range and lyre-leaved rockcress (*Arabidopsis lyrata,* formerly *Arabis lyrata*) at Grand Bend.

OVERWINTERING STAGE: Chrysalis.

HABITAT: Mostly very dry habitats, such as alvars, Canadian Shield rock barrens and sandy meadows, and also open woodlands.

DISTRIBUTION AND ABUNDANCE: Mainly a species of the Great Plains from the Canadian Prairies south through the United States and east through the Great Lakes Region with an isolated population in the Appalachians. In Ontario, at its easternmost distribution, an uncommon and local resident, ranging through south-central Ontario from Manitoulin Island east to the Ottawa valley, most commonly along the southern edge of the Canadian Shield. An isolated population occurs near southern Lake Huron, an extension of colonies in Michigan.

COMMENTS: The Olympia Marble first appeared in the Ottawa area in the 1970s as it expanded its range eastward. The reasons for this range shift are unknown.

MUSTARD WHITE *Pieris oleracea*

32–50 mm

ETYMOLOGY: *Pieris* is the name of an ancient country in Greece whose inhabitants were called *Pieres*. In Latin, *oleracea* means "pertaining to kitchen gardens either as a vegetable or pot-herb".

ADULT: Small to medium-sized. **Upperside:** Chalky white surface with some black dusting close to the body and on the tip of the FW. **Underside:** HW is yellowish in the spring form, with dark green scaling along the veins. The summer form has almost none of this dark scaling and appears nearly pure white on all surfaces.

SIMILAR SPECIES: See West Virginia White and Plate 3.

BEHAVIOUR: Flies slowly, close to the ground, but if frightened can fly quickly and high up into the trees.

FLIGHT SEASON: Two generations per year.

	MAR	APR	MAY	JUN	JUL	AUG	SEP	OCT	NOV
Boreal/Tundra									
Mixed Forest									
Carolinian Zone									

Summer form

Spring form

CATERPILLAR: Green with a yellow stripe down each side. **Foodplants:** Members of the Mustard family (Brassicaceae), particularly toothworts (*Cardamine* spp., formerly *Dentaria* spp.) and rockcresses (*Turritis* spp., *Arabis* spp.).

OVERWINTERING STAGE: Chrysalis.

HABITAT: Deciduous and mixed woodlands or forests.

DISTRIBUTION AND ABUNDANCE: Occurs across much of Canada and south into the northeastern United States. In Ontario, a common and widespread resident found as far north as the coastal tundra of Hudson Bay.

COMMENTS: Early literature on eastern North American butterflies usually described the Mustard White as very common. Biologists speculate that the Mustard White, which has been outcompeted for mustard food sources by the introduced Cabbage White, has retreated more into woodlands.

WEST VIRGINIA WHITE *Pieris virginiensis*

32–40 mm

ETYMOLOGY: *Virginiensis* refers to the American state of the same name where this butterfly was first encountered.

ADULT: Small to medium-sized. The wings on this species are somewhat more rounded than other whites. **Upperside:** Dingy white and thinly scaled, which gives the wings a translucent appearance. Females are duskier on the forewings. **Underside:** White with broad, diffuse grey-brown scaling along the HW veins.

SIMILAR SPECIES: The Mustard White is very similar in size and appearance, but the underside HW veins are narrowly lined with dark green scales in the spring form and very few scales in the summer form. The Cabbage White tends to be larger with less translucent wings and black tips and one to two black spots on the FW. The Checkered White and the Western White have heavy black markings on both the uppersides and undersides of the FW. See Plate 3.

BEHAVIOUR: Tends to be a slow flyer, staying close to the ground.

FLIGHT SEASON: One generation per year.

CATERPILLAR: Green with fine, white lateral lines. **Foodplants:** In Ontario, recorded only on two-leaved toothwort (*Cardamine diphylla*) but females have been laying eggs on the introduced invasive garlic mustard (*Alliaria petiolata*) which is leading to population declines of the butterfly since their caterpillars cannot survive on this plant.

OVERWINTERING STAGE: Chrysalis.

HABITAT: Rich deciduous forests where its larval foodplant grows.

DISTRIBUTION AND ABUNDANCE: The West Virginia White is a species of the Great Lakes Region and the central Appalachians. In Ontario, an uncommon and local resident with several isolated populations across southern Ontario as well as on Manitoulin Island and in the area around Sault Ste. Marie.

COMMENTS: The West Virginia White was originally listed as Endangered in Ontario in 1977 but in 1990, after it was found to be more widespread than previously known, it was downlisted to Vulnerable (now called Special Concern).

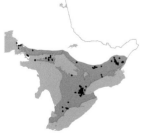

CABBAGE WHITE *Pieris rapae*

♀

32–47 mm

ETYMOLOGY: *Rapae* refers to the larval mustard foodplants, specifically turnip, *rapa* in Latin.

ADULT: Small to medium-sized. **Upperside:** Clear white with a black tip on the FW. The male has one black spot in the middle of the FW, whereas the female has two. **Underside:** The FW has two black spots and the HW is yellowish.

SIMILAR SPECIES: Best distinguished from other whites by black tips and one or two round black spots on the dorsal FWs.

BEHAVIOUR: The Cabbage White tends to be a very deliberate flyer, but can also flit about in open areas.

FLIGHT SEASON: Multiple generations per year.

	MAR	APR	MAY	JUN	JUL	AUG	SEP	OCT	NOV
Boreal/Tundra									
Mixed Forest									
Carolinian Zone									

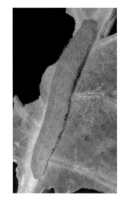

CATERPILLAR: Bluish-green with faint lateral yellow stripes or dashes and a yellow dorsal stripe. A glandular fluid that collects on the fine hairs is known to repel ants and possibly other predators. **Foodplants:** Many species of the Mustard family (Brassicaceae), including many garden plants, such as cabbage, cauliflower and broccoli, all of which are cultivars of *Brassica oleracea*.

OVERWINTERING STAGE: Chrysalis.

HABITAT: Many habitats, from gardens to isolated woodland clearings. Most common in disturbed areas where wild mustards grow.

DISTRIBUTION AND ABUNDANCE: The Cabbage White is one of the most widely distributed butterflies in North America. In Ontario, a common and widespread resident, much more common in southern Ontario but ranging all the way to the coast of Hudson Bay.

COMMENTS: The Cabbage White was introduced from Europe where it is also called the Small White. First recorded near Quebec City in the 1860s, it has spread across North America likely because of its ability to colonize almost any type of habitat and its ability to feed on a wide variety of foodplants.

CHECKERED WHITE *Pontia protodice*

♂

33–49 mm

ETYMOLOGY: *Pontia* refers to the Black Sea region. In Greek, *proto* means the "first, earliest or original". *Dice* was the personification of justice in Greek mythology.

ADULT: Small to medium-sized. **Upperside:** FW of the male is white with black markings giving a checkered look to the outside margin. HW is clear white. The female is much more heavily checkered brownish-black overall. **Underside:** The male HW ranges from clear to a vague greyish checkering whereas the female HW varies from black-brown to greenish checkering.

SIMILAR SPECIES: The Checkered White is similar to the Western White, but the HW on the male of the latter has some black markings near the margin. The Western White has heavier checkered markings along the FW margins. Female Western Whites tend to have darker markings than those of the Checkered White. However, there is a great deal of variability, so identification can be difficult where the two species occur together. See Plate 3.

BEHAVIOUR: The Checkered White migrates into the province from the south in some years and establishes temporary colonies, but these often disappear after a year or two.

FLIGHT SEASON: Two generations per year.

Boreal/Tundra				—					
Mixed Forest		•	•						
Carolinian Zone		•							
	MAR	APR	MAY	JUN	JUL	AUG	SEP	OCT	NOV

CATERPILLAR: Alternating yellowish-green and greyish-blue lateral stripes with tiny black dots. **Foodplants:** Many different mustards (Brassicaceae) including cabbage (*Brassica oleracea*) and turnip (*Brassica rapa*).

OVERWINTERING STAGE: Chrysalis.

HABITAT: Open fields and disturbed areas, including roadsides.

DISTRIBUTION AND ABUNDANCE: A permanent resident in northern Mexico and the southern United States appearing infrequently northward to southern Canada where it sometimes establishes temporary breeding colonies. In Ontario, a rare to uncommon breeding migrant and temporary resident that has been recorded as far north as the Pickle Lake area of Kenora District.

141

WESTERN WHITE *Pontia occidentalis*

♀

33–48 mm

ETYMOLOGY: In Latin, *occidentalis* means "western".

ADULT: Small to medium-sized. **Upperside:** Male is relatively lightly checkered with black. Females are more heavily checkered than males with all spring individuals darker than the summer form. In both sexes, the marginal spots on the FW are grey. **Underside:** Heavy greenish checkering on the HW.

SIMILAR SPECIES: Similar to Checkered White, but Western White has heavier checkered markings along the FW margins. In addition, male Western has some black near the HW margin and female Western tends to have darker markings than those of Checkered. There is, however, a great deal of variability, so identification can be difficult where the two species occur together. See Plate 3.

BEHAVIOUR: Males are known to hilltop looking for females. The females can be more difficult to find. The flight is rapid and erratic.

FLIGHT SEASON: Two generations per year.

	MAR	APR	MAY	JUN	JUL	AUG	SEP	OCT	NOV
Boreal/Tundra									
Mixed Forest									
Carolinian Zone									

CATERPILLAR: Alternating yellowish-green and greyish-blue lateral stripes with tiny black dots. **Foodplants:** Many different mustards (Brassicaceae) including cabbage (*Brassica oleracea*) and turnip (*Brassica rapa*). At James Bay it seems to be most common in areas with wormseed wallflower also known as treacle mustard (*Erysimum cheiranthoides*).

OVERWINTERING STAGE: Chrysalis.

HABITAT: Prefers open areas, including woodland clearings, roadsides and even tundra. Along James Bay it occurs above the supratidal line along gravel/sand beach ridges, and in drier meadows.

DISTRIBUTION AND ABUNDANCE:
Mainly a species of western North America ranging from Alaska to northwestern Ontario and south to California and New Mexico. In Ontario, mostly a rare to uncommon sporadic breeder/migrant that has been found throughout northwestern Ontario as far east as Moosonee and to the Quebec border and north to the coast of Hudson Bay. There may be a few resident populations.

143

GREAT SOUTHERN WHITE *Ascia monuste*

♂

47–56 mm

ETYMOLOGY: *Ascia* is "axe" in Latin. In Greek mythology, *Monuste* was one of Danaus's forty-nine daughters who killed their husbands.

ADULT: The largest of the white butterflies recorded in Ontario. The FW is relatively pointed. **Upperside:** Male clear white FW with a narrow black border, the inside of which forms a zig-zag pattern. Females are similar but range from off-white to smoky grey with a more prominent dark border on both the FW and HW. **Underside:** Varies from white to creamy yellow with females having darker markings along the veins.

SIMILAR SPECIES: Looks like a large version of other whites that have few black markings on the wings.

BEHAVIOUR: This butterfly has periodic, massive emergences and migrates north where it may reach Ontario.

FLIGHT SEASON: Migrants to Ontario could occur from June to October.

Boreal/Tundra									
Mixed Forest									
Carolinian Zone				•					
	MAR	APR	MAY	JUN	JUL	AUG	SEP	OCT	NOV

CATERPILLAR: Has not been recorded in Canada. Longitudinally striped greyish and yellow with many small black dots. Head yellow. **Foodplants:** A large number of cultivated mustards (Brassicaceae).

OVERWINTERING STAGE: Does not overwinter in Ontario.

HABITAT: In the U.S., mainly coastal, disturbed habitats.

DISTRIBUTION AND ABUNDANCE:
Widespread in tropical America into Mexico and the extreme southern United States. In Ontario, a very rare, non-breeding migrant known from only a single individual observed on June 16, 1981 at Point Pelee National Park.

145

Mating Eastern Tailed Blues

THE GOSSAMER-WINGS
Family Lycaenidae

The butterflies in this family are small, delicate and most hold their wings completely closed over their backs while perched. Many species are specialists, with the caterpillars feeding on a single foodplant or a group of closely related foodplants, quite often specializing on the floral parts.

Worldwide, this family is extremely diverse with estimates of 4,000-6,000 species. A total of 36 species have been recorded in Ontario.

Many species overwinter as eggs, which allows the young caterpillars to be ready to feed on early spring plants. Other species overwinter as chrysalides; the adults emerge in early spring, breed and then lay their eggs upon freshly emerging flower buds.

Due to the extreme environmental specificity of some members of this family, many are quite rare and local. In Ontario, two such species—both lupine (*Lupinus* spp.) feeders—are now extirpated from the province—Karner Blue and Frosted Elfin.

HARVESTERS (page 152)
Subfamily: Miletinae

Although this subfamily has about 50 species worldwide, there is only a single species in North America, with most of the others occurring in Asia and Africa. Their caterpillars are unique in that they are carnivorous, feeding on other insects such as aphids.

COPPERS (page 154)
Subfamily: Lycaeninae

This subfamily is found mainly in the northern hemisphere. There are 12 species in Canada with half of those occurring in Ontario. They are mostly brownish above with some degree of dark spotting and usually some coppery-orange patches. The males of many species also have a purplish iridescence. The undersides are usually paler (whitish, grey or yellow/orange) with many dark spots. Adults often rest with their wings partially open but are also seen regularly with their wings completely closed over their backs. Most species tend to be quite local, favouring wet areas. Species' flights vary from weak to strong, but they tend to be erratic and low to the vegetation.

Summer Azures mudpuddling

HAIRSTREAKS (page 166)
Subfamily: Theclinae

A hugely diverse, although mostly tropical, subfamily found worldwide. Thirty-one species have been recorded in Canada, 18 of which have been found in Ontario; they are uncommon-to-rare and tend to be fairly local. Most are dark brown or grey on the upperside but this is rarely seen, except in flight, as they always perch with wings held completely closed over their backs (with the exception of the Gray Hairstreak which often holds its wings partially open). The underside HW is usually richly patterned with a combination of spots, streaks, wavy lines or chevrons. Many species have a dark eye-spot (called a thecla) on the margin of the HW and a large blue spot (called a lunule) below this, with hair-like "tails" projecting from below, and sometimes also from above, the eye-spot. This pattern creates the impression of a head and is thought to lure predators such as birds away from the real head. Most species sit upside-down and slowly rub their wings together, further creating the impression of a head with moving antennae.

BLUES (page 202)
Subfamily: Polyommatinae

The blues are largely a family of the northern hemisphere with 20 species recorded in Canada, 11 of which have been found in Ontario. Most of our species are uncommon-to-common residents with one species (Marine Blue) occurring only as a very rare migrant and another species (Karner Blue) formerly so rare and local that it is now extirpated from the province. As their name suggests, all of our species are mostly blue on the uppersides except for some females. They also share a similar pattern on the underside of the wings being white or pale grey with darker grey-to-black spots or smudges.

Eggs

The eggs of lycaenids are very ornate and are laid singly on the foodplant.

Banded Hairstreak

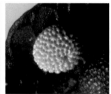

Bronze Copper

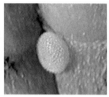

Spring Azure

Eastern Pine Elfin

Eastern Tailed Blue

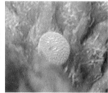

Summer Azure

Caterpillars

The caterpillars are unique among butterflies, being short, wide and somewhat flattened, similar to a sow-bug or wood-louse. They are often green but can also be grey, brown, pink or reddish. Lycaenid caterpillars are usually very difficult to find as they are extremely well camouflaged and often burrow into flowerheads. Many species secrete a sweet "honeydew" that attracts certain ant species. These ants gather the honeydew and in turn provide protection to the otherwise defenceless caterpillars from predators and parasites.

Eastern Tailed Blue

Green form of Spring Azure

Red form of Cherry Gall Azure

Chrysalides

The chrysalides are short and rounded at both ends and are usually cryptically coloured. Gossamer-wings usually pupate in the leaf litter or attach themselves to a branch where they resemble a leaf-bud.

Acadian Hairstreak

Bronze Copper

Eastern Tailed Blue

Banded Hairstreak

Coral Hairstreak

Silvery Blue

Spring Azure

Striped Hairstreak

Summer Azure

Harvester

151

HARVESTER *Feniseca tarquinius*

23–32 mm

ETYMOLOGY: *Feniseca* is from Latin *fenisex*, a mower or harvester. *Tarquinius* was the name of two kings of Rome; *Lucius Tarquinius Superbus* was a tyrant and the last king of Rome before it became a Republic.

ADULT: Small. **Upperside:** FW orange, framed with irregularly shaped blackish-brown marks and a central blackish spot. HW mostly orange, often with a row of blackish submarginal spots. **Underside:** Orange-brown to purplish-brown with many darker spots finely edged in white.

SIMILAR SPECIES: Superficially similar to some coppers, but the pattern on both the upperside and underside is unique.

BEHAVIOUR: When at rest, the adults usually hold their wings closed. Most often seen perched upon vegetation (usually on alders, *Alnus* spp.) and when disturbed have a very fast and erratic flight. Adults do not nectar at flowers but are known to feed on the honeydew produced by aphids. They can also be seen mudpuddling on the ground or feeding on carrion or dung.

FLIGHT SEASON: One to two generations per year.

	MAR	APR	MAY	JUN	JUL	AUG	SEP	OCT	NOV
Boreal/Tundra									
Mixed Forest									
Carolinian Zone									

Caterpillar ready to pupate

Caterpillar surrounded by woolly aphids

CATERPILLAR: Has relatively long hairs that are usually covered with the waxy secretions from the aphids it feeds on. If clean, the body is greenish-grey but is variable and can be marked with yellow and/or reddish tones. There is also a broad waxy white area with lobes on each segment that runs the length of the body. **Food:** Our only carnivorous butterfly caterpillar, it feeds on several species (in fact several genera) of woolly aphids (e.g., *Prociphilus* spp. and *Neoprociphilus* spp.); in much of Ontario the colonies are usually on alders. In the Carolinian Zone, however, where alders are very rare and local, Harvester larvae very likely feed on woolly aphids that feed on other tree and shrub species such as ash, beech, hawthorn and wild currant.

OVERWINTERING STAGE: Unconfirmed, but likely as a mature caterpillar or chrysalis.

HABITAT: In most of Ontario, wet areas with alders, such as alder swamps and along riverbanks. In the Carolinian Zone, deciduous and mixed woodlands along riverbanks.

DISTRIBUTION AND ABUNDANCE: Eastern North America. In Canada, ranging from southern Manitoba east to Nova Scotia. In Ontario, an uncommon and local resident found north to at least 52° N latitude.

AMERICAN COPPER *Lycaena phlaeas*

21–30 mm

ETYMOLOGY: *Lycaenus* was a mountain sacred to the Greek god Zeus. *Phlaeas* may be from the Greek *phlego* "to burn up" or from the Latin *floreo*, "to flourish".

ADULT: A small to medium-sized copper. **Upperside:** FW most boldly patterned of all our coppers—bright orange with dark spots of variable size and a brownish margin. HW dark brown with a bright orange submarginal band within which are dark spots. **Underside:** FW bright orange with white-rimmed black spots and a pale grey margin. HW pale grey with small black spots and usually a thin orange submarginal band.

SIMILAR SPECIES: When perched with wings closed, most likely to be confused with Bronze Copper which is larger and has a much wider orange submarginal band on the underside HW. No other coppers have bright orange on the upperside of the FW, although female Bronze Coppers are similarly patterned but are never bright coppery-orange.

BEHAVIOUR: Males are very aggressive and actively defend small, well defined territories. Commonly seen nectaring with half-open wings. When at rest, their wings are held completely closed.

FLIGHT SEASON: At least two overlapping generations, possibly as many as three or four in southern Ontario.

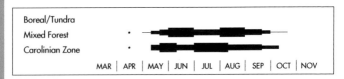

Boreal/Tundra									
Mixed Forest									
Carolinian Zone									
	MAR	APR	MAY	JUN	JUL	AUG	SEP	OCT	NOV

Form fasciata with larger black spots

CATERPILLAR: Usually pale green, with many short whitish hairs as well as tiny white dots; can sometimes be reddish and/or have white or reddish lateral stripes. **Foodplants:** Primarily docks (*Rumex* spp.) including sheep sorrel (*R. acetosella*) and curled dock (*R. crispus*).

OVERWINTERING STAGE: Not entirely certain, but likely as a chrysalis.

HABITAT: Meadows and disturbed areas including roadsides, hydro rights-of-way and vacant lots. Also found in pine-oak barrens.

DISTRIBUTION AND ABUNDANCE: A holarctic species found throughout temperate regions of North America, Europe and Asia and into the Arctic. Also found in some east African mountains. In Ontario, an uncommon-to-common resident that tends to be quite local. Mostly found south of the Sault Ste. Marie/Sudbury area but records also exist as far north as Moosonee, Thunder Bay and Atikokan.

155

GRAY COPPER *Lycaena dione*

31–36 mm

ETYMOLOGY: In Greek mythology, *Dione* was a titan, beloved by *Zeus* and the mother of *Aphrodite*.

ADULT: A large copper. **Upperside:** Relatively uniform grey. FW with two central dark spots in males and a variable number of dark spots in females. Also with a partial orange submarginal band. HW with an orange submarginal band dotted with black spots. **Underside:** Whitish-grey with many black spots. HW with an orange submarginal band.

SIMILAR SPECIES: Bronze Coppers are similar but have a wider, orange submarginal band on the HW and are orange (not whitish) on the underside FW.

BEHAVIOUR: Rapid, erratic flight, often chasing other butterflies.

FLIGHT SEASON: One generation per year.

Boreal/Tundra								
Mixed Forest			———					
Carolinian Zone								
MAR	APR	MAY	JUN	JUL	AUG	SEP	OCT	NOV

CATERPILLAR: Usually green with an orange-to-maroon stripe; can also be orange or maroon. **Foodplants:** Docks (*Rumex* spp.).

OVERWINTERING STAGE: Egg.

HABITAT: Mostly wet areas including roadside ditches and along riverbanks.

DISTRIBUTION AND ABUNDANCE: The Great Plains of the United States north into the Canadian prairies. In Ontario, a rare and local resident, restricted to the Rainy River/Lake of the Woods area.

BRONZE COPPER *Lycaena hyllus*

♂

25–38 mm

ETYMOLOGY: In Greek mythology, *Hyllus* was a giant of the kingdom of Lydia.

ADULT: A large copper. **Upperside:** Male FW coppery-brown often showing a purplish iridescence. Female FW pale orange with blackish spots and a coppery-brown margin. HW in both sexes coppery-brown with a wide orange submarginal band. **Underside:** FW orange with black spots and a grey margin. HW pale grey with many white-rimmed black spots and a wide, bright orange submarginal band.

SIMILAR SPECIES: Similar to but larger than American Copper. Female Bronze Copper has a paler orange upperside FW than the bright coppery-orange American Copper. Bronze Copper has a wider, orange submarginal band on the HW and is orange (not whitish) on the underside FW compared with Gray Copper.

BEHAVIOUR: Low, floppy flight. Usually very approachable. Commonly seen nectaring on a variety of flowers including milkweeds (*Asclepias* spp.) and smartweeds (*Persicaria* spp. and *Aconogonon* spp.).

FLIGHT SEASON: Two overlapping generations per year.

	MAR	APR	MAY	JUN	JUL	AUG	SEP	OCT	NOV
Boreal/Tundra									
Mixed Forest									
Carolinian Zone									

♀

CATERPILLAR: Yellow-green with a darker mid-dorsal stripe and typically more slender than other coppers. **Foodplants:** Mostly docks (*Rumex* spp.) including greater water dock (*R. britannica*), curled dock (*R. crispus*) and common dock (*R. occidentalis*), as well as knotweeds (*Polygonum* spp.).

OVERWINTERING STAGE: Egg.

HABITAT: Meadows, ditches and the borders of wetlands and streams.

DISTRIBUTION AND ABUNDANCE: Ranges from Colorado to Virginia north to the southern edge of the Northwest Territories and east to New Brunswick. In Ontario, an uncommon and local resident, most commonly found in southern Ontario south of the Canadian Shield, as well as in the Rainy River/Lake of the Woods area. Much rarer and very locally distributed in the north but with records extending as far as southern James Bay.

COMMENTS: Declining in urbanized areas due to the draining of wetlands.

BOG COPPER *Lycaena epixanthe*

♂

17–22 mm

ETYMOLOGY: From Greek, *epi-* means "beyond the normal, above, over"; *xanth-* means "yellow".

ADULT: Our smallest copper. **Upperside:** Greyish-brown with orange marks along the margin of the HW. FW with a few dark spots in males (more in females). Males have a purplish iridescence. **Underside:** Variable among populations. Pale whitish-grey (white form) to creamy-yellow (yellow form) with many black spots and a thin zigzag submarginal band of orange.

SIMILAR SPECIES: Both Dorcas and Purplish coppers are similar, but the underside HW is a darker orange-brown in these two species. In addition, males of these two species have more black spots on the upperside FW. Dorcas can be found in the same habitat as Bog Copper but the two tend to occupy different niches. Dorcas prefers shrubbier areas, whereas Bog tends to be found in more open areas with lower vegetation. Purplish Copper does not occur in peatlands.

BEHAVIOUR: Low, slow and weak flight. Adults almost exclusively nectar on cranberry flowers.

FLIGHT SEASON: One generation per year.

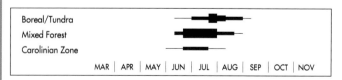

	MAR	APR	MAY	JUN	JUL	AUG	SEP	OCT	NOV
Boreal/Tundra									
Mixed Forest									
Carolinian Zone									

White form

Yellow form

CATERPILLAR: Blue-green with a darker mid-dorsal stripe and covered in many short whitish hairs. **Foodplants:** Large cranberry (*Vaccinium macrocarpon*) and small cranberry (*V. oxycoccos*).

OVERWINTERING STAGE: Egg.

HABITAT: Restricted to bogs with cranberries.

DISTRIBUTION AND ABUNDANCE:
Northeastern North America, ranging from Manitoba to Newfoundland and south to Indiana and Virginia. In Ontario, generally an uncommon and local resident but it can be common at some sites. Widely distributed in the province with populations as far south as London and as far north as Polar Bear Provincial Park.

161

DORCAS COPPER *Lycaena dorcas*

♂

19–27 mm

ETYMOLOGY: *Dorcas* was a Christian disciple; she was raised from the dead by Saint Peter. The name *dorkas* means "gazelle" or "antelope" in Greek.

ADULT: A small to medium-sized copper. **Upperside:** Brown with many scattered blackish spots (larger in females). HW with few to no orange submarginal markings, restricted to the inner portion when present. Males have a purplish iridescence. **Underside:** FW yellow-orange with many prominent dark spots. HW is a darker orange-brown with fewer and smaller dark spots and a faint orange zigzag submarginal band.

SIMILAR SPECIES: Very similar to Purplish Copper but Purplish has a much more prominent orange submarginal band on the upperside HW. Also, female Purplish is more boldly patterned on the upper FW with much more orange.

BEHAVIOUR: Fast and direct flight. Nectars on a variety of flowers, sometimes straying beyond the usual habitat in order to do so.

FLIGHT SEASON: One generation per year.

	MAR	APR	MAY	JUN	JUL	AUG	SEP	OCT	NOV
Boreal/Tundra									
Mixed Forest									
Carolinian Zone									

162

CATERPILLAR: Pale green with faint wavy lines along its length. Similar to Purplish Copper. Image not available. **Foodplants:** Shrubby cinquefoil (*Dasiphora fruticosa*, formerly *Potentilla fruticosa*).

OVERWINTERING STAGE: Egg.

HABITAT: Peatlands, as well as fields containing the foodplant.

DISTRIBUTION AND ABUNDANCE: Ranges from Alaska through most of Canada to Newfoundland and into the Great Lakes states and Maine. In most of Ontario, an uncommon-to-common but very local resident found throughout northern Ontario. In the south, it is largely confined to fens on the Bruce Peninsula and southern Georgian Bay with scattered localities as far south as Grand Bend. There are also a few isolated populations in fens in the Cambridge and Brantford area.

PURPLISH COPPER *Lycaena helloides*

♂

22–33 mm

ETYMOLOGY: In Greek, *helloides* means "growing in marshy places".

ADULT: A medium-sized copper. **Upperside:** A prominent orange, scalloped submarginal band on the HW. Male brown with a purplish iridescence, many scattered blackish spots. Female largely orange with black spots and dark brown wing margins. **Underside:** FW yellow-orange with many prominent dark spots. HW is a darker orange-brown with fewer and smaller dark spots and an orange, scalloped submarginal band.

SIMILAR SPECIES: Similar to Dorcas and Bog coppers. Underside HW is darker orange-brown than Bog Copper. Males have more black spots on dorsal FW than Bog Copper. Purplish has a much more prominent orange submarginal band on the upperside HW than Dorcas. Female Purplish is more boldly patterned on the dorsal FW with much more orange. Purplish Copper does not occur in peatlands..

BEHAVIOUR: Fast and direct flight. Nectars on many different flowers, sometimes straying far from the usual habitat.

FLIGHT SEASON: Two overlapping generations per year.

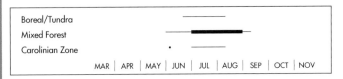

	MAR	APR	MAY	JUN	JUL	AUG	SEP	OCT	NOV
Boreal/Tundra									
Mixed Forest									
Carolinian Zone									

CATERPILLAR: Green with faint wavy lines along its length, very similar to Dorcas Copper, but note foodplant differences. **Foodplants:** Mostly knotweeds (*Polygonum* spp.) and docks (*Rumex* spp.).

OVERWINTERING STAGE: Egg.

HABITAT: Open, moist meadows, roadsides, and prairie remnants.

DISTRIBUTION AND ABUNDANCE: Largely a species of western and central portions of North America from Baja California to southern British Columbia east to the Great Lakes states. In Ontario, a rare and local resident confined to the Rainy River/Lake of the Woods area with seemingly disjunct populations on Manitoulin Island and along the north shore of Lake Huron. There are also four additional reports from scattered localities in Cochrane District and the northern portions of Algoma and Sudbury districts. Other disjunct populations once occurred in southern Ontario (Toronto, Hamilton, Paris and the Kitchener-Waterloo area) but these now appear to be extirpated.

ACADIAN HAIRSTREAK *Satyrium acadica*

24–32 mm

ETYMOLOGY: *Satyrium* is a derivative of *satyr*, a goat-like woodland deity in Greek mythology. *Acadica* is named for the old French colony of Acadia which included parts of Quebec, the Maritime provinces and northern Maine.

ADULT: Larger than most other hairstreaks. Tailed. **Upperside:** Rarely seen but uniform greyish-brown with a prominent orange spot near the tails (see Plate 6). **Underside:** HW and FW pale-grey to bluish-grey with a postmedian band of round white-rimmed black spots and a submarginal band of orange spots, including a prominent orange cap above the blue lunule on the HW.

SIMILAR SPECIES: Coral Hairstreak has brownish (not greyish) wings, no tails and lacks a blue lunule. Edwards' Hairstreak is also similar but the spots are more oval-shaped and there is little to no orange cap above the blue lunule; it is also browner on the underside. None of the other hairstreaks in Ontario have rounded spots.

BEHAVIOUR: Males perch on low vegetation, such as the tips of grasses or sedges, awaiting females. Nectars on a variety of flowers.

FLIGHT SEASON: One generation per year.

	MAR	APR	MAY	JUN	JUL	AUG	SEP	OCT	NOV
Boreal/Tundra									
Mixed Forest									
Carolinian Zone									

Light variant

Purplish form caterpillar

Green form caterpillar

CATERPILLAR: Body somewhat flattened and green or purplish with a pair of white dorsal stripes and whitish-to-yellowish diagonal dashes along the sides. **Foodplants:** Willows (*Salix* spp.).

OVERWINTERING STAGE: Egg.

HABITAT: Open, often wet, habitats including fields, riverbanks, and roadside ditches; always near willows.

DISTRIBUTION AND ABUNDANCE:
Ranges across the central and eastern portions of the northern United States and southern Canada. In Ontario, an uncommon resident found throughout southern and central Ontario as far north as Timiskaming District and Sault Ste. Marie. Also found in the Rainy River/ Lake of the Woods area as far north as Kenora.

CORAL HAIRSTREAK *Satyrium titus*

♂

23–33 mm

ETYMOLOGY: In Greek and Latin, a titan is a person or thing of enormous size or power. This species was named for the Roman Emperor *Titus* from the first century AD.

ADULT: Relatively large for a hairstreak. Lacks the tails found in other similar hairstreaks. Females have rounder wings. **Upperside:** Rarely seen but dark brown. **Underside:** HW and FW light brown with a postmedian band of small, oval, white-rimmed black spots. HW with a submarginal band of large red-orange spots and no blue lunule.

SIMILAR SPECIES: No other similar hairstreaks lack tails. See Acadian Hairstreak and Plate 6.

BEHAVIOUR: Males often perch high above ground, as much as three to four metres, defending a territory from other males and watching for females. Both sexes are avid flower visitors, most often seen nectaring on milkweeds (*Asclepias* spp.).

FLIGHT SEASON: One generation per year.

	MAR	APR	MAY	JUN	JUL	AUG	SEP	OCT	NOV
Boreal/Tundra									
Mixed Forest									
Carolinian Zone									

CATERPILLAR: Pale green or yellowish-green with bright pink patches at each end. **Foodplants:** The developing fruits of sweet cherries and plums (*Prunus* spp.) including black cherry (*P. serotina*) and chokecherry (*P. virginiana*).

OVERWINTERING STAGE: Egg.

HABITAT: Open habitats including old fields, pastures, roadsides and areas of secondary growth.

DISTRIBUTION AND ABUNDANCE: Most of the United States and southern Canada from British Columbia to Quebec. In Ontario, an uncommon resident found throughout southern and central Ontario, as far north as Timiskaming District and Sault Ste. Marie where it is decidedly rarer. Also found in the vicinity of Thunder Bay as well as in the Rainy River/Lake of the Woods area.

169

EDWARDS' HAIRSTREAK *Satyrium edwardsii*

19–31 mm

ETYMOLOGY: Named for the American entomologist William H. Edwards.

ADULT: Small to medium-sized, tailed hairstreak. **Upperside:** Rarely seen but light grey-brown and often with a small orange spot near the tail (see Plate 6). **Underside:** HW and FW light grey-brown with a postmedian band of oval white-rimmed black spots. In some individuals, this band is reduced or even absent. HW with a submarginal band of orange markings and a prominent orange, spear-shaped patch below the blue lunule and along the anal margin.

SIMILAR SPECIES: See Acadian Hairstreak. Banded and Hickory hairstreaks are similar but the postmedian bands in both species are rectangular and fused forming true bands, not ovals or spots. Also, the orange, spear-shaped patch is far less extensive in those species.

BEHAVIOUR: Males are highly territorial, defending their territories from low perches, often on oak leaves. Both sexes are avid flower visitors, often seen nectaring on milkweeds (*Asclepias* spp.) and white sweet-clover (*Melilotus albus*).

FLIGHT SEASON: One generation per year.

	MAR	APR	MAY	JUN	JUL	AUG	SEP	OCT	NOV
Boreal/Tundra									
Mixed Forest									
Carolinian Zone									

Individual with reduced spots

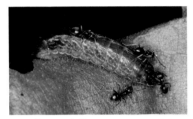

Caterpillar attended by ants (see page 150)

CATERPILLAR: Greenish-brown to reddish-brown with numerous pale diagonal dashes along the sides. **Foodplants:** The buds and leaves of various oaks (*Quercus* spp.) including both white (*Q. alba*) and black (*Q. velutina*) oaks.

OVERWINTERING STAGE: Egg.

HABITAT: Oak-forest edges as well as oak and pine-oak woodlands and barrens.

DISTRIBUTION AND ABUNDANCE:
Most of the eastern United States into Canada from southeastern Saskatchewan to Quebec. In Ontario, an uncommon resident mostly restricted to the Carolinian Zone but with some records as far north and east as Ottawa.

BANDED HAIRSTREAK *Satyrium calanus*

23–34 mm

ETYMOLOGY: *Kalanos* was an Indian sage (gymnosophist) who accompanied Alexander the Great to Greece; he died by burning himself alive.

ADULT: Medium-sized to large, tailed hairstreak. **Upperside:** Rarely seen but dark blackish-brown. **Underside:** HW and FW dark grey with a narrow postmedian band with the white edging most prominent on the outer side. HW blue lunule extends only slightly farther inward on the wing than the adjacent orange submarginal spot.

SIMILAR SPECIES: See both Edwards' and Hickory hairstreaks.

BEHAVIOUR: Males defend territories from perches, anywhere from ground level to high into the canopy. They often engage in ascending swirling "combat" flight with other males. Both sexes are avid flower visitors, often seen nectaring on milkweeds (*Asclepias* spp.), spreading dogbane (*Apocynum androsaemifolium*) and white sweet-clover (*Melilotus albus*).

FLIGHT SEASON: One generation per year.

Boreal/Tundra									
Mixed Forest									
Carolinian Zone									
	MAR	APR	MAY	JUN	JUL	AUG	SEP	OCT	NOV

Weak-patterned individual

Variant with somewhat rounded bands

CATERPILLAR: Light green or brownish with light and dark diagonal dashes along the sides and dark dorsal blotches on both ends.
Foodplants: Buds and leaves of oaks (*Quercus* spp.), hickories (*Carya* spp.) and walnuts, especially butternut (*Juglans cinerea*).

OVERWINTERING STAGE: Egg.

HABITAT: Clearings and edges within deciduous and mixed forests.

DISTRIBUTION AND ABUNDANCE: Most of the eastern United States north into Canada from southeastern Saskatchewan to Nova Scotia. In Ontario, a relatively common resident although numbers can vary, sometimes dramatically, from year to year. Primarily found in southern Ontario south of the Canadian Shield, but with records extending as far north as Sudbury and Sault Ste. Marie. Also found in the Rainy River/Lake of the Woods area.

COMMENTS: With the dramatic decline of butternut (*Juglans cinerea*) in Ontario due to butternut canker (a fungus), there could also be a decline in Banded Hairstreak since butternut is one of its preferred foodplants.

173

HICKORY HAIRSTREAK *Satyrium caryaevorus*

22–29 mm

ETYMOLOGY: *Carya* is the genus of hickory trees, *-vorus* is Latin for "eating".

ADULT: Medium-sized, tailed hairstreak. **Upperside:** Rarely seen but dark brown. **Underside:** HW and FW greyish-brown with the postmedian band gradually widening toward the top and with white edging on both sides of the band. HW blue lunule usually extends farther inward on the wing than the adjacent orange submarginal spot.

SIMILAR SPECIES: Similar to Banded Hairstreak, especially worn individuals. Hickory tends to be greyish-brown, not dark or blackish-grey. Both sides of the postmedian underside HW band tend to be edged in white in Hickory and usually only on the outer side in Banded. The postmedian band widens toward the top in Hickory, with the topmost portion (offset toward the wing's centre) as wide as the partial inner second band. In Banded, the postmedian band does not widen as dramatically toward the top; the topmost spot is typically narrower than the partial inner second band. The blue lunule on the HW typically extends farther inward in Hickory.

FLIGHT SEASON: One generation per year.

	MAR	APR	MAY	JUN	JUL	AUG	SEP	OCT	NOV
Boreal/Tundra									
Mixed Forest									
Carolinian Zone									

Worn individual

BEHAVIOUR: Breeding behaviour is little known but presumed to be similar to Banded. Nectars on milkweeds (*Asclepias* spp.) and white sweet-clover (*Melilotus albus*).

CATERPILLAR: Similar to that of Banded Hairstreak but with a complete dark mid-dorsal stripe, not just dark dorsal patches at either end as in Banded. Image not available. **Foodplants:** Mostly hickories (*Carya* spp.) but also oaks (*Quercus* spp.), ashes (*Fraxinus* spp.) and butternut (*Juglans cinerea*).

OVERWINTERING STAGE: Egg.

HABITAT: Rich deciduous forests; in clearings or along forest edges.

DISTRIBUTION AND ABUNDANCE: Most of the northeastern United States ranging into Canada only in Ontario and extreme southern Quebec. In Ontario, an uncommon resident mostly restricted to areas south of the Canadian Shield. Normally much less common than the similar Banded Hairstreak; in some years, however, Hickory Hairstreak can become quite abundant during which time it greatly outnumbers the Banded Hairstreak.

STRIPED HAIRSTREAK *Satyrium liparops*

21–28 mm

ETYMOLOGY: In Greek, *liparos* means "sleek, oily, shiny with oil" and *ops* means "eye or face".

ADULT: Medium-sized, tailed hairstreak. **Upperside:** Rarely seen but dark brown. **Underside:** HW and FW greyish-brown sometimes with a purplish tinge. The two bands are very widely spaced creating a striped appearance. HW blue lunule capped with orange.

SIMILAR SPECIES: Somewhat similar to Banded and Hickory hairstreaks but with much wider bands and with the blue lunule capped in orange.

BEHAVIOUR: Frequently seen perched relatively low on thick shrubbery near forest edge. Nectars on a wide variety of flowers.

FLIGHT SEASON: One generation per year.

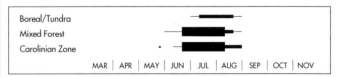

	MAR	APR	MAY	JUN	JUL	AUG	SEP	OCT	NOV
Boreal/Tundra									
Mixed Forest									
Carolinian Zone									

Variant

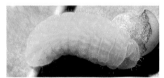

Green form caterpillar

Red form caterpillar

CATERPILLAR: Green or red with a dark mid-dorsal line and sometimes with faint diagonal yellow lines along the sides. **Foodplants:** The flowers, seeds and young leaves of trees and shrubs mostly in the Rose family (Rosaceae), including cherries and plums (*Prunus* spp.) and hawthorns (*Crataegus* spp.); also blueberries (*Vaccinium* spp.).

OVERWINTERING STAGE: Egg.

HABITAT: Deciduous and mixed forests and swamps, and open areas adjacent to them.

DISTRIBUTION AND ABUNDANCE: Most of the central and eastern United States, as well as most of southern Canada east of the Rocky Mountains east to Nova Scotia. In Ontario, an uncommon resident found throughout much of Ontario as far north as southern Cochrane District with an isolated record from Stout Lake (located at approximately 52° N in Kenora District).

OAK HAIRSTREAK *Satyrium favonius*

24–38 mm

ETYMOLOGY: In Roman mythology, *Favonius* was the personification of the west wind (*Zephryus*, in Greek mythology).

ADULT: Relatively large for a hairstreak. Tailed. **Upperside:** Rarely seen but grey-brown. **Underside:** HW and FW light grey-brown with a thin postmedian band forming a "W" near the tails. HW with a relatively small and dull blue lunule as well as reduced orange submarginal spots (compared to other *Satyrium* hairstreaks).

SIMILAR SPECIES: Unlike all other *Satyrium* hairstreaks in having an extremely thin postmedian band with the "W" near the tails. May be easily confused with the Gray Hairstreak and the rare immigrant White-M Hairstreak but note the much more extensive and brighter orange patch between the tails in the latter two species.

BEHAVIOUR: Little behavioural information is known about this species, but it is frequently seen nectaring on milkweeds (*Asclepias* spp.) and dogbanes (*Apocynum* spp.) with other hairstreaks.

FLIGHT SEASON: One generation per year.

Boreal/Tundra									
Mixed Forest									
Carolinian Zone				———					
	MAR	APR	MAY	JUN	JUL	AUG	SEP	OCT	NOV

CATERPILLAR: Variable but usually green with short reddish hairs and a yellowish lateral stripe. **Foodplants:** Buds and young leaves of oaks (*Quercus* spp.).

OVERWINTERING STAGE: Egg.

HABITAT: Oak forests and pine-oak barrens.

DISTRIBUTION AND ABUNDANCE: Largely the southeastern United States, much more isolated in the north but with populations extending as far as the New England states, Michigan and Ontario. In Ontario, a very rare and local resident with only two small colonies currently known to exist, both in Lambton County. These may be recent colonies established by migrants but they have been observed annually since 2008. A presumed stray was recorded at Point Pelee in 1999.

COMMENTS: Comprises two subspecies once considered separate species: *S. f. favonius* and *S. f. ontario* (formerly called Southern Hairstreak and Northern Hairstreak, respectively). The only entity in Ontario is the subspecies *ontario,* named so because it was described from a specimen collected at Port Stanley, Ontario in July 1868. The two subspecies were combined relatively recently and the common name Southern Hairstreak took precedence. This has been regarded by many, however, as confusing since the two subspecies would then be referred to as "Northern" Southern Hairstreak and "Southern" Southern Hairstreak. As a result, many authorities are now using the common name Oak Hairstreak.

JUNIPER HAIRSTREAK *Callophrys gryneus*

20–25 mm

ETYMOLOGY: *Callophrys* appears to be a combination of Greek words: *callo-* from *kalos* meaning "beautiful" and *ophrys* meaning "eyebrow"—perhaps a reference to the delicate band on the underwings. In Greek mythology, *Gryneus* was the surname of Apollo, one of the great gods.

ADULT: Small to medium-sized, tailed hairstreak. Our only hairstreak that is green on the underside. **Upperside:** Rarely seen but tawny in females and bronzy in males. **Underside:** A unique bright apple-green. FW with a white postmedian band edged with purplish-brown on the inside. HW with a similar postmedian band but it is broken and not straight as in the FW. HW also with two white dashes near the base.

SIMILAR SPECIES: None in Ontario.

BEHAVIOUR: Does not stray far from its larval foodplant and is most often found perched upon medium-sized eastern red cedars. Shaking the tree often causes the butterfly to fly, thus revealing its presence. After darting around for a moment, they usually land on the same perch. Nectars on a variety of flowers.

FLIGHT SEASON: One generation per year in eastern Ontario. Two generations per year at Point Pelee and Pelee Island.

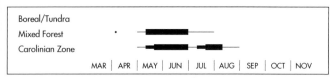

Worn individual

CATERPILLAR: Green to blue-green and bumpy with prominent white to pale yellow spots along each side of a very faint, pale mid-dorsal line. Also with white to pale yellow diagonal dashes along the sides. **Foodplants:** Eastern red cedar (*Juniperus virginiana*).

OVERWINTERING STAGE: Chrysalis.

HABITAT: Open dry habitats containing mid-sized eastern red cedar including old fields, pastures and alvars.

DISTRIBUTION AND ABUNDANCE: Widespread in the United States. In Canada, appears only in southern Saskatchewan, Ontario and extreme southern Quebec. In Ontario, a rare and local resident with two widely disjunct populations. One occurs at Point Pelee National Park and on Pelee Island. The other, larger population, occurs in eastern Ontario from the Campbellford area of Northumberland County east to the Frontenac Axis (Charleston Lake, Mallorytown Landing).

COMMENTS: Due to its relatively narrow ecological niche and habitat preference, this species is sensitive to habitat succession. When the eastern red cedars become too large and/or the habitat becomes less open due to succession, it normally disappears.

BROWN ELFIN *Callophrys augustinus*

19–26 mm

ETYMOLOGY: The species was named for the Inuit, Augustus, who guided the early 19th-century Franklin expeditions.

ADULT: Small to medium-sized, tailless elfin. **Upperside:** Rarely seen but brown to grey-brown. **Underside:** A rich reddish-brown when fresh, with the basal area much darker, especially on the HW. Worn individuals are a more uniform pale brown.

SIMILAR SPECIES: This is our most uniform elfin and the only one without any whitish frosting on the outer half of the underside HW. Very worn Hoary Elfins might be confused for Browns but they usually retain some level of whitish frosting. Very worn Henry's Elfins may also be confused for Browns but the ends of the postmedian line usually retain some white and they have a blunt tail.

BEHAVIOUR: Most often seen perched on low vegetation or directly upon the ground. Nectars on the flowers of its hostplant and often also seen mudpuddling.

FLIGHT SEASON: One generation per year.

	MAR	APR	MAY	JUN	JUL	AUG	SEP	OCT	NOV
Boreal/Tundra									
Mixed Forest									
Carolinian Zone									

Worn individual

CATERPILLAR: Yellow-green to olive-green, often unmarked but sometimes with yellowish or reddish chevrons down the back.
Foodplants: The flowers, fruits and leaves of many different plants, mostly those in the Heath family (Ericaceae) including blueberries (*Vaccinium* spp.), leatherleaf (*Chamaedaphne calyculata*), common Labrador tea (*Rhododendron groenlandicum,* formerly *Ledum groenlandicum*), common bearberry (*Arctostaphylos uva-ursi*) and laurels (*Kalmia* spp.).

OVERWINTERING STAGE: Chrysalis.

HABITAT: Habitats with acidic substrates and heath plants, including open coniferous woods, pine-oak barrens, peatlands and clearcuts.

DISTRIBUTION AND ABUNDANCE: Ranges from Alaska through most of Canada to Newfoundland and south into the eastern and western United States. In Ontario, a common and widespread resident throughout central and northern Ontario all the way to the Hudson Bay coast, much less common and more local south of the Canadian Shield.

HOARY ELFIN *Callophrys polios*

19–26 mm

ETYMOLOGY: In Greek, *polios* means "grey".

ADULT: A small, tailless elfin. **Upperside:** Rarely seen, but reddish-brown. See Plate 6. **Underside:** FW brown and narrowly frosted along the margin with a thin white postmedian band. HW dark brown basally, lighter brown on the outer half and extensively frosted (especially in fresh individuals).

SIMILAR SPECIES: Most likely to be confused with Frosted (extirpated from Ontario) and Henry's elfins, but both of these species have short tails and neither is frosted on the margin of the FW. Also note the small dark spot inward of the tail on Frosted and the white bars on either end of the postmedian band on the HW of Henry's.

BEHAVIOUR: Always perches on or very close to the ground. Often seen nectaring on common bearberry (*Arctostaphylos uva-ursi*) and other members of the Heath family (Ericaceae).

FLIGHT SEASON: One generation per year.

	MAR	APR	MAY	JUN	JUL	AUG	SEP	OCT	NOV
Boreal/Tundra									
Mixed Forest									
Carolinian Zone									

Worn individual

Burnt Lands alvar – Almonte

CATERPILLAR: Bright green with an indistinct pale lateral stripe.
Foodplants: Primarily the flowers and leaf buds of common bearberry (*Arctostaphylos uva-ursi*) but also reported from trailing arbutus (*Epigaea repens*).

OVERWINTERING STAGE: Chrysalis.

HABITAT: Open habitats including coniferous woodlands, alvars, shoreline dunes, bog edges and clear-cuts.

DISTRIBUTION AND ABUNDANCE: Ranges from Alaska through most of Canada to Nova Scotia and south into the eastern and western United States. In Ontario, an uncommon-to-common but local resident largely restricted to areas north of the southern edge of the Canadian Shield as far north as Timmins and Geraldton. Also found on Manitoulin Island and the Bruce Peninsula with an isolated population at Pinery Provincial Park and surrounding area.

FROSTED ELFIN *Callophrys irus*

22–24 mm

ETYMOLOGY: In Greek mythology, *Irus* was the father of Eurydamas (an Argonaut) and Eurytion; Irus was killed during the Calydonian boar hunt.

ADULT: A small to medium-sized elfin with a stubby tail. **Upperside:** Rarely seen, but brown to grey-brown in males and reddish-brown in females. **Underside:** A relatively uniform dark brown to reddish-brown with less contrast between the inner and outer HW than in other similar elfins. The outer HW is frosted and there is a dark spot slightly inward of the tail.

SIMILAR SPECIES: Similar to Hoary Elfin which lacks the short tails and is frosted along the FW margin. Hoary does not have the small dark spot on the underside of the HW. See Plate 6.

BEHAVIOUR: Flight low, but usually seen perched on or very near the ground.

FLIGHT SEASON: One generation per year.

Boreal/Tundra									
Mixed Forest									
Carolinian Zone			————						
	MAR	APR	MAY	JUN	JUL	AUG	SEP	OCT	NOV

Dark variant

CATERPILLAR: Pale green with a pale lateral stripe and covered in short white hairs. **Foodplants:** In Ontario, known to have fed only on the inflated seedpods of sundial lupine, also known as wild lupine (*Lupinus perennis*), but elsewhere in its range, yellow wild indigo (*Baptisia tinctoria*).

OVERWINTERING STAGE: Chrysalis.

HABITAT: Open, dry disturbed areas. In Ontario, was confined to openings in pine-oak woodlands with sandy soils.

DISTRIBUTION AND ABUNDANCE: Ranges throughout the eastern United States but it is very local, and populations are often small. Extirpated from Ontario. Prior to extirpation, this globally rare and highly local butterfly was known in Ontario only from a single site—St. Williams Forest in Norfolk County where it was last recorded in 1988.

COMMENTS: This species is conservation-listed in most of the northern portion of its range. This status is related to the fact that most colonies occur in barrens or other dry, disturbed areas that historically have been kept open by occasional ground fires. Fire suppression, leading to succession of the habitat and decline of the foodplants, combined with development, and the negative effects of grazing by White-tailed Deer, have had a serious negative impact on this specialized butterfly.

HENRY'S ELFIN *Callophrys henrici*

20–25 mm

ETYMOLOGY: Possibly named for Henry Edwards, an English-born American entomologist.

ADULT: A small to medium-sized elfin with a stubby tail. **Upperside:** Rarely seen but usually dark brown. **Underside:** Strongly two-toned, the inner wing dark blackish-brown (especially on the HW), the outer wing reddish-brown and frosted on the HW. The postmedian line that separates the two halves is white at either end.

SIMILAR SPECIES: Similar to Brown and Hoary elfins. Hoary does not have the short tail nor the white bars on either end of the postmedian band on the HW underside. Brown Elfin lacks the whitish frosting on the HW underside and has no tail. Very worn Henry's Elfins may be confused for Brown Elfins but the ends of the postmedian line usually retain some white and they have a tail. See Plate 6.

BEHAVIOUR: Usually perches on, or near, the ground up to about eye level. Often seen nectaring or mudpuddling.

FLIGHT SEASON: One generation per year.

	MAR	APR	MAY	JUN	JUL	AUG	SEP	OCT	NOV
Boreal/Tundra									
Mixed Forest									
Carolinian Zone									

Worn individual

CATERPILLAR: Variable from pale-to-dark green to reddish, with a pale mid-dorsal stripe bordered by wide diagonal dashes and with a pale lateral line. **Foodplants:** The flower buds, young fruits and leaves of a diversity of plants including blueberries (*Vaccinium* spp.) and plums (*Prunus* spp.). Also known to feed on the invasive exotic glossy buckthorn (*Frangula alnus*, formerly *Rhamnus frangula*).

OVERWINTERING STAGE: Chrysalis.

HABITAT: Openings in or near dry forested areas. Its adaptation to feed on glossy buckthorn has also enabled it to colonize small urban woodlots and wetter habitats than were previously considered typical.

DISTRIBUTION AND ABUNDANCE: Most of the eastern United States and from southern Manitoba east to Nova Scotia. In Ontario, an uncommon and local resident mostly found in eastern and central Ontario as far north as Parry Sound District and Algonquin Provincial Park where it is very rare. There are also some local populations in areas of sandy soil in the southwest in Norfolk County. Recorded from the Rainy River District in the northwest part of the province.

BOG ELFIN *Callophrys lanoraieensis*

16–19 mm

ETYMOLOGY: This species was named for the Lanoraie Bog, east of Montréal, Québec, where it was first collected.

ADULT: A tiny, tailless elfin. **Upperside:** Rarely seen, but dark orange-brown. **Underside:** FW dull brown with a narrow dark postmedian band edged in white and small black chevrons closer to the margin. HW with a complex pattern of both dark and light brown patches broken by irregular dark bands edged in white and dark, weakly developed chevrons closer to the margin. Margin with a frosted band extending inward to the dark chevrons

SIMILAR SPECIES: Very similar to Eastern Pine Elfin but the very small size and habitat (Eastern Pine is very rarely found in open spruce bogs) help identification. Bog Elfin tends to be darker and duller (not the reddish and yellowish-brown of Eastern Pine), less boldly marked and with a wider frosted band on the margin of the HW. Western Pine Elfin has more sharply pointed chevrons on the under HW.

BEHAVIOUR: Males often perch on the highest parts of black spruce and are most easily detected by shaking trees and watching individuals fly out. Less commonly, they are seen lower, nectaring on flowers of heath plants or obtaining moisture from the ground.

FLIGHT SEASON: One generation per year.

		MAR	APR	MAY	JUN	JUL	AUG	SEP	OCT	NOV
Boreal/Tundra										
Mixed Forest			·	▬▬						
Carolinian Zone										

Worn individual

Newington Bog in eastern Ontario

CATERPILLAR: Green with prominent white mid-dorsal and lateral stripes. Essentially identical to the caterpillars of the two pine elfins. Image not available. **Foodplants:** The needles of black spruce (*Picea mariana*).

OVERWINTERING STAGE: Chrysalis.

HABITAT: Mature spruce bogs, usually in the more open parts of the bog where there is some open water and short black spruce (*Picea mariana*), but they can also be found along the edges of stands of taller trees.

DISTRIBUTION AND ABUNDANCE: Very restricted range in eastern North America, the majority of the sites in a band from eastern New Hampshire through Maine to New Brunswick with isolated sites in Nova Scotia, southern Quebec and eastern Ontario. In Ontario, a very rare and highly local resident restricted to a few spruce bogs in far eastern Ontario.

191

EASTERN PINE ELFIN *Callophrys niphon*

22–27 mm

ETYMOLOGY: *Niphon* is a Japanese island and also a variation of "Nippon" which means Japan.

ADULT: A medium-sized, tailless elfin. **Upperside:** Rarely seen, but dark brown to tawny brown (see Plate 6). **Underside:** FW grey-brown to reddish-brown with a relatively wide dark postmedian band that is offset and edged in white and two short dark dashes on the inner part of the wing. FW also with small black chevrons close to a checkered margin. HW with a complex pattern of both dark and light grey-brown to reddish-brown patches broken by irregular dark bands edged in white and dark shallow chevrons close to the margin. There is a narrow frosted band before a checkered margin.

SIMILAR SPECIES: See Bog and Western Pine elfins, and Plate 6.

BEHAVIOUR: Commonly found perched on the ground along sandy trails and roadsides. Males often mudpuddle and both sexes nectar from a variety of flowers.

FLIGHT SEASON: One generation per year.

	MAR	APR	MAY	JUN	JUL	AUG	SEP	OCT	NOV
Boreal/Tundra									
Mixed Forest									
Carolinian Zone									

Worn individual

CATERPILLAR: Green with prominent white mid-dorsal and lateral stripes. Essentially identical to those of Bog and Western Pine elfins. **Foodplants:** The needles of both jack pine (*Pinus banksiana*) and eastern white pine (*P. strobus*).

OVERWINTERING STAGE: Chrysalis.

HABITAT: Jack pine forests, pine-oak woodlands and barrens.

DISTRIBUTION AND ABUNDANCE: Found in most of the eastern United States; in Canada, recorded from the Maritimes to Alberta. In Ontario, a common and widespread resident throughout central and northern Ontario, as far north as the Sandy Lake area in Kenora District but probably occurring throughout the Boreal Forest Region coincident with the range of jack pine. Less common in southwestern Ontario; locally distributed as far south as Norfolk County and the vicinity of Pinery Provincial Park.

193

WESTERN PINE ELFIN *Callophrys eryphon*

22–28 mm

ETYMOLOGY: *Eryphon* is possibly a variation of *Euryphon,* who was a celebrated Greek physician from the fifth century BCE.

ADULT: A medium-sized, tailless elfin. **Upperside:** Rarely seen, but dark chocolate-brown (see Plate 6). **Underside:** FW reddish-brown with a dark postmedian band that is usually only slightly offset and edged in white and with a single short dark dash on the inner part of the wing. FW also with prominent black chevrons close to the margin. HW with a complex pattern of both dark and light reddish-brown patches broken by irregular dark bands edged in white and usually very prominent, deeply cut chevrons close to the margin.

SIMILAR SPECIES: Very similar to Eastern Pine Elfin, especially when worn. Characters to examine: chevrons tend to be much more prominent and deeply cut in Western; HW usually has a narrow frosted margin in Eastern, unfrosted in Western; inner FW of Eastern has two short bars, usually only one in Western; FW postmedian band is usually noticeably offset in Eastern, only slightly so in Western.

BEHAVIOUR: Commonly found perched on the ground along sandy trails and roadsides. Males often mudpuddle and both sexes nectar from a variety of flowers.

FLIGHT SEASON: One generation per year.

Boreal/Tundra								
Mixed Forest								
Carolinian Zone								
	MAR	APR	MAY	JUN	JUL	AUG	SEP	OCT	NOV

Worn variant

CATERPILLAR: Green with prominent white mid-dorsal and lateral stripes. Essentially identical to those of Bog and Eastern Pine elfins. **Foodplants:** In Ontario, feeding habits are not fully understood but most likely feeds on the needles of jack pine (*Pinus banksiana*). However, in locations where jack pine is absent (e.g., parts of Algonquin Park to the south and in the Hudson Bay Lowlands to the north), it likely feeds on black spruce (*Picea mariana*), or possibly eastern white pine (*Pinus strobus*) in the south.

OVERWINTERING STAGE: Chrysalis.

HABITAT: Jack pine or other pine forests, and treed peatlands.

DISTRIBUTION AND ABUNDANCE: Largely a western species found throughout the western United States and Canada, but also across the Boreal Forest Region as far east as New Brunswick. In Ontario, an uncommon and local resident found throughout northern Ontario from the Hudson Bay Lowlands as far south as Algonquin Provincial Park with some records from Haliburton County. There is a specimen in the Canadian National Collection of Insects, Arachnids and Nematodes in Ottawa labelled Port Hope, 1912.

GRAY HAIRSTREAK *Strymon melinus*

23–29 mm

ETYMOLOGY: There is a river *Strymon* in northern Greece. In Greek, *melinos* means "ashen"; this is likely a reference to the grey colour.

ADULT: A medium-sized hairstreak with a long and a short tail.
Upperside: Dark, dull bluish-grey with a prominent orange-and-black spot between the tails. **Underside:** Both wings pale grey with a narrow tri-coloured postmedian band (white, black and reddish-orange). HW with a large orange patch between the tails containing a smaller black spot near the margin. There is also a small blue lunule below the tails.

SIMILAR SPECIES: See White-M and Oak hairstreaks.

BEHAVIOUR: One of the few hairstreaks that regularly perch with their wings open. Males have a territorial perch and are often seen in upward-spiralling flights with other intruding males.

FLIGHT SEASON: Two generations per year.

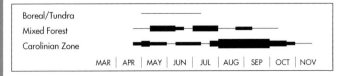

CATERPILLAR: Colour variable green, but usually with a pale lateral line. May or may not also have pale-to-purplish diagonal markings along the sides. **Foodplants:** Two populations: the resident population appears to feed only on sweet-fern (*Comptonia peregrina*), whereas the migrant population feeds on the flowers, fruits and seeds of many plants, primarily mallows (Malvaceae) and legumes (Fabaceae).

OVERWINTERING STAGE: Chrysalis.

HABITAT: The resident population is restricted to areas of sandy soil where sweet-fern grows. The migrant population is usually associated with open, disturbed areas.

DISTRIBUTION AND ABUNDANCE: Widespread, from northern South America to southern Canada, from British Columbia to Nova Scotia. In Ontario, this species comprises two populations, one of which is an uncommon and local resident, the other an uncommon breeding migrant. The resident population occurs throughout eastern and central Ontario (largely on the Canadian Shield) north to Timiskaming District. The migrant population appears to be mostly restricted to southwestern Ontario as far northeast as Toronto. What are presumably migrants have also been recorded in the Rainy River area, in southern Bruce County and in the southern portions of eastern Ontario such as Prince Edward County and Amherst Island.

COMMENTS: Why the resident population seems restricted to a single foodplant when the migrant population feeds on so many different plants is a mystery.

WHITE-M HAIRSTREAK *Parrhasius m-album*

27–34 mm

ETYMOLOGY: *Parrhasius* was a surname of the Greek god Apollo. *Albus* in Latin is "white"; *m-album* refers to the shape of the white band on the HW.

ADULT: A large hairstreak with a long and a short tail. **Upperside:** A brilliant metallic blue, easily seen in flight, but also visible during wing-rubbing at a perch. **Underside:** Both wings dark grey with a narrow white postmedian band edged in black. The HW band forms an "M" near the tails. HW also with a short white line nearer the base. There is a blue lunule on the margin below the tails and a bright reddish-orange patch between the tails and the "M".

SIMILAR SPECIES: Most similar to Gray Hairstreak but the underside postmedian line in Gray is usually tri-coloured (white, black and reddish-orange), not bi-coloured. Also, the orange spot on the HW is larger, closer to the margin and contains a black spot in Gray. The bright metallic blue upperside of the White-M is also distinctive. Also see Oak Hairstreak.

BEHAVIOUR: Fast and erratic flight. Nectars on a variety of flowers, although earlier generations are reported to spend much of their time in the canopy nectaring on the flowers of trees.

FLIGHT SEASON: Most Ontario records are from August and September but migrants have arrived as early as June.

	MAR	APR	MAY	JUN	JUL	AUG	SEP	OCT	NOV
Boreal/Tundra									
Mixed Forest						• •			
Carolinian Zone				—		———			

CATERPILLAR: Never recorded in Ontario, but olive to yellow-green sometimes with dark rusty-brown spots on the dorsum of both ends. **Foodplants:** Oaks (*Quercus* spp.).

OVERWINTERING STAGE: Chrysalis, but does not overwinter in Ontario.

HABITAT: Migrants could occur in any habitat but typical breeding habitat is deciduous forest edge and nearby clearings.

DISTRIBUTION AND ABUNDANCE: The eastern United States from Texas and Florida north to Connecticut and Iowa, occasionally straying northward. In Ontario, a very rare migrant that likely occasionally breeds in extreme southwestern Ontario, most records coming from Point Pelee and Pelee Island. There is also one record from Toronto in 1999, a record from Whitby and two records from Prince Edward County in August 2012.

COMMENTS: This species has been gradually extending its range northward and is a relatively regular breeding species in Ohio, where it produces three generations. Some individuals at Point Pelee National Park have been very fresh and it is possible that they were the offspring of migrants that arrived earlier in the season. Early generations reportedly tend to feed largely in the canopy; so it is possible that they go mostly undetected.

EARLY HAIRSTREAK *Erora laeta*

21–24 mm

ETYMOLOGY: *Erora* may be a variation of Latin *aurora* meaning "sunrise", a reference to its bright colour. It could also be a variant of *Eros*, the god of love in Greek mythology. In Latin, *laeta* means "happy".

ADULT: A small, tailless hairstreak. **Upperside:** Male dingy grey-blue with a small blue patch on the trailing edge of the HW. Female bright metallic blue with wide black borders on the FW and narrower black borders on the HW. **Underside:** Blue-green with an orange-red margin and a postmedian row of orange-red spots, straight in the FW and irregularly placed on HW. HW also has a submarginal row of orange-red chevron-shaped spots.

SIMILAR SPECIES: None.

BEHAVIOUR: Adults are thought to spend the majority of their time in the forest canopy, flying only occasionally down to the ground where they are most often encountered sipping at damp soil. During such encounters, they are often very approachable.

FLIGHT SEASON: Usually only one generation per year in Ontario (two farther south), but in 2011 a second-generation individual was photographed in Haliburton County.

Boreal/Tundra									
Mixed Forest			———	•					
Carolinian Zone									
	MAR	APR	MAY	JUN	JUL	AUG	SEP	OCT	NOV

Dorsal view

CATERPILLAR: Green to rusty-brown with dark reddish blotches.
Foodplants: First-generation individuals feed on the nuts of American beech (*Fagus grandifolia*) and possibly beaked hazelnut (*Corylus cornuta*). Early instars eat the husk before boring into the nut in order to feed on the developing seeds. Second-generation individuals are thought to feed on galls or catkins.

OVERWINTERING STAGE: Chrysalis.

HABITAT: Usually mature maple-beech forests, but some Ontario records are from younger, earlier successional forests.

DISTRIBUTION AND ABUNDANCE: Rare and local in its range from northern Wisconsin to the Maritime provinces and south through the Appalachians to Georgia. In Ontario, a rarely encountered resident. The majority of Ontario records are from eastern and central Ontario as far north as Algonquin Provincial Park. The type specimen was described from an individual collected in the early 1860s in the vicinity of London, Ontario, but this species has not been recorded since, from there or anywhere else in southwestern Ontario.

201

MARINE BLUE *Leptotes marina*

`16–25 mm`

ETYMOLOGY: In Greek, *leptotes* means "thin or delicate". In Latin, *marina* is the feminine of *marinus* meaning "of the sea".

ADULT: Usually a very small blue, but it is variable and can be medium-sized. **Upperside:** Violet-blue with white fringes and two black spots—that can often be faint—on anal margin of HW. **Underside:** Grey to grey-brown with a series of wavy white bands from the inner wing to the margin creating a zebra-stripe pattern. HW with two black spots rimmed with pale metallic blue and then orange.

SIMILAR SPECIES: No other blues in our area have such an underside pattern.

BEHAVIOUR: Fast erratic flight, usually within a small area close to the ground, for minutes before landing. Often basks with wings partially open. One of only a few gossamer-wings that regularly migrate long distances.

FLIGHT SEASON: Migrants have been recorded as early as May 19 and are capable of producing several generations per year.

Boreal/Tundra								
Mixed Forest								
Carolinian Zone		•	—	—	—			
	MAR	APR	MAY	JUN	JUL	AUG	SEP	OCT	NOV

CATERPILLAR: Extremely variable, often matching the colour of the flowers on which they feed. Vary from light green to maroon to brownish and often with pale and/or dark blotches or diagonal stripes. **Foodplants:** The flowers and fruits of legumes (Fabaceae).

OVERWINTERING STAGE: Chrysalis.

HABITAT: Woodland clearings and many disturbed habitats, e.g., fields, roadsides, and vacant lots.

DISTRIBUTION AND ABUNDANCE:
Permanent range extends from
Guatemala to the southern United
States. Wanders northward,
temporarily colonizing areas as far
north as Wisconsin. In Ontario, a
very rare migrant that has established
temporary breeding colonies twice:
once at Point Pelee National Park in
1993 resulting in three generations; and
once in Toronto in 2008.

EASTERN TAILED BLUE *Cupido comyntas*

16–26 mm

ETYMOLOGY: *Cupido* in Latin means "desire". Species may have been named for John III Comyn, Lord de Badenoch, a Scottish nobleman.

ADULT: A small to medium-sized blue, with a thin tail. **Upperside:** Male iridescent purplish-blue bordered with black with a whitish fringe and 1-3 (usually 2) orange spots near the tail. Female similar but dark brownish-grey, sometimes bluish. **Underside:** Pale greyish-white with blackish spots and dashes edged in white. Two to three orange spots, containing smaller black spots, near the tail.

SIMILAR SPECIES: Western Tailed Blue is extremely similar. Best distinguished by examining several characters: 1) the orange spots are usually much smaller in Western, sometimes non-existent on the upperside; 2) especially in males, the underside tends to be whiter in Western with smaller and paler spots; and 3) Western females are greyer above and almost always have some blue basally.

BEHAVIOUR: Often basks with wings partially open. When closed, they often rub their wings. Their flight is typically low, slow, and erratic. Nectars on a wide variety of flowers and are avid mudpuddlers.

FLIGHT SEASON: Two to three overlapping generations per year.

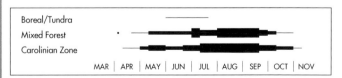

	MAR	APR	MAY	JUN	JUL	AUG	SEP	OCT	NOV
Boreal/Tundra									
Mixed Forest									
Carolinian Zone									

Fourth instar caterpillar

CATERPILLAR: Highly variable, ranging from yellow to green to pink to purplish-brown. Often with a darker mid-dorsal line and a pale lateral line. **Foodplants:** The flowers and seeds, sometimes also the leaves, of many different plants in the Legume family (Fabaceae) including vetches (*Vicia* spp.) and clovers (*Trifolium* spp.).

OVERWINTERING STAGE: Mature caterpillar, often inside a seed pod.

HABITAT: Open, often disturbed habitats, ranging from old fields and woodland clearings to roadsides and vacant lots.

DISTRIBUTION AND ABUNDANCE: Ranges from Costa Rica north through Central America and the eastern United States into Canada from southeastern Saskatchewan to New Brunswick. There is a disjunct population in the west from California north to southern British Columbia where it might have been introduced. In Ontario, a common and widespread resident, most common in southern Ontario south of the Canadian Shield. Less common and more local throughout central and northern Ontario as far north as Nakina, Cochrane District and west to the border with Manitoba. In the last fifteen years, it increased from rare to locally common in the Ottawa area.

WESTERN TAILED BLUE *Cupido amyntula*

♂

17–27 mm

ETYMOLOGY: *Amyn* means "honest, faithful and trustworthy" in Arabic.

ADULT: A small to medium-sized blue with a short, thin tail on the HW. **Upperside:** Male iridescent purplish-blue bordered with black and with a pale bluish-white fringe. There may be a small single orange spot near the tail, often none. Female is similar but is grey, usually with some blue basally. **Underside:** Whitish with small and rather dull blackish spots and dashes and one to two small orange spots, containing smaller black spots, near the tail.

SIMILAR SPECIES: See Eastern Tailed Blue.

BEHAVIOUR: Often basks with wings partially open. When perched with their wings closed, they often rub their wings, creating a distraction display for would-be predators. Their flight is typically low, slow, and erratic. Nectar on a wide variety of flowers and are avid mudpuddlers.

FLIGHT SEASON: One to two overlapping generations per year.

	MAR	APR	MAY	JUN	JUL	AUG	SEP	OCT	NOV
Boreal/Tundra									
Mixed Forest									
Carolinian Zone									

CATERPILLAR: Indistinguishable from Eastern Tailed Blue. **Foodplants:** Flowers and pods of several different legumes (Fabaceae) including peas (*Lathyrus* spp.) and milk-vetches (*Astragalus* spp.).

OVERWINTERING STAGE: Mature caterpillar.

HABITAT: Unlike Eastern Tailed Blue, seldom found in disturbed areas, but tends to favour forest clearings and shrub thickets.

DISTRIBUTION AND ABUNDANCE: Ranges from Alaska across Canada to Ontario and south through the western United States to northern Mexico. There is also an isolated population in the Gaspé Peninsula of Quebec and northern New Brunswick. In Ontario, an uncommon-to-common resident throughout the north from Hudson Bay south to Timiskaming District, south of which it becomes far less common, with records as far south as Algonquin Provincial Park where it is decidedly rare. Also seems relatively common on Manitoulin Island.

SPRING AZURE *Celastrina lucia*

18–28 mm

ETYMOLOGY: In Greek, *kelastros* is the name of an evergreen tree. The plant genus, *Celastrus* (bittersweet) and *Celastrina* are derived from this name. In Latin, *lucia* is "light".

ADULT: A small to medium-sized blue. **Upperside:** Male pale blue with a black-and-white checkered fringe. Female similar but the FW has a wide, blackish margin. **Underside:** Variable, being one of three forms: 1) "lucia" is the darkest form, with a medium grey ground colour, a large darker grey patch in the central HW, numerous large darker grey blotches on the FW that typically bleed into one another, and darker grey margins on both wings; 2) "marginata" has a medium grey ground colour with numerous blackish spots on both the FW and HW and a dark margin on the HW; 3) "violacea" is the rarest of the three forms and is pale grey with scattered blackish spots and streaks of varied shapes and a row of paler blackish submarginal spots inwardly bordered by equally pale crescents.

SIMILAR SPECIES: See Summer and Cherry Gall azures, and Plate 5.

BEHAVIOUR: Flight is usually fast and erratic. Often perches on or very close to the ground, with wings completely closed. Less commonly seen with wings partially open, at which times they are usually perched upon a leaf. Regularly seen mudpuddling.

FLIGHT SEASON: One generation per year.

	MAR	APR	MAY	JUN	JUL	AUG	SEP	OCT	NOV
Boreal/Tundra									
Mixed Forest									
Carolinian Zone									

Form "violacea"

♀

Form "lucia"

Form "marginata"

CATERPILLAR: Essentially identical to that of Summer Azure (see page 213). **Foodplants:** Flowers and developing fruits of a variety of early-flowering trees and shrubs including cherries (*Prunus* spp.), viburnums such as hobblebush (*Viburnum lantanoides*) and nannyberry (*V. lentago*), as well as blueberries (*Vaccinium* spp.).

OVERWINTERING STAGE: Chrysalis.

HABITAT: Woodland clearings and along forest edges.

DISTRIBUTION AND ABUNDANCE: Alaska through most of Canada and into the northern United States. Common and widespread resident throughout Ontario.

COMMENTS: The genus *Celastrina* is currently in a state of taxonomic flux. Some experts believe that what was once considered a single species actually comprises at least three species in Ontario: Spring, Summer and Cherry Gall azures. We have chosen to follow this arrangement. The spring-flying species that is still called Spring Azure has been further split by some experts: the northern form, *C. lucia*, that we call Spring Azure is now referred to by some authors as Northern Azure; and a more southern form, *C. ladon*, that has not been recorded in Ontario but likely occurs in the Carolinian Zone.

CHERRY GALL AZURE *Celastrina serotina*

♀

25–29 mm

Female laying eggs on cherry galls

ETYMOLOGY: S*erotina* is the feminine form of the Latin adjective *serus* meaning "coming late". This is a reference to their appearance in late spring.

ADULT: A small to medium-sized blue. **Upperside:** Male FW pale blue with a slightly checkered fringe. HW also pale blue but usually with a white margin and sometimes with white scaling along the veins. Female similar but the FW has a wide black margin and the HW has extensive whitish scaling with a row of black submarginal spots. **Underside:** Usually somewhere between the very white and poorly marked pattern of Summer Azure and the more heavily patterned Spring Azure.

SIMILAR SPECIES: Individuals fall somewhere in between those of Spring and Summer azures, being more similar to Spring Azure. Due to the difficulty of identifying adults, most if not all individuals are probably only identifiable when one follows closely the flights of azures in a given area, in any given year. Proximity to cherry trees with leaf galls is also helpful. See Plate 5.

BEHAVIOUR: Poorly known, but presumably like that of Spring and Summer azures.

FLIGHT SEASON: One generation per year. Adults generally fly between the flight periods of the Spring and Summer azures.

	MAR	APR	MAY	JUN	JUL	AUG	SEP	OCT	NOV
Boreal/Tundra									
Mixed Forest									
Carolinian Zone									

Reared on cherry galls

Green form

♀

♂

Reared on cherry galls

CATERPILLAR: Essentially identical to those of Spring and Summer azures (see page 213). Identifiable mostly by foodplant associations. **Foodplants:** Thought to feed primarily on the leaf galls created by eriophyid mites, mostly on cherries (*Prunus* spp.).

OVERWINTERING STAGE: Chrysalis.

HABITAT: Poorly known, but presumably anywhere cherries grow and are infested with eriophyid mites.

DISTRIBUTION AND ABUNDANCE: Distribution poorly known due to its similarity to both Spring and Summer azures and the fact that it has only relatively recently been described as a distinct species. Appears to be restricted to the northeastern United States and southeastern Canada from Ontario to Nova Scotia. In Ontario, it is likely an uncommon (perhaps common) resident and is currently known to occur throughout southern and central Ontario as far north as southern Sudbury District.

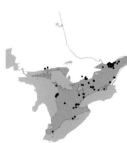

SUMMER AZURE *Celastrina neglecta*

♀

23–29 mm

ETYMOLOGY: *Neglecta* is Latin for "not chosen, neglected or overlooked". This may be a reference to its small size or the difficulty of identifying closely related species of *Celastrina*.

ADULT: A small to medium-sized blue. **Upperside:** Male FW pale blue with a black or checkered fringe, HW with extensive white scaling and usually a white fringe. Female similar but the FW has a black margin extending in from the fringe and, like the HW, has extensive whitish scaling. **Underside:** Almost always like "violacea" form of Spring Azure but usually whiter than Spring Azure with smaller and duller blackish markings.

SIMILAR SPECIES: Spring Azure form "violacea" very similar but tends to be greyer with larger and bolder blackish markings on the underside. Spring Azure also lacks the extensive white scaling on the upperside. In addition, these two species rarely, if ever, overlap in flight time in any given area. See also Cherry Gall Azure, and Plate 5.

BEHAVIOUR: Like that of Spring Azure. See photo of mudpuddlers on page 148.

FLIGHT SEASON: Two to three generations per year.

	MAR	APR	MAY	JUN	JUL	AUG	SEP	OCT	NOV
Boreal/Tundra									
Mixed Forest									
Carolinian Zone									

Pink form of caterpillar   Green form of caterpillar

CATERPILLAR: Usually green but can be pink with mid-dorsal and dark lateral stripes. Identifiable from almost identical Spring Azure by timing and foodplant associations. **Foodplants:** The flowers and developing fruit of shrubs including dogwoods (*Cornus* spp.), New Jersey tea (*Ceanothus americanus*), meadowsweets (*Spiraea* spp.) and viburnums (*Viburnum* spp.), such as northern wild raisin (*V. cassinoides*) and highbush cranberry (*V. trilobum*).

OVERWINTERING STAGE: Chrysalis.

HABITAT: Woodland clearings and along forest edges, but also found in open disturbed sites.

DISTRIBUTION AND ABUNDANCE: Found in most of the eastern and central United States and in southern Canada from southeastern Saskatchewan to Nova Scotia. A common and widespread resident throughout southern and central Ontario with a few scattered records along the north shore of Lake Superior and then west through the Rainy River/Lake of the Woods area. Appears to be largely absent from the Boreal Forest Region.

SILVERY BLUE *Glaucopsyche lygdamus*

18–28 mm

ETYMOLOGY: In Latin, *glaucus* (in Greek *glaukos*) means "bluish-green or grey" as well as "silvery, gleaming". In Greek mythology, *Psyche* was the companion of Eros and sometimes is represented as a butterfly. *Lygdamus* was a slave of Cynthia, a mistress of the Roman poet Propertius.

ADULT: A small to medium-sized blue. **Upperside:** Male silvery-blue with narrow black margins on wings. Females are brown often with some extensive bluish scaling at the wing bases. **Underside:** Medium grey with a row of very round black spots ringed in white on both the wings.

SIMILAR SPECIES: No other blues have very round spots ringed in white with a lack of any other wing markings (e.g., marginal bands, orange spots, etc.). Poorly marked Greenish Blues can be superficially similar, but always have a row of submarginal and usually also marginal markings on the undersides and a black spot in the centre of the upperside FW. See Plate 5.

BEHAVIOUR: Flight is usually low to the ground but very active. Perches mostly on or near the ground and often seen nectaring or mudpuddling.

FLIGHT SEASON: One generation per year.

	MAR	APR	MAY	JUN	JUL	AUG	SEP	OCT	NOV
Boreal/Tundra									
Mixed Forest									
Carolinian Zone									

Green form of caterpillar   Pink form of caterpillar

CATERPILLAR: Variable depending on the food source. Green when feeding on leaves. Whitish to pink to purplish when feeding on flowers. Always with a dark dorsal stripe often bordered by pale diagonal stripes. Often accompanied by ants. **Foodplants:** The flowers and leaves of legumes (Fabaceae), including tufted vetch (*Vicia cracca*), white sweet-clover (*Melilotus albus*) and alfalfa (*Medicago sativa*).

OVERWINTERING STAGE: Chrysalis.

HABITAT: Open woodland, meadows, old fields, roadsides and vacant lots.

DISTRIBUTION AND ABUNDANCE: Alaska through most of Canada and the western United States, as well as the northeastern United States and south through the Appalachians to Georgia. In Ontario, common resident throughout but, until relatively recently, largely absent from southwestern Ontario (there is a single record from Brant County in 1936 and a few scattered records in the 1970s to 1990s). Currently, this species is expanding its range southwestward in the province; research is being done to determine factors in this expansion.

215

NORTHERN BLUE *Plebejus idas*

17–28 mm

ETYMOLOGY: In Latin, *plebeius* means "common, of the common people". In Greek mythology, *Idas* was an Argonaut and a participant in the Calydonian boar hunt.

ADULT: A small to medium-sized blue. **Upperside:** Male bright iridescent blue with a thin black margin, white fringe and sometimes faint black spots along the trailing edge of the HW. Female greyish-brown, sometimes with some blue scaling, and usually with orange-capped blackish spots along the trailing edge of the HW. **Underside:** Pale grey with many prominent black spots. HW also with a marginal row of black and metallic blue spots capped with orange.

SIMILAR SPECIES: Similar to Karner Blue but the ranges of these two species do not overlap.

BEHAVIOUR: Often basks with wings partially open.

FLIGHT SEASON: One generation per year.

	MAR	APR	MAY	JUN	JUL	AUG	SEP	OCT	NOV
Boreal/Tundra									
Mixed Forest									
Carolinian Zone									

CATERPILLAR: Greenish-blue with a pale lateral stripe. **Foodplants:** Heaths (Ericaceae) including black crowberry (*Empetrum nigrum*), dwarf bilberry (*Vaccinium caespitosum*), common Labrador tea (*Rhododendron groenlandicum*, formerly *Ledum groenlandicum*) and sheep laurel (*Kalmia angustifolia*).

OVERWINTERING STAGE: Egg.

HABITAT: Open habitats including coastal tundra, peatlands, open spruce forest, clear-cuts, burns and roadsides.

DISTRIBUTION AND ABUNDANCE:
Holarctic. In North America ranging from Alaska through most of Canada to Newfoundland and south into the northwestern United States and the northern Great Lakes states. In Ontario, an uncommon resident found throughout the Boreal Forest Region from the Hudson Bay Lowlands south to the Wawa area.

217

KARNER BLUE *Plebejus samuelis*

18–28 mm

ETYMOLOGY: Vladimir Nabokov, the famous author and lepidopterist, honoured the pioneer American lepidopterist Samuel Scudder with *samuelis*.

ADULT: A small to medium-sized blue. **Upperside:** Male pale blue with very narrow black margins and a whitish fringe. Female dark brown to blackish with blue on the inner portions of both the HW and FW and a submarginal row of black-centred orange spots on the HW. **Underside:** Whitish to pale grey with numerous black spots. HW with a submarginal row of prominent orange spots margined by a row of blue-centred black spots.

SIMILAR SPECIES: The Northern Blue is similar but the ranges of these two species do not overlap in Ontario. Also similar to the introduced European Common Blue that occurs in Quebec, but has not yet been found in Ontario. See Plates 4 and 5.

BEHAVIOUR: A largely sedentary species with a weak flight, not straying far from patches of sundial lupine.

FLIGHT SEASON: Two generations per year.

Boreal/Tundra										
Mixed Forest										
Carolinian Zone										
	MAR	APR	MAY	JUN	JUL	AUG	SEP	OCT	NOV	

Sundial lupine

CATERPILLAR: Body green with a darker green mid-dorsal stripe and whitish lateral stripes. **Foodplants:** Feeds only on sundial lupine also known as wild lupine (*Lupinus perennis*).

OVERWINTERING STAGE: Egg.

HABITAT: Open dry pine-oak woodland with sandy soils and sundial lupine.

DISTRIBUTION AND ABUNDANCE: Restricted to the northeastern United States from Wisconsin to southern New Hampshire. In Ontario, formerly a rare and highly local species known from a few sites in the southwest as far north as Toronto and thought likely to have occurred also in the Rice Lake Plains of Northumberland County. This species is now extirpated from Ontario, with the last two populations (Port Franks, Lambton County and St. Williams Forest, Norfolk County) surviving until a serious drought occurred in 1988. Efforts are underway to consider re-introducing this species to Ontario from populations in the United States.

COMMENTS: The Karner Blue was considered a subspecies of the more western Melissa Blue (*Plebejus melissa*) but recent taxonomic work suggests that it is a separate species.

GREENISH BLUE *Plebejus saepiolus*

21–28 mm

ETYMOLOGY: *Saepiolus* may be from the Latin *saepio*, to "limit, protect, delineate".

ADULT: A small to medium-sized blue, with strongly angled FWs.
Upperside: Male pale metallic blue with a narrow blackish margin and a white fringe. Female is dusky brown with some blue on the inner portions of the wings and a faint submarginal row of black-capped orange spots on HW. Both sexes have a black spot in the middle of the FW. **Underside:** Male whitish-grey with numerous black spots narrowly outlined in white. Females are similar but tend to be slightly darker grey with more prominent spots.

SIMILAR SPECIES: The "violacea" form of male Spring Azure is similar but lacks the central dark spot on the upperside of the FW and has less angled FWs than Greenish Blue. See also Silvery Blue and Plate 5.

BEHAVIOUR: Usually flies low to the ground; and are avid mudpuddlers.

FLIGHT SEASON: One generation per year.

	MAR	APR	MAY	JUN	JUL	AUG	SEP	OCT	NOV
Boreal/Tundra									
Mixed Forest									
Carolinian Zone									

CATERPILLAR: Green with a white lateral stripe edged with pink.
Foodplants: The flowerheads of clovers, including white clover (*Trifolium repens*) and Alsike clover (*T. hybridum*).

OVERWINTERING STAGE: Late instar caterpillar.

HABITAT: A variety of open, often wet, habitats.

DISTRIBUTION AND ABUNDANCE: In North America, ranges from Alaska through most of Canada into the northern Great Lakes states and Maine, also south through the mountains of the western United States to New Mexico. In Ontario, an uncommon resident found from the Hudson Bay Lowlands south to Manitoulin Island.

COMMENTS: Sometime in early 1900s this species began expanding its range southward and was collected relatively commonly in the 1920s and 1930s in Parry Sound, Nipissing and Muskoka districts, and in Renfrew and Victoria (now City of Kawartha Lakes) counties. This expansion south of the Boreal Forest Region has retracted, however, since there are no records from most of this area since 1968 and not from Algonquin Park since 1998. Why this species first expanded its range southward and has since retracted is a mystery.

ARCTIC BLUE *Plebejus glandon*

17–23 mm

ETYMOLOGY: Unknown.

ADULT: A small blue. **Upperside:** Male dark greyish-blue with dusky wing margins and usually with dark spots along the trailing edge of the HW. There are short dark bars often ringed in white in the middle of each wing. Female similar but dark grey to greyish-brown. **Underside:** FW grey with black spots ringed in white. HW grey with large white patches, some of which have grey or blackish spots in the centres.

SIMILAR SPECIES: None.

BEHAVIOUR: Fast, erratic flight very low to the ground. Its grey coloration creates the impression of a small moth.

FLIGHT SEASON: One generation per year.

Boreal/Tundra				▬■▬				
Mixed Forest								
Carolinian Zone								
	MAR	APR	MAY	JUN	JUL	AUG	SEP	OCT	NOV

CATERPILLAR: Green with reddish dorsal marks and covered in long, fine hairs. **Foodplants:** The buds and flowers of many different plants in the Primrose family (Primulaceae), Legume family (Fabaceae) and Saxifrage family (Saxifragaceae). In Ontario, it has been recorded ovipositing only on black crowberry (*Empetrum nigrum*).

OVERWINTERING STAGE: Chrysalis.

HABITAT: Dry open places including tundra and old beach ridges.

DISTRIBUTION AND ABUNDANCE: Holarctic. In North America, ranges from Alaska through most of western and northern Canada east to Newfoundland. Also ranges through the mountains of the western United States to New Mexico. In Ontario, an uncommon resident restricted to the far north. Although there are records 40 km south of the Hudson Bay coast, most records are from coastal or near-coastal areas. This is, however, probably an artifact of accessibility, with inland sites being much more difficult to access and therefore seldom surveyed. The true southernmost extent of the range is yet to be determined.

223

Painted Ladies

THE BRUSHFOOTS
Family Nymphalidae

One of the most diverse families with many well known species, brushfoots are usually medium-sized to large. Whereas a number are highly localized due to their habitat and foodplant needs, some are widespread and common and often visit gardens. One thing they all have in common is that they have only two pairs of functional legs as the third, frontal pair (the brushfooted forelegs) is small and held under the head. A number of these butterflies are also our strongest and most highly visible migrants. A total of 51 brushfoot species have been recorded in Ontario.

Many of the twelve global subfamilies of brushfoots were formerly considered families; the common character of brushfooted forelegs has resulted in their being combined into one family. There are seven subfamilies represented in Ontario: Snouts (Libytheinae), Monarchs (Danainae), Admirals (Limenitidinae), Longwings and Fritillaries (Heliconiinae), Emperors (Apaturinae), Anglewings, Tortoiseshells, Thistle Butterflies, Peacocks, Checkerspots and Crescents (Nymphalinae), Satyrs and Wood-nymphs (Satyrinae). In Ontario, the species in this family overwinter as caterpillars or adults.

In addition to the Monarch, one other brushfoot species recorded from Ontario is considered at risk by the federal *Species at Risk Act*. Weidemeyer's Admiral is listed as Special Concern, but it has been recorded only once in Ontario as a stray.

SNOUTS (page 234)
Subfamily: Libytheinae

This is a very small worldwide family of 12 species. The sole North American species is, like all members of the subfamily, noted for its long "snout" formed by an extension of the labial palps on the head. The humpbacked caterpillar has no spines and the chrysalis is quite plain.

MILKWEED BUTTERFLIES (page 236)
Subfamily: Danainae

This is a mostly tropical subfamily of large butterflies with four representatives in North America; only the Monarch reaches Ontario. The caterpillars are mostly distasteful, acquiring toxins from their hostplants. This toxicity is passed on to the adults. The smooth caterpillars are brightly coloured often with filaments. Chrysalides are smooth with metallic spotting.

ADMIRALS (page 238)
Subfamily: Limenitidinae

The admirals are a diverse group; found worldwide. The eggs are laid singly on tree leaves. Young caterpillars mimic bird droppings. Mature caterpillars have an expanded thorax with two branching spines. As winter approaches, partly grown caterpillars roll up a leaf for a shelter. Adults are usually woodland species and feed on rotting fruit and animal dung. They are often seen sipping moisture on dirt roads. Some admirals are so closely related that they regularly hybridize, and intermediate forms can be seen. Some members, such as the Viceroy and Red-spotted Purple, belong to mimicry associations with other species, some of which are in other families.

LONGWINGS AND FRITILLARIES (page 246)
Subfamily: Heliconiinae

The longwings or heliconians are found throughout tropical America with a few species occurring in southern

North America. Only one species, the Gulf Fritillary, is known to stray occasionally as far north as Canada.

The fritillaries have about 35 species in North America, but only 11 have been recorded in Ontario. These species fall into two main groups, the greater fritillaries (genus *Speyeria*) and the lesser fritillaries (genus *Boloria*). There is also a single member in the genus *Euptoieta*. All are orange with intricate dark brown to black markings on the uppersides. They are best identified by the complex underside HW patterns.

Eggs are laid singly, often away from the foodplants—mainly violets for all of the greater fritillaries and for many of the more southerly lesser fritillaries. The caterpillars feed at night and are seldom seen. They have branching spines but not on the head. The greater fritillaries hibernate as first instar larvae while the lesser fritillaries mostly overwinter in the fourth instar. A few northern species take two years to develop and overwinter both years as caterpillars. Chrysalides have small dorsal cones.

The members of this subfamily occupy a wide range of habitats in Ontario, some general and some highly specialized.

EMPERORS (page 270)
Subfamily: Apaturinae

This is a small worldwide subfamily with 12 species in North America, only two of which are found in Ontario, Tawny Emperor and Hackberry Emperor. The adult females are larger and lighter than the males.

The smooth caterpillars have two tails on the hind end and two horns on the head. They overwinter as caterpillars in rolled-up leaf tents. The unusual chrysalides of both our species are flattened and lie flat on a leaf rather than hanging from vegetation as in most other species.

The butterflies are found in forests with hackberry trees (*Celtis* spp.), the larval foodplants, and are often seen resting on trunks and branches.

THISTLE BUTTERFLIES, TORTOISESHELLS, ANGLEWINGS, PEACOCKS, CHECKERSPOTS AND CRESCENTS (page 274)
Subfamily: Nymphalinae

This is a large and varied subfamily with about 130 species in North America. Twenty species have been recorded from Ontario. The caterpillars have branching rows of spines along the body; chrysalides are angular, often with metallic spots. Ontario Nymphalinae fall into five groups.

1. The three Ontario thistle butterflies (genus *Vanessa*) are all migrants. The Painted Lady is probably the most cosmopolitan of all butterflies, flying on every continent except Antarctica.

2. There are three tortoiseshells (genus *Nymphalis*) found in Ontario. They have similar, scalloped wing-edges and undersides, but the patterning and colour of the uppersides are unique. These are among the longest-lived of Ontario butterflies with only one generation per year and all overwinter as adults.

3. The seven Ontario anglewings (genus *Polygonia*) are orange with black spots above and all have uniquely angled and lobed wing margins and very cryptically marked underwings, giving them the appearance of a dead leaf when at rest with wings closed. The bright silver mark in the centre of the lower HW varies from species to species. Anglewing caterpillars are the only brushfoots with a pair of spines on the head, with the exception of Compton Tortoiseshell which also has these spines. The adults and caterpillars of the *Polygonia* species are highly variable and can be difficult to tell apart. They overwinter as adults.

4. There is only one member of the mainly tropical group of peacock butterflies (genus *Junonia*) that migrates to Ontario—the Common Buckeye.

5. The 50 species in the checkerspot and crescent group (genera *Euphydryas*, *Chlosyne* and *Phyciodes*) are restricted to the Western Hemisphere with seven members in Ontario. They are all orange with black or brown markings on the

uppersides, and each species has relatively distinctive markings on the underside of the HW. The eggs are mostly laid in large numbers on plants of the Sunflower family (Asteraceae) where the caterpillars often live in colonies in spun webs. The caterpillars have six rows of branching spines and overwinter partially grown; after emerging in the spring they tend to live singly.

SATYRS AND WOOD-NYMPHS (page 314)
Subfamily: Satyrinae

The species in this subfamily are usually drab orange to dark brown, several also having prominent eye-spots. There are 50 species in North America, with 12 found in Ontario. The FW veins of all Satyrinae have enlargements at their bases which are thought to be hearing organs. The caterpillars are smooth, green or brown, with short, forked tails. They all feed on grasses and sedges in Canada. Satyrinae hibernate as caterpillars; some in the north take two years to develop. Chrysalides are unornamented, but often have two horns. Except for several fast-flying members of the genus *Oeneis* (the arctics), they have a weak, bouncy flight. None migrate and all usually rest with wings closed.

Mourning Cloak and Question Mark

Eggs

The eggs of this family are ovoid to barrel-shaped and, in keeping with the diverse nature of the group, are laid singly or in clusters on or near the larval foodplants.

Milbert's Tortoiseshell

Baltimore Checkerspot

Meadow Fritillary

Common Buckeye

Painted Lady

Variegated Fritillary

Northern Pearly Eye

Monarch

Mourning Cloak

Northern Crescent

Pearl Crescent

Question Mark

Red-spotted Purple

Silvery Checkerspot

Red Admiral

Caterpillars

The caterpillars mostly have branched spines all along the body or just on the thorax and live either on their own or in large groups.

Mourning Cloak, first instars

Mourning Cloak communal early instars

American Lady

Question Mark – dark form

Gorgone Checkerspot – communal nesting

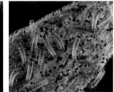
Pearl Crescent – first instars

Chrysalides

The chrysalides are mostly hung by a hook, called a
cremaster, from a pad of silk.

Milbert's Tortoiseshell

Baltimore Checkerspot

Common Buckeye

Silvery Checkerspot

Painted Lady

Meadow Fritillary

Viceroy

Northern Pearly Eye

Monarch

Arctic Fritillary

Mourning Cloak

Northern Crescent

Pearl Crescent

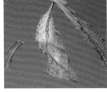
Eastern Comma

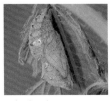
Red Admiral

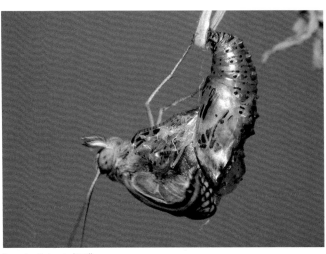
Emerging Variegated Fritillary

AMERICAN SNOUT *Libytheana carinenta*

41–51 mm

ETYMOLOGY: In Hebrew, *Liby* means "god's promise", *thea* is a Greek word for goddess. *Libythea* is an old world genus; the *na* was added to the end to create the New World (North American) genus. *Carinenta* is a derivative of the Latin *carina* or "keel".

ADULT: Medium-sized. This butterfly gets its common name from the "snout" on its head. It also has cut-off edges to the FW tips giving it an unusual silhouette when seen from the side. **Upperside:** Brown with orange towards the base and with four largish, white spots towards the tips of the FW. **Underside:** HW is mottled purplish-grey and the white spots on the FW mirror those on the upperside.

SIMILAR SPECIES: None.

BEHAVIOUR: A very strong migratory species. Often perch on tree limbs with wings closed appearing to be a dead leaf, the snout looking like the stem. This camouflage likely provides some protection from predators.

FLIGHT SEASON: Two to three generations.

	MAR	APR	MAY	JUN	JUL	AUG	SEP	OCT	NOV
Boreal/Tundra									
Mixed Forest									
Carolinian Zone									

CATERPILLAR: Pale green with a thin, pale yellow, mid-dorsal line and thicker lateral lines. **Foodplants:** Various hackberries (*Celtis* spp.). In Ontario, it has been recorded feeding only on common hackberry (*Celtis occidentalis*).

OVERWINTERING STAGE: Not known to overwinter in Canada, but as an adult in the southern United States.

HABITAT: Woodland edges usually close to hackberry trees. Migrants can be found in many different habitats.

DISTRIBUTION AND ABUNDANCE: Permanent range extends from Argentina north to the southern United States and migrates north throughout most of the eastern United States. In Ontario, a rare-to-uncommon breeding migrant regularly appearing in the Carolinian Zone of southwestern Ontario, with occasional strays north of their breeding range (e.g., Manitoulin Island and Algonquin Park). Since 2008, small numbers of adults have appeared every year in the same small grove of isolated common hackberries in the Fletcher Wildlife Garden in Ottawa where they likely have successfully bred. There are other stands of common hackberry in eastern Ontario which may also support local breeding populations.

COMMENTS: The American Snout used to be considered a member of its own very small butterfly family, the Libytheidae, with separate species scattered on different continents and islands around the world. The North American form was once considered a different species from that which occurred from Mexico south, but these are now considered to be the same species.

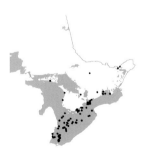

MONARCH *Danaus plexippus*

93–105 mm

ETYMOLOGY: *Danaus* refers to a mythical king of Argos in ancient Greece. *Plexippus* was Danaus' nephew who was killed by his wife, Amphicomone, one of Danaus' daughters.

ADULT: One of the largest butterflies in Ontario. **Upperside:** Bright orange broken up by black along the veins with a black marginal band punctuated by many small, white spots. The males have a black scent patch along a vein towards the bottom of the HW. **Underside:** Similar to upperside but the HW a lighter orange.

SIMILAR SPECIES: The Viceroy is very similar in coloration but is generally smaller and has a black postmedian band crossing the HW.

BEHAVIOUR: Most often seen gliding in open areas, nectaring on large flowers or clusters of flowers, often with its wings beating. During migration, seen moving deliberately in a north or south direction depending on the season. In late summer and fall, they gather along the north shores of the Great Lakes and can often be seen clinging, sometimes in large concentrations, to trees before heading across the waters.

FLIGHT SEASON: Two overlapping generations, sometimes three, in the southern parts of the province.

	MAR	APR	MAY	JUN	JUL	AUG	SEP	OCT	NOV
Boreal/Tundra									
Mixed Forest									
Carolinian Zone									

CATERPILLAR: Banded black, white and yellow with two fleshy filaments at both ends. **Foodplants:** Milkweeds (*Asclepias* spp.). In Ontario, most often common milkweed (*A. syriaca*), swamp milkweed (*A. incarnata*), and butterfly milkweed (*A. tuberosa*).

OVERWINTERING STAGE: Does not overwinter in Ontario, but migrates to a few sites in the mountains of central Mexico where adults have been known to concentrate in the tens of millions.

HABITAT: Open areas, such as meadows, roadsides, gardens and woodland clearings.

DISTRIBUTION AND ABUNDANCE: While Central and North American in its origins, the Monarch has spread to, and now breeds on, most other continents, even the Pacific islands. The North American population that takes part in the annual return migration, occurs throughout the United States and southern Canada. In Ontario, a common breeding migrant but numbers fluctuate from year to year depending on many factors, particularly its overwintering success in Mexico. In good years, they flourish with very large numbers building up from late summer to early fall. In poor years, far fewer individuals arrive but if conditions are good for breeding, their numbers can rise quickly.

COMMENTS: Listed as a species of Special Concern by SARA and ESA 2007.

WHITE ADMIRAL *Limenitis arthemis arthemis*

47–78 mm

ETYMOLOGY: *Limenitis* may come from the Latin *limus* meaning "a priestly apron trimmed with purple" and *itus* meaning "a movement or departure". *Arthemis* was the Greek goddess of the hunt.

ADULT: Medium-sized to large. **Upperside:** Purplish-black with a broad white band crossing all four wings. The HW has rows of bluish spots along the margin and in some individuals a row of red spots as well. **Underside:** Blackish with bluish-green marginal spots and red submarginal and basal spots. There is also a broad white band crossing the wings.

SIMILAR SPECIES: Besides the Weidemeyer's Admiral (with a single Ontario record), there are no other Ontario species similar to this one.

BEHAVIOUR: Usually not flower visitors, but can be seen feeding on animal dung and rotting fruit. They also like to perch on leaves or on the ground soaking up the warmth of the sun.

FLIGHT SEASON: Two overlapping generations.

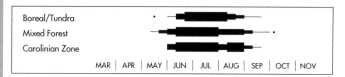

	MAR	APR	MAY	JUN	JUL	AUG	SEP	OCT	NOV
Boreal/Tundra									
Mixed Forest									
Carolinian Zone									

Brown form

White Admiral/Red-spotted Purple hybrid

CATERPILLAR: Brown or olive, and humpbacked, with two branching spines and a white saddle. **Foodplants:** Mainly willows (*Salix* spp.), aspens and poplars (*Populus* spp.) and birches (*Betula* spp.).

OVERWINTERING STAGE: Partly grown caterpillar.

HABITAT: Forest edges and openings.

DISTRIBUTION AND ABUNDANCE: Found across the northern United States and throughout the forested regions of Canada. In Ontario, a common resident recorded from Norfolk County on Lake Erie north to Hudson Bay.

COMMENTS: In Ontario, there are two very different-looking subspecies of *L. arthemis*, the White Admiral and the Red-spotted Purple (pages 240–241). In the broad zone of overlap of these two subspecies, hybrid forms can be found regularly with varying portions of the white bands present.

RED-SPOTTED PURPLE *Limenitis arthemis astyanax*

47–78 mm

ETYMOLOGY: In Greek mythology, *Astyanax* was the son of Hector and Andromache. The young child was thrown from a wall and killed by the Greeks after the Trojan War.

ADULT: Medium-sized to large. **Upperside:** Purplish-black but the hindwings are usually iridescent blue; no white bands. Some individuals have a row of red spots on HW. **Underside:** Purplish-black with marginal blue spots and a submarginal row of red spots and basal red spots.

SIMILAR SPECIES: The Red-spotted Purple is part of a mimicry complex which includes the Pipevine Swallowtail. In Ontario, the Red-spotted Purple is the only member of that mimicry complex that lacks tails and has basal red spots. See Plate 1.

BEHAVIOUR: Most often seen on the ground with open wings absorbing heat from the sun. Feeds on sap, rotting fruit and dung.

FLIGHT SEASON: Two overlapping generations per year.

	Boreal/Tundra								
Mixed Forest								
Carolinian Zone								
	MAR	APR	MAY	JUN	JUL	AUG	SEP	OCT	NOV

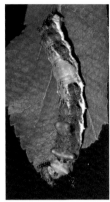

Brown form

Variant with red spots on HW

Olive form

CATERPILLAR: Brown or olive, and humpbacked, with two branching spines and a whitish saddle. **Foodplants:** Mainly willows (*Salix* spp.), aspens and poplars (*Populus* spp.) and birches (*Betula* spp.).

OVERWINTERING STAGE: Partly grown caterpillar.

HABITAT: Forest edges.

DISTRIBUTION AND ABUNDANCE:
Widespread in the eastern United States to southern Ontario, where it is a common resident, largely restricted to the Carolinian Zone, but also found on the Bruce Peninsula to Manitoulin Island, and east to Prince Edward County.

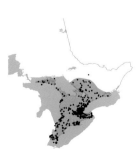

COMMENTS: Both subspecies of *L. arthemis* occasionally hybridize with the Viceroy producing a number of varying-coloured forms (page 244).

WEIDEMEYER'S ADMIRAL *Limenitis weidemeyerii*

55–72 mm

ETYMOLOGY: Named in 1861 by the lepidopterist, W. H. Edwards, in honour of his friend, J. W. Weidemeyer.

ADULT: Medium-sized to large. **Upperside:** Black with broad white bands across the middle of all wings and with small submarginal white spots. **Underside:** Similar broad white median band and marginal whitish spots on all wings. HW base is banded grey and white.

SIMILAR SPECIES: This species is unlikely to be seen in Ontario. Similar to White Admiral dorsally but Weidemeyer's has white submarginal spots. Best distinguished by examining the undersides, especially the HW base: banded grey and white in Weidemeyer's, dark with red spots in White Admiral.

BEHAVIOUR: Often seen flying around thickets at water's edge.

FLIGHT SEASON: One generation per year.

Boreal/Tundra									
Mixed Forest				•					
Carolinian Zone									
	MAR	APR	MAY	JUN	JUL	AUG	SEP	OCT	NOV

CATERPILLAR: Not likely to be found in Ontario. Mottled grey and white with a brown saddle and a humped back. **Foodplants:** Willows (*Salix* spp.) and poplars (*Populus* spp.).

OVERWINTERING STAGE: Partially grown caterpillar, but not known to overwinter in Ontario.

HABITAT: River edges and stream sides.

DISTRIBUTION AND ABUNDANCE: Western United States from New Mexico to the extreme southwestern edge of Alberta and east to Iowa. There is only one Ontario record; the specimen is in the Canadian National Collection of Insects, Arachnids and Nematodes in Ottawa. It is labelled Rainy River, Ontario, 14 July, 1960 and is not thought to be mislabelled but likely a stray.

COMMENTS: Listed as a species of Special Concern under the federal *Species at Risk Act.*

VICEROY *Limenitis archippus*

53–81 mm

ETYMOLOGY: *Archippus* means "master of horses" in Greek; the name may refer to the Greek comic poet Archippus.

ADULT: Medium-sized to large. **Upperside:** Dark orange with black veins and a thick dark border with white spots. There are three other large white spots in a black leading-edge FW patch. The HW has a black postmedian line crossing the veins (faint or missing in some individuals). **Underside:** Similar to the upperside but the HW and tip of the FW are a lighter orange.

SIMILAR SPECIES: The Monarch is larger with a more pointed FW and lacks the black postmedian line on the HW.

BEHAVIOUR: Often nectars on milkweeds (*Asclepias* spp.), thistles (*Cirsium* spp. and *Carduus* spp.) and other common flowers. The males usually patrol a territory awaiting females.

FLIGHT SEASON: Two generations.

244

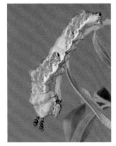

Green caterpillar

White Admiral-Viceroy hybrid

Brown caterpillar

CATERPILLAR: Light brown or greenish-white with a humpbacked thorax with two branching spines. There is a light saddle crossing the body giving it the appearance of a bird dropping. **Foodplants:** The leaves of mainly willows (*Salix* spp.) and poplars (*Populus* spp.).

OVERWINTERING STAGE: Half-grown caterpillar.

HABITAT: Wet meadows, marsh edges and roadsides.

DISTRIBUTION AND ABUNDANCE: Widespread from central Mexico through most of the United States and Canada to the southern Northwest Territories. In Ontario, a common resident found from southern Ontario north to central James Bay and Favourable Lake near the Manitoba border.

COMMENTS: The Viceroy was previously thought to be palatable but gained protection from predators by looking like the distasteful Monarch—an example of Batesian mimicry. It is now known that the Viceroy is also distasteful—an example of Mullerian mimicry.

GULF FRITILLARY *Agraulis vanillae*

72–100 mm

ETYMOLOGY: *Vanilla* is Spanish for "little pod". *Agraulis* – origin of name unknown.

ADULT: Large, with elongated forewings. **Upperside:** Bright orange with black veins and marginal black markings. There are three black spots with white centres near the leading edge of the FW. **Underside:** The brownish-orange undersides have striking elongated, bright silvery-white markings.

SIMILAR SPECIES: Superficially resembles the greater fritillaries, but the elongated wings are distinctive.

BEHAVIOUR: Often seen rapidly beating its wings and hovering over flowers.

FLIGHT SEASON: In the southern United States, this butterfly is on the wing year-round, but strays north between June and October. The three Canadian records were all recorded in June.

Boreal/Tundra								
Mixed Forest								
Carolinian Zone			•					
MAR	APR	MAY	JUN	JUL	AUG	SEP	OCT	NOV

CATERPILLAR: Has not been recorded in Canada. Orange with several dark lines running along the body and black spines. **Foodplants:** Passion flowers (*Passiflora* spp.) which do not grow in Canada, except as indoor ornamentals.

OVERWINTERING STAGE: Does not overwinter in Ontario, but as an adult in the southern United States.

HABITAT: Migrants could occur in any open areas.

DISTRIBUTION AND ABUNDANCE: Widespread and common in the tropical Americas, ranging north into the southern United States. In Ontario, a very rare non-breeding migrant known only from a single record—June 20, 2010 when one was photographed at Rondeau Provincial Park.

COMMENTS: This species should not be expected in Ontario, but should still be looked for along the shore of Lake Erie.

VARIEGATED FRITILLARY *Euptoieta claudia*

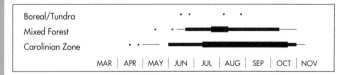

44–60 mm

ETYMOLOGY: *Euptoieta* is derived from the Greek for "easily scared", whereas *claudia* likely refers to one of the Roman Emperors named Claudius.

ADULT: Medium-sized, with somewhat pointed forewings. **Upperside:** Tawny-orange with a complex pattern of black spots and dashes including a row of dark submarginal spots and a paler creamy-orange median band. **Underside:** HW is mottled light brown with a pale median patch, a row of smudgy submarginal dark spots and a greyish margin.

SIMILAR SPECIES: Superficially similar to the greater fritillaries (*Speyeria* spp.) but Variegated lacks the silver underside HW spots.

BEHAVIOUR: An active and rapid-flying butterfly, often keeping low and nectaring on a variety of flowers.

FLIGHT SEASON: Several generations per year.

	MAR	APR	MAY	JUN	JUL	AUG	SEP	OCT	NOV
Boreal/Tundra									
Mixed Forest									
Carolinian Zone									

Darker variant

CATERPILLAR: Reddish-orange with alternating dorsal patches of black and white and rows of black spines. **Foodplants:** A wide variety of plants from many families, including violets (*Viola* spp.), flaxes (*Linum* spp.) and plantains (*Plantago* spp.).

OVERWINTERING STAGE: Likely as an adult, but not known to overwinter in Ontario. See COMMENTS below.

HABITAT: A variety of open, often disturbed, habitats.

DISTRIBUTION AND ABUNDANCE: Mainly a tropical butterfly ranging from Argentina north into the southern United States. Migrates northward and regularly colonizes most of the United States as well as the prairie provinces. In Ontario, a rare breeding migrant with the possibility of becoming more common later in the summer if several generations are produced. It has been found as far north as the Albany River in extreme northeast Thunder Bay District. In 2012, this species was locally common in southwestern Ontario.

COMMENTS: Since 1996, a colony has been recorded on the Ile-d'Orléans, near Québec City. It is obviously overwintering which means it could possibly do the same in parts of Ontario.

BOG FRITILLARY *Boloria eunomia*

32-40 mm

ETYMOLOGY: *Boloria* may refer to an Asian mountain, Mount Bolor. *Eunomia* was a daughter of the Greek god Zeus.

ADULT: Small to medium-sized. **Upperside:** Dark orange with a complicated pattern of black spots and lines. The wing bases are covered in long, dark scales creating a dark, fuzzy appearance. The HW often, but not always, has a row of whitish marginal spots. **Underside:** HW reddish with bands of pearly-white spots, including a distinctive submarginal band of small, round, dark-rimmed spots.

SIMILAR SPECIES: Dorsally, very similar to all other lesser fritillaries but the whitish marginal spots are distinctive, when present. Ventrally, most similar to the Silver-bordered Fritillary but Silver-bordered lacks the submarginal row of round, dark-rimmed pearly-white spots.

BEHAVIOUR: Tends to be a strong flyer, regularly visiting bog flowers. Usually stays low to the ground and stays close to peatlands.

FLIGHT SEASON: One generation per year.

Boreal/Tundra								
Mixed Forest								
Carolinian Zone								
	MAR	APR	MAY	JUN	JUL	AUG	SEP	OCT	NOV

CATERPILLAR: Silvery-grey with whitish spines and fine white dotting. **Foodplants:** Willows (*Salix* spp.) are preferred but in bogs near Ottawa, caterpillars have been recorded feeding on small cranberry (*Vaccinium oxycoccos*) and creeping snowberry (*Gaultheria hispidula*).

OVERWINTERING STAGE: Caterpillar.

HABITAT: In much of Ontario, acidic peatlands dominated by sphagnum moss, but also wet tundra on the Hudson Bay coast. While regularly seen in some peatlands, it can be absent from similar-looking sites in the same area.

DISTRIBUTION AND ABUNDANCE: Holarctic, found in colder climates around the Northern Hemisphere, including most of Canada south through the Rocky Mountains to Colorado and into bordering areas of the northeastern United States.

In Ontario, an uncommon and local resident (more common in the north), ranging from the Hudson Bay Lowlands to isolated bogs in northern Peterborough County.

COMMENTS: Once a resident of the Mer Bleue Bog just east of Ottawa, but has not been seen there since 1908.

SILVER-BORDERED FRITILLARY *Boloria selene*

35–51 mm

ETYMOLOGY: *Selene* was the Titan goddess of the moon in Greek mythology.

ADULT: Small to medium-sized, the largest of the Ontario members of this genus. **Upperside:** Bright orange with black margins containing small orange spots, a row of black submarginal spots and a complex pattern of zigzag lines on the inner halves of the wings and little dark basal colouring. **Underside:** HW is patterned with cream and brick-red and has numerous bright silvery-white markings, including along the margin. The silver margin is also present in the FW. There is a distinctive silver-rimmed black spot near the base of the HW.

SIMILAR SPECIES: Dorsally, similar to the other *Boloria* species, but note the more complete dark margin of Silver-bordered containing small orange spots. The greater fritillaries (*Speyeria* spp.), with their bright silver markings on the undersides, are superficially similar but are all considerably larger. See Bog Fritillary.

BEHAVIOUR: An avid flower visitor, particularly on asters and daisies, it can be a quick flyer.

FLIGHT SEASON: Two overlapping generations in most of Ontario; one in northern areas.

| | MAR | APR | MAY | JUN | JUL | AUG | SEP | OCT | NOV |

Boreal/Tundra
Mixed Forest
Carolinian Zone

CATERPILLAR: Colour variable from greyish to black and has four rows of spines running along the body. The first two spines are longer than the others. **Foodplants:** Violets (*Viola* spp.).

OVERWINTERING STAGE: Half-grown caterpillar.

HABITAT: Open wet meadows and wetland edges.

DISTRIBUTION AND ABUNDANCE: Widespread throughout the Holarctic region. Found across Canada from Yukon to Newfoundland and south into the northern United States. In Ontario, it is a common resident in wetter habitats throughout most of the province. Uncommon to rare and local in extreme southwestern Ontario.

COMMENTS: Recent taxonomic work suggests that the North American and Eurasian populations are distinct. If so, our species would be renamed *Boloria myrina*. The common name in North America, Silver-bordered Fritillary, would, however, likely still stand as the species in Europe is commonly called Pearl-bordered Fritillary.

MEADOW FRITILLARY *Boloria bellona*

35–44 mm

ETYMOLOGY: *Bellona* was the goddess of war in Roman mythology.

ADULT: Small to medium-sized, with the FW squared off at tip.
Upperside: Orange with black markings as follows: a marginal
row of faint chevrons, an inner marginal row of elongated spots, a
submarginal row of round spots and inner bands of zigzag lines.
Black dusting towards the wing bases. **Underside:** HW lacks silver or
white spots and is mottled orange and purplish-brown with a lighter
anvil-shaped marking towards the forward edge and frosted with pale
violet along the outer half when fresh.

SIMILAR SPECIES: Ventrally, very similar to Frigga Fritillary but note
the squared-off wing tips of Meadow. Also, Frigga has much darker
wing bases when viewed dorsally. The lack of silver or pearly-white
spots on the underside HW combined with a lack of a black border
on the uppersides distinguish this species from all other *Boloria*
species in Ontario.

BEHAVIOUR: Flight low and slow, visits many open-area flowers,
preferring those that are yellow.

FLIGHT SEASON: Two to three generations in southern Ontario; two
generations in much of the rest of the province with the exception of
the far north where there is likely only one.

CATERPILLAR: Purplish-black to dark brown with yellow dots at the bases of brown to yellow-brown spines. Each segment has spines. **Foodplants:** Violets (*Viola* spp.).

OVERWINTERING STAGE: Caterpillar.

HABITAT: Open, often wet, habitats, including meadows, roadsides, pastures, forest clearings and sometimes peatlands.

DISTRIBUTION AND ABUNDANCE: Widespread across most of southern Canada from eastern British Columbia to Newfoundland and into the northern and eastern United States. In Ontario, considered the most common *Boloria* species in southern Ontario, but becomes less common farther north and west in the province ranging all the way to the Hudson Bay Lowlands.

COMMENTS: The nominate subspecies *bellona* is found in the more southerly parts of the province; the darker subspecies *toddi* is found in the north.

FRIGGA FRITILLARY *Boloria frigga*

32–41 mm

ETYMOLOGY: In Norse mythology, *Frigga* was the goddess of clouds, sky, love and marriage; she was the wife of Odin.

ADULT: Small to medium-sized. **Upperside:** Orange with a marginal row of elongated black spots and a submarginal row of round black spots and extensive black scaling towards the base, particularly on the HW. **Underside:** HW is frosted pale violet on the outer edge and mottled orange and brown towards the base. There is a prominent pale patch along the leading edge toward the base.

SIMILAR SPECIES: Dorsally, most similar to Freija Fritillary as both have dark wing bases but Freija has chevrons along the wing margins rather than the elongated spots of Frigga. See Meadow Fritillary and Plate 8.

BEHAVIOUR: Males patrol most of the day searching for females.

FLIGHT SEASON: One generation per year. Flight season is relatively short.

	MAR	APR	MAY	JUN	JUL	AUG	SEP	OCT	NOV
Boreal/Tundra									
Mixed Forest									
Carolinian Zone									

CATERPILLAR: Black with black spines and light purplish or white lines running down the sides. **Foodplants:** Willows (*Salix* spp.) and possibly birches (*Betula* spp.).

OVERWINTERING STAGE: Mature caterpillar.

HABITAT: Willow thickets in the boreal forest, bogs and wet areas on the tundra.

DISTRIBUTION AND ABUNDANCE: Holarctic. In North America, ranges across most of Canada and south into the northern Great Lakes states and through the Rocky Mountains to Colorado. In Ontario, an uncommon and local resident limited to the northern parts of the province, north of a line from the shore of Lake Superior east to northern Timiskaming District.

COMMENTS: As this butterfly is found in remote parts of the province, its seeming rarity may be an artifact of few observers.

FREIJA FRITILLARY *Boloria freija*

28–38 mm

ETYMOLOGY: *Freija* was the Norse goddess of love and fertility as well as war and death.

ADULT: Small to medium-sized. **Upperside:** Tawny-orange, individuals usually have alternating black and orange wing margins, an inner marginal row of black chevrons, a submarginal row of black spots and an inner pattern of black zigzag lines with dark basal scaling, especially on the HW which can look quite hairy. **Underside:** HW reddish-brown with a jagged silvery-white line across the centre of the wings bordered on the inside by black chevrons and with several larger silvery-white markings in the basal area, the most distinctive of which is a hook-shaped marking nearest the base.

SIMILAR SPECIES: Of the northern *Boloria* species, the Arctic Fritillary is closest in appearance. Dorsally, the marginal black markings of the inner row are triangle-shaped in Arctic, not chevrons as in Freija and the inner HW is not as dark in Arctic. Ventrally, Freija usually has a more prominent, silvery, irregular band across the underside HW and large silvery markings in the basal area of the wings. See Frigga Fritillary and Plate 8.

BEHAVIOUR: The earliest flyer among the northern *Boloria* species.

FLIGHT SEASON: One generation per year.

	MAR	APR	MAY	JUN	JUL	AUG	SEP	OCT	NOV
Boreal/Tundra									
Mixed Forest									
Carolinian Zone									

CATERPILLAR: Spined, brown with light spotting. **Foodplants:** Blueberries (*Vaccinium* spp.) and common bearberry (*Arctostaphylos uva-ursi*).

OVERWINTERING STAGE: Caterpillar.

HABITAT: Willow-dominated bogs and open jack pine woodlands of the Boreal Forest Region.

DISTRIBUTION AND ABUNDANCE: Holarctic. In North America, ranges across most of Canada and south into the northern Great Lakes states and through the Rocky Mountains to New Mexico. In Ontario, an uncommon-to-common resident found throughout northern Ontario south to Wawa and northern Timiskaming District.

COMMENTS: This species was recorded from an extensive and largely inaccessible bog near Ottawa, called the Mer Bleue that features a great deal of blueberry on open sphagnum but has not been recorded there since June 1911.

ARCTIC FRITILLARY *Boloria chariclea*

32–44 mm

ETYMOLOGY: *Chariclea* was the heroine of the Greek romance, *Aethiopica*, by Heliodorus.

ADULT: Small to medium-sized. **Upperside:** Dark orange with black patterning as follows: thin black margin, inner marginal row of triangle-shaped spots, submarginal row of rounded spots and an inner pattern of zigzag lines with relatively little dark basal scaling. **Underside:** HW is dark reddish to purplish with marginal silvery-white dashes capped by purple triangles, particularly in the boreal subspecies *grandis*, and a submarginal row of black spots. The tundra subspecies *arctica* has very reduced or absent purple triangles on the underside margins and usually a more prominent row of silvery markings in the centre of the underside HW.

SIMILAR SPECIES: See Freija Fritillary and Plate 8.

BEHAVIOUR: Flies rapidly, close to the ground, and will chase after other butterflies coming into its territory.

FLIGHT SEASON: One generation every one to two years. It probably has a one-year life cycle in most of the province, but may take up to two years in the far north.

	MAR	APR	MAY	JUN	JUL	AUG	SEP	OCT	NOV
Boreal/Tundra									
Mixed Forest									
Carolinian Zone									

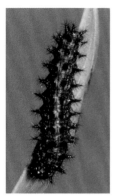

CATERPILLAR: Grey and black with orange spines. **Foodplants:** Willows (*Salix* spp.) and smartweeds (*Aconogonon* spp. and *Persicaria* spp.).

OVERWINTERING STAGE: Caterpillar.

HABITAT: A range of habitats from wet, moist meadows in the tundra to boreal woodlands and peatlands farther south.

DISTRIBUTION AND ABUNDANCE: Widespread across Canada and south into the Rocky Mountains as far as northern New Mexico, the western Great Lakes states and northern Maine and New Hampshire. In Ontario, a common northern resident, as far south as the north shore of Lake Superior and Timiskaming District with several scattered records in southern Algoma District.

COMMENTS: This butterfly has a complicated taxonomic history. At one time, most experts agreed that there were two Holarctic species—*Boloria chariclea*, a tundra species, and *Boloria titania*, a species of the Boreal regions. Today, however, most experts agree that the Eurasian and North American populations are separate species with *B. titania* being restricted to Eurasia and *B. chariclea* being restricted to North America. Evidence suggests that the tundra and boreal subspecies in North American may be different species.

GREAT SPANGLED FRITILLARY *Speyeria cybele*

62–88 mm

ETYMOLOGY: *Speyeria* refers to Adolph Speyer, a noted eighteenth-century German lepidopterist; *cybele* refers to the Greek earth goddess, Cybele.

ADULT: The largest of the four Ontario greater fritillaries, particularly the females. **Upperside:** Male bright orange with extensive black markings and extensive black veining. Females are a yellowish-brown with extensive blackish scaling basally. **Underside:** HW pale-brown to orange-brown with a wide yellow submarginal band and many large silvery-white spots.

SIMILAR SPECIES: Atlantis Fritillary, and especially Aphrodite Fritillary, are similar, but both have a narrower yellow submarginal band on the underside HW. See Plate 7.

BEHAVIOUR: A very active butterfly that feeds on large multi-headed flowers, such as milkweeds (*Asclepias* spp.), thistles (*Cirsium* spp. and *Carduus* spp.) and spotted Joe Pye weed (*Eutrochium maculatum* var. *maculatum*).

FLIGHT SEASON: One generation per year.

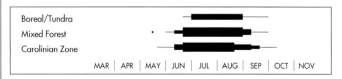

Boreal/Tundra			
Mixed Forest			
Carolinian Zone			
	MAR APR MAY JUN JUL AUG SEP OCT NOV		

CATERPILLAR: Black on the back and brown on the sides. The many spines are yellow at the base. **Foodplants:** Many species of violets (*Viola* spp.).

OVERWINTERING STAGE: Newly hatched caterpillars.

HABITAT: Open meadows, roadsides and forest clearings; also recorded from urban habitats.

DISTRIBUTION AND ABUNDANCE:
Widespread in North America, ranging from interior British Columbia to Nova Scotia and south throughout most of the United States. In Ontario, a common resident (often the most numerous of the greater fritillaries in southern Ontario) found across the province as far north as Sioux Lookout and southern James Bay.

APHRODITE FRITILLARY *Speyeria aphrodite*

♂

51–73 mm

ETYMOLOGY: In Greek mythology, *Aphrodite* is the goddess of love and beauty.

ADULT: Medium-sized to large with yellow-green eyes. **Upperside:** Male bright orange with many black markings including a black spot (sometimes small) close to the body near the trailing edge of upper FW. The margins are usually orange, bordered on each side by a thin black line. Female similar but usually duller orange with darker basal scaling. **Underside:** HW cinnamon-brown to brick-red with many silvery-white spots and a narrow, yellow submarginal band. The darker ground colour bleeds into the yellow band.

SIMILAR SPECIES: See Great Spangled Fritillary. Can be very similar to Atlantis Fritillary. Examine several characters to confirm identity: 1) Eye colour yellow-green in Aphrodite, blue-grey in Atlantis; 2) HW underside typically dark brown in Atlantis, reddish-brown in Aphrodite; 3) upperside wing margins, especially the FW, usually dark and solid in Atlantis, orange-bordered with black in Aphrodite; and 4) upperside FW veins typically thickened by black scales in male Atlantis, not so in Aphrodite. See Plate 7.

BEHAVIOUR: Regularly visits large flowers.

FLIGHT SEASON: One generation per year.

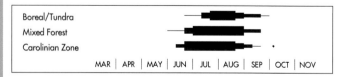

	MAR	APR	MAY	JUN	JUL	AUG	SEP	OCT	NOV
Boreal/Tundra									
Mixed Forest									
Carolinian Zone									

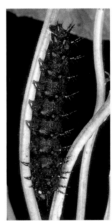

CATERPILLAR: Brownish-black with light striations and spines with black bases. **Foodplants:** Violets (*Viola* spp.).

OVERWINTERING STAGE: First instar caterpillar, before they feed.

HABITAT: Open areas in or near forests, but can also be found in open meadows.

DISTRIBUTION AND ABUNDANCE:
Widespread across southern Canada and northern United States, east of the Rocky Mountains to the Atlantic coast. In Ontario, a common resident that may be found throughout the province. Much less common in extreme southwestern Ontario and the far north.

REGAL FRITILLARY *Speyeria idalia*

66–92 mm

...

ETYMOLOGY: *Idalia* is from the Greek meaning "behold the sun".

ADULT: A large and distinctive fritillary, and the most easily identified of Ontario's greater fritillaries. **Upperside:** FW is typical of fritillaries except the black markings are reduced in size. Most of HW is black with an orange-spotted submarginal band (white in female) and a white-dotted medial band. **Underside:** HW is dark brown with the largest silver/white spots of any greater fritillary.

SIMILAR SPECIES: None.

BEHAVIOUR: Males patrol their grassland habitat often stopping for nectar. Mating occurs in early summer, but females do not lay eggs until August.

FLIGHT SEASON: One generation per year.

	MAR	APR	MAY	JUN	JUL	AUG	SEP	OCT	NOV
Boreal/Tundra									
Mixed Forest					—	—			
Carolinian Zone					—		•		

CATERPILLAR: Brown with yellow lines and black spots. Unlike other greater fritillaries, they feed in daytime. **Foodplants:** Violets (*Viola* spp.).

OVERWINTERING STAGE: First instar caterpillar, before they feed.

HABITAT: Restricted to grasslands such as tallgrass prairies.

DISTRIBUTION AND ABUNDANCE: In the United States, the Regal Fritillary was formerly found in grasslands from Maine west to Colorado, but it has now disappeared from most of the eastern United States due, at least in part, to loss of habitat. In Canada, it has been recorded in Manitoba, Saskatchewan (one record), and extreme southwestern Ontario. There were likely breeding colonies in appropriate habitat in southwestern Ontario but, if so, they are all now extirpated. The only recent record is a female observed at Holiday Beach on Lake Erie on October 2, 2000, likely a stray from elsewhere.

COMMENTS: While not to be expected in Ontario, butterfly watchers should always consider this species when they are in native grasslands in the summer. In addition, strays could show up in any open habitat.

ATLANTIS FRITILLARY *Speyeria atlantis*

50–64 mm

ETYMOLOGY: In Greek mythology, Atlantis was a mythical lost continent.

ADULT: The smallest and darkest of the three resident greater fritillaries. Eyes blue-grey. **Upperside:** Variable: dark orange to yellowish-orange with heavy black markings. The outer margins are usually solid black, at least on the FW, and the FW veins are thickened in males by black scales. **Underside:** HW dark purplish to chocolate-brown with a narrow yellow submarginal band and many large silvery-white spots.

SIMILAR SPECIES: See Great Spangled Fritillary. Can be very similar to Aphrodite Fritillary. Examine several characters to confirm identity: 1) Eye colour yellow-green in Aphrodite, blue-grey in Atlantis; 2) HW underside typically dark brown in Atlantis, reddish-brown in Aphrodite; 3) upperside wing margins, especially the FW, usually dark and solid in Atlantis, orange-bordered with black in Aphrodite; and 4) upperside FW veins typically thickened by black scales in male Atlantis, not so in Aphrodite. See Plate 7.

BEHAVIOUR: A rapid-flying butterfly that often visits spotted Joe Pye weed (*Eutrochium maculatum* var. *maculatum*), its favourite nectar source.

FLIGHT SEASON: One generation per year.

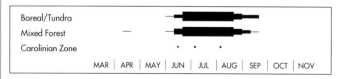

	MAR	APR	MAY	JUN	JUL	AUG	SEP	OCT	NOV
Boreal/Tundra									
Mixed Forest									
Carolinian Zone									

Bright variant

CATERPILLAR: Mostly black with grey or brown stripes and orange spines. **Foodplants:** Violets (*Viola* spp.).

OVERWINTERING STAGE: First instar caterpillar, before they feed.

HABITAT: Open clearings in or near woodlands and forests.

DISTRIBUTION AND ABUNDANCE: Widely distributed across Canada (south of the Territories) and south through the Rocky Mountains to Colorado and into the northeastern United States. In Ontario, a common resident (mostly north of the southern edge of the Canadian Shield) north to the coast of Hudson Bay. Less common south of the Shield and absent from extreme southwestern Ontario.

COMMENTS: In western Canada, there is a great deal of confusion in the taxonomy of this species and former subspecies have been reclassified as species.

HACKBERRY EMPEROR *Asterocampa celtis*

♂

39–47 mm

ETYMOLOGY: *Asterocampa* is from Greek *aster* meaning "star" and from Latin *campus* meaning "of or pertaining to fields"; so "star of the fields". *Celtis* is the generic name for hackberry trees, the larval foodplant.

ADULT: Medium-sized, but females are larger and paler brown than males. **Upperside:** Brown to tawny above with white spots on the FW and a row of black submarginal spots on the HW. A distinctive feature is the single dark spot toward the outside edge of the FW, below the white spots. **Underside:** The single dark spot can be seen on the FW. Paler grey-brown with a row of submarginal white-centred dark spots with yellow rims on the HW.

SIMILAR SPECIES: Tawny Emperor is more orange-looking on the upperside with yellowish rather than white spots and lacks the single marginal black spot on the FW. Underside HW of Tawny is less well marked, the eye-spots are smaller or non-existent.

BEHAVIOUR: They regularly and aggressively patrol their territories in woodland clearings and along trails, even sometimes pursuing people. The adults feed on ripe fruit, animal dung and tree sap and often sit on trunks or on leaves high up in trees.

FLIGHT SEASON: One generation per year.

	MAR	APR	MAY	JUN	JUL	AUG	SEP	OCT	NOV
Boreal/Tundra									
Mixed Forest									
Carolinian Zone									

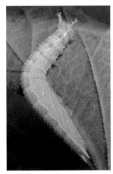

CATERPILLAR: Bright green with yellow stripes and two short horns at the rear end. Head with yellow, branching spines. **Foodplants:** The leaves of hackberry trees including common hackberry (*Celtis occidentalis*) and, at Point Pelee, dwarf hackberry (*Celtis tenuifolia*).

OVERWINTERING STAGE: Mature caterpillar.

HABITAT: Forests with hackberry trees.

DISTRIBUTION AND ABUNDANCE: Found locally from southern Mexico north through the central and eastern United States into extreme southern Quebec. In Ontario, a rare and local resident with the exception of Point Pelee where it is quite common. Although largely restricted to the Carolinian Zone, it is also found north of this zone where there are stands of common hackberry (*Celtis occidentalis*), including the Kingston area and as far north as Petrie Island in the Ottawa River within the city of Ottawa.

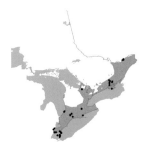

271

TAWNY EMPEROR *Asterocampa clyton*

♂

40–64 mm

ETYMOLOGY: *Clyton* is from the Greek *klytos* meaning "heard of, famous or renowned".

ADULT: Medium-sized; females larger than males. FW pointed, particularly in the males. **Upperside:** Bright tawny-orange to reddish-brown, FW with yellowish spots and two prominent black bars on the leading edge. HW has a row of submarginal black spots, often ringed in orange. There is a female form with dark HWs. **Underside:** A mix of tawny- and light brown (somewhat purplish in some individuals). HW variable, from prominent submarginal rows of spots to unmarked.

SIMILAR SPECIES: Similar to Hackberry Emperor but this species is more orange-looking on the upperside with yellowish rather than white spots and lacks the single marginal black spot on the FW. Underside HW of Tawny is less well marked, the eye-spots are smaller or non-existent.

BEHAVIOUR: Tends to fly and rest higher in trees than Hackberry Emperor. Males also patrol clearings and trails looking for females.

FLIGHT SEASON: One generation per year.

| | MAR | APR | MAY | JUN | JUL | AUG | SEP | OCT | NOV |

Boreal/Tundra
Mixed Forest
Carolinian Zone

Dark variant

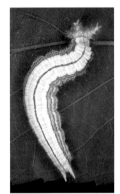

CATERPILLAR: Similar to the Hackberry Emperor. Bright green with yellow stripes along the body. There are two short horns at the rear and yellow, branching spines on the head. **Foodplants:** The leaves of hackberry trees including common hackberry (*Celtis occidentalis*) and, at Point Pelee, dwarf hackberry (*Celtis tenuifolia*).

OVERWINTERING STAGE: Mature caterpillar.

HABITAT: Forests with hackberry trees.

DISTRIBUTION AND ABUNDANCE: Northern Mexico through the eastern United States. In Ontario, a rare and local resident restricted to the southwest with records as far north as Goderich, Huron County and Toronto. May occur in eastern Ontario as it has been found in southwestern Quebec south of Montreal.

COMMENTS: Whereas Tawny Emperor caterpillars feed on mature hackberry leaves, Hackberry Emperor caterpillars tend to feed on younger leaves. This better allows these two extremely similar species to co-exist.

AMERICAN LADY *Vanessa virginiensis*

37–56 mm

ETYMOLOGY: *Vanessa* was a goddess of the Orphic rites in ancient Greece. *Virginiensis* refers to the type locality in the state of Virginia.

ADULT: Medium-sized. **Upperside:** Tawny-orange and blackish-brown with white spots at the FW tips, the larger, inner spot pale orange in females. A small white submarginal spot on top of orange midway along the FW is distinctive, though not always present. HW with a submarginal row of blue-centred eye-spots. **Underside:** FW mirrors the upperside but with pink replacing the orange. Two large eye-spots toward the outer margin of the HW.

SIMILAR SPECIES: Painted Lady is very similar. The shape of the FW (slightly more pointed in Painted) and upper wing coloration (brighter orange in American, larger black areas in Painted) help to distinguish between the two species. When present, the small white submarginal spot midway along the FW is diagnostic for American. The two large spots on the HW underside in American immediately differentiate it from the five, small spots on Painted.

BEHAVIOUR: An active, rapid-flying butterfly that often alights on flowers to nectar.

FLIGHT SEASON: Several generations per year.

	MAR	APR	MAY	JUN	JUL	AUG	SEP	OCT	NOV
Boreal/Tundra									
Mixed Forest									
Carolinian Zone									

CATERPILLAR: Banded with narrow black and white lines interspersed with black or orange bands each containing two white-to-yellow spots. The spines running down the body are red or orange at the base. Solitary, living in leaf nests on the foodplants. **Foodplants:** A number of members of the Sunflower family (Asteraceae), including pussytoes (*Antennaria* spp.) and cudweeds (*Gnaphalium* spp.).

OVERWINTERING STAGE: Does not normally overwinter in Ontario.

HABITAT: Open areas such as gardens, meadows, woodland clearings, disturbed sites, that have plenty of flowers.

DISTRIBUTION AND ABUNDANCE: A wide-ranging resident from Colombia through central America into the southern United States, regularly migrating north to breed in most of the United States and southern Canada, but more common in the east. In Ontario, in most years, a common breeding migrant throughout the province as far north as Hudson Bay. This is probably the most consistent migrant of the genus as its numbers do not fluctuate nearly so dramatically from year-to-year as in Red Admiral and Painted Lady.

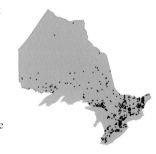

COMMENTS: The American Lady is considered more cold-tolerant than the other members of this genus. Small numbers of this species migrate southward in the fall.

PAINTED LADY *Vanessa cardui*

42–66 mm

ETYMOLOGY: *Cardui* comes from the Latin *carduus* meaning "thistle" and is also the name of a genus of thistles.

ADULT: Medium-sized. FW has a slightly pointed appearance. **Upperside:** Orange to salmon-pink and blackish-brown above with white spots near the wing tips. HW with a submarginal row of black spots, sometimes but not usually with blue centres. **Underside:** Large pink patch on FW often hidden by HW. The complex greyish-and-white patterning on the HW leads to a row of five small eye-spots along the wing margin.

SIMILAR SPECIES: See American Lady.

BEHAVIOUR: Often nectars at flowers and perches on the ground with its wings laid flat.

FLIGHT SEASON: Migrants usually arrive in May sometimes as early as mid-April.

	MAR	APR	MAY	JUN	JUL	AUG	SEP	OCT	NOV
Boreal/Tundra									
Mixed Forest									
Carolinian Zone									

CATERPILLAR: Black to purple with dense yellow spots and dashes and yellowish-to-white, branched spines. **Foodplants:** Feeds in leaf nests on a range of composite plants (Asteraceae)—almost 100 different species have been recorded worldwide. In Ontario, they include thistles (*Cirsium* spp. and *Carduus* spp.), knapweeds (*Centaurea* spp.), and burdocks (*Arctium* spp.).

OVERWINTERING STAGE: While not thought to overwinter in Canada or even most of the United States, fresh individuals have been seen in parts of Ontario following especially warm winters suggesting that some may occasionally overwinter as pupae.

HABITAT: Primarily open areas, such as vacant lots, gardens and roadsides, but can be found in almost any habitat.

DISTRIBUTION AND ABUNDANCE: The most cosmopolitan of any butterfly species—found regularly on all continents except Antarctica. Highly migratory throughout its range; it moves toward the equator from northerly or southerly latitudes to escape cold weather. In North America, it is a year-round resident in northern Mexico and possibly the southwestern United States. From this region, it migrates north each spring reaching as far as the Canadian territories. In Ontario, it varies from a rare-to-common breeding migrant. Numbers fluctuate widely from year to year, being superabundant in some years (often associated with El Niño years in the Pacific Ocean) and rare to absent in others.

RED ADMIRAL *Vanessa atalanta*

45–57 mm

ETYMOLOGY: *Atalanta* is from the mythological Greek huntress Atalanta.

ADULT: Medium-sized. **Upperside:** Striking red/orange bands on black/brown wings and bright white FW spots. **Underside:** FW has a red band with some blue markings, whereas the HW is mottled greyish and brown.

SIMILAR SPECIES: Milbert's Tortoiseshell might be mistaken while flying, but it has bright orange-yellow bands and a more angular wing shape. Ventral HWs lack eye-spots of other members of this genus.

BEHAVIOUR: Active and often lands to nectar on a wide variety of flowering plants. Quite territorial, it will chase after other butterflies, birds and even humans.

FLIGHT SEASON: Two to three overlapping generations in Ontario.

	MAR	APR	MAY	JUN	JUL	AUG	SEP	OCT	NOV
Boreal/Tundra									
Mixed Forest									
Carolinian Zone									

CATERPILLAR: Variable from black to greenish with branched spines and a broken yellow line along the sides. **Foodplants:** Plants of the Nettle family (Urticaceae) including stinging nettle (*Urtica dioica*) and Canada wood nettle (*Laportea canadensis*).

OVERWINTERING STAGE: As an adult, but does not usually overwinter in Ontario.

HABITAT: Almost anywhere from urban areas to northern forests and even tundra.

DISTRIBUTION AND ABUNDANCE: Holarctic. In the Americas, ranges from Central America to the south-central United States and migrates each year throughout the northern United States and most of Canada north to the southern territories. In Ontario, varies from an uncommon-to-common breeding migrant. Numbers fluctuate widely from year to year. In some years, such as 1981, 2010 and 2012, thousands were noted passing at a single location during migration and they were commonly found in very large numbers everywhere in the province. In some years, they do not range much beyond the central parts of the province and there have been other years with very few records.

COMMENTS: This species may overwinter in Ontario since fresh individuals occasionally appear in early spring.

MILBERT'S TORTOISESHELL *Aglais milberti*

34–52 mm

ETYMOLOGY: *Aglaia* means "splendour or beauty" in Greek. Jacques-Gérard Milbert was a French naturalist and friend of the entomologist Jean Baptiste Godart who described the species.

ADULT: Medium-sized. **Upperside:** Very striking with dark brown bases, a broad submarginal band, yellow on the inside, grading to bright orange toward the dark margins. FW with two orange patches on the leading edge. HW with a row of blue spots along the dark margin. **Underside:** Striated brown, darker in the basal portion.

SIMILAR SPECIES: The undersides resemble other tortoiseshells and anglewings, but the uppersides are unique among Ontario butterflies.

BEHAVIOUR: An active, sometimes pugnacious, defender of its territory, often along woodland roads. Regularly seen perched on dirt roads with the wings spread flat or sipping tree sap or moisture from animal dung. Commonly nectars at a variety of flowers.

FLIGHT SEASON: One generation per year.

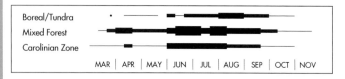

	MAR	APR	MAY	JUN	JUL	AUG	SEP	OCT	NOV
Boreal/Tundra									
Mixed Forest									
Carolinian Zone									

CATERPILLAR: Early instar caterpillars feed communally in silken nests, but eventually wander off on their own and feed from folded-leaf shelters. The mature caterpillars are black with branching spines along the body. **Foodplants:** Nettles (*Urtica* spp.) recorded in Ontario, but other plants, such as willows (*Salix* spp.) and sunflowers (*Helianthus* spp.), in other parts of Canada.

OVERWINTERING STAGE: Adult.

HABITAT: Open habitats, often wet areas near forests and fields.

DISTRIBUTION AND ABUNDANCE: Widespread across most of North America with the exception of the southeastern United States. In Ontario, an uncommon-to-common resident found throughout the province and tends to be localized. Reported as becoming less common in many areas around the Great Lakes.

COMMENTS: While previously placed in the genus *Nymphalis* with other North American tortoiseshells, it is now placed in the genus *Aglais*, which is a genus of largely Eurasian tortoiseshells.

COMPTON TORTOISESHELL *Nymphalis l-album*

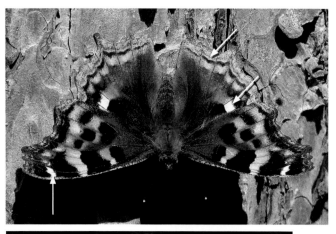

45–79 mm

ETYMOLOGY: *Nympha* refers to the mythological Greek nymphs (minor deities of land, sky or water). *Album*, meaning "white" in Latin, refers to the white central wing mark on the ventral HWs.

ADULT: Medium-sized to large. **Upperside:** Black, gold, brown and white. The golden margin of the HW and the white spots on the leading edges of both the HW (often concealed by the FW) are distinguishing features. **Underside:** Variable dark-grey to brown, basal half darker, with a wavy, green submarginal line on both wings.

SIMILAR SPECIES: Similar to many of the anglewings (genus *Polygonia*) but the golden colour and white spots on the upperside and larger size distinguish this species.

BEHAVIOUR: Males patrol woodland roads, trails and clearings awaiting females. Most often perched directly on the ground with wings flat or on tree trunks, often upside-down. They regularly feed on dung, animal carcasses or on the sap from tree wounds or Yellow-bellied Sapsucker holes. This is probably the longest-lived adult butterfly in the province, sometimes surviving for up to 10 months.

FLIGHT SEASON: One generation per year.

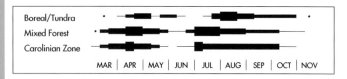

Dark-grey variant

Brown variant

CATERPILLAR: Variable; may be green, yellow or reddish-brown with rows of white dots on the dorsal surface and black or white spines. **Foodplants:** Birches (*Betula* spp.), willows (*Salix* spp.) and trembling aspen (*Populus tremuloides*).

OVERWINTERING STAGE: Adult, with individuals emerging from hibernation as early as March or even February when the temperature ranges above 10°C.

HABITAT: Woodland and forest clearings or along forest edges.

DISTRIBUTION AND ABUNDANCE: Holarctic. Can be found across Canada and the northern United States. In Ontario, a common resident although its numbers fluctuate from year to year. Most often encountered singly.

COMMENTS: The common name is derived from the town of Compton in the Eastern Townships of Quebec, where the famous English naturalist, Philip Henry Gosse, studied it in the mid-nineteenth century. Recent taxonomic evidence suggests that the North American and Eurasian species are distinct. If so, our species would be renamed *Nymphalis j-album*. The common name would, however, likely still stand as the species in Europe is commonly called False Comma.

MOURNING CLOAK *Nymphalis antiopa*

Form "hyperborea"

45–79 mm

ETYMOLOGY: In Greek mythology, *Antiope* was a princess, the mother of twins.

ADULT: Medium-sized to large. **Upperside:** Rich maroon to brown with a yellow band along the outside edges of the wings. There is also a row of bright purple to blue spots along the inside of the yellow band. **Underside:** A dark brown, wavy pattern with pale margins.

SIMILAR SPECIES: The underside is similar to that of tortoiseshells and anglewings, but note the pale margins. The upperside is unique.

BEHAVIOUR: Males often seen patrolling woodland roads in their chosen territory, chasing off intruders of its own species, but will even make dashes at passing humans. Often perched on the ground. Adults commonly feed on sap and decaying matter, but occasionally nectar at flowers.

FLIGHT SEASON: Two generations per year in Ontario.

	MAR	APR	MAY	JUN	JUL	AUG	SEP	OCT	NOV
Boreal/Tundra									
Mixed Forest									
Carolinian Zone									

Form "lintnerii"

CATERPILLAR: Black with white spots and rows of black spines when mature. There is also a row of orange spots running down the back. Early instars live communally (see page 231). **Foodplants:** Many different kinds of trees including willows (*Salix* spp.), elms (*Ulmus* spp.), cottonwoods (*Populus* spp.) and hackberries (*Celtis* spp.).

OVERWINTERING STAGE: Adult.

HABITAT: Woodlands but can wander into a broad range of habitats, from backyard gardens to northern bogs.

DISTRIBUTION AND ABUNDANCE: Holarctic. In the Americas found from arctic regions south to central Mexico. In Ontario, this is one of the most widespread and common of butterflies.

COMMENTS: In North America, there are two forms: a northern maroon form (hyperborea) and a larger southern dark brown form (lintnerii). These could be separate subspecies or species, but more study is required. In Ontario, hyperborea predominates, but the form lintnerii (presumably migrants from farther south) have been recorded in southern Ontario.

QUESTION MARK *Polygonia interrogationis*

45–68 mm   Overwintering form

ETYMOLOGY: *Polygonia* is from the Greek words *poly* meaning "many" and *gonia* meaning "angle", in reference to the shape of the wing margins. *Interrogationis* is from the Greek word for "questioning".

ADULT: The largest and longest-tailed of Ontario's anglewings. FW tips are strongly hooked. **Upperside:** Two colour forms—the pale overwintering form is usually mostly orange with large black spots. The dark summer form differs in having a mostly black HW. Both forms have a diagnostic elongated spot at the upper end of the FW spots and pale violet margins when fresh. **Underside:** Can appear either as a blotchy light and dark brown or a more uniform purplish-brown. There is a silver "question mark" in the centre of the HW.

SIMILAR SPECIES: The combination of larger size, longer tails, the elongated spot on the upper FW and the silver question mark on the underside HW help to distinguish this species from the other anglewings, but some Eastern Commas have a weakly defined elongated spot and/or a broken comma. See Plate 9.

BEHAVIOUR: Often seen sunning on the ground, sipping tree sap, feeding on dung and mudpuddling.

FLIGHT SEASON: Summer form migrants appear in spring and breed. The overwintering generation appears in mid- to late-summer and flies into the fall before presumably migrating south.

	MAR	APR	MAY	JUN	JUL	AUG	SEP	OCT	NOV
Boreal/Tundra									
Mixed Forest									
Carolinian Zone									

Summer form

Light caterpillar

CATERPILLAR: Variable colour with white dots and yellow-to-orange, branched spines. See page 231 for dark form. **Foodplants:** Stinging nettle (*Urtica dioica*), elms (*Ulmus* spp.), common hop (*Humulus lupulus*) and hackberries (*Celtis* spp.).

OVERWINTERING STAGE: Adult, although it probably does not overwinter in Ontario, or rarely does.

HABITAT: Woodlands, but also seen in open areas, towns and even urban areas.

DISTRIBUTION AND ABUNDANCE:
Widespread from Mexico north through the eastern United States to southeastern Canada. In Ontario, usually a common breeding migrant but in some years it can be scarce. Most commonly found north to Algonquin Park, but there are scattered records as far north as Lake Nipigon and Kapuskasing.

287

EASTERN COMMA *Polygonia comma*

37–56 mm

Overwintering form

ETYMOLOGY: *Comma* refers to the silver spot on the underside HW.

ADULT: Medium-sized. **Upperside:** Two forms. Overwintering form orangey-brown with black margins and large black spots. Wing margins violet when fresh. Summer form similar but has a mostly black HW. **Underside:** Highly variable, ranging from heavily mottled to more uniform brown. HW with a silvery-white comma, slightly enlarged at each end, often shaped like a fish hook.

SIMILAR SPECIES: All the anglewings are similar; however, the two forms of Question Mark may more closely resemble this species. Satyr, Green, and Hoary commas all tend to have more heavily scalloped wing margins. The innermost FW spot in Satyr and Green commas is doubled (single in Eastern). In addition, Satyr is a distinctive golden-orange dorsally often without a very dark HW margin. The FW spots in Gray tend to be smaller. See Plate 9.

BEHAVIOUR: Males often set up territories along woodland roads or edges awaiting females. They sip moisture from the soil or animal dung or perch upside-down on tree trunks resembling dead leaves.

FLIGHT SEASON: Overwintering form individuals appear in early spring and breed resulting in the summer form generation. These then breed producing another generation of overwintering form individuals in late summer/fall.

288

Brown form

Mottled dark form

Summer form

Greenish-brown caterpillar

Greenish-white caterpillar

CATERPILLAR: Two forms, one greenish-white, one greenish-brown, both with white-to-yellow spines. **Foodplants:** Wood nettle (*Laportea canadensis*) is preferred, but also elms (*Ulmus* spp.) and common hop (*Humulus lupulus*).

OVERWINTERING STAGE: Adult.

HABITAT: Moist woodlands and nearby open areas.

DISTRIBUTION AND ABUNDANCE: Widespread in the eastern United States and southeastern Canada. In Ontario, a common resident throughout southern Ontario, becoming less common north of the southern edge of the Canadian Shield where it ranges into southern Cochrane and Kenora districts.

SATYR COMMA *Polygonia satyrus*

39–54 mm

ETYMOLOGY: In Greek mythology, Satyrs were woodland deities that were half-man, half-goat.

ADULT: Medium-sized. Wing margins very scalloped. **Upperside:** Golden-orange with black spots. Two black, sometimes joined, spots on FW inner margin. Submarginal row of golden spots on the HW merges into a band and the margin is often quite pale. **Underside:** Striated light and dark reddish-brown. Dark streaks near the leading edge of the FW are lozenge-shaped. HW with a silvery-white comma.

SIMILAR SPECIES: Dorsally, similar to other anglewings but the combination of a double inner FW spot, and the overall golden colour, especially the relatively pale HW margin, are distinguishing features. Ventrally, extremely similar to the mottled form of Eastern Comma, but the dark bands in Satyr tend to be straighter and more organized-looking than in Eastern. Also note the more heavily scalloped wing margin of Satyr. See Plate 9.

BEHAVIOUR: A woodland anglewing that sips sap from trees and moisture from the ground.

FLIGHT SEASON: One generation in Ontario.

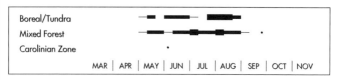

	MAR	APR	MAY	JUN	JUL	AUG	SEP	OCT	NOV
Boreal/Tundra									
Mixed Forest									
Carolinian Zone									

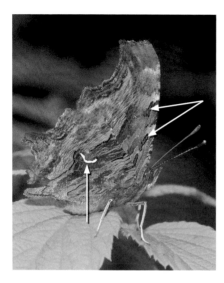

CATERPILLAR: Black with a broad, greenish-white dorsal stripe. The rows of spines on the top are white and black-tipped, whereas the spines on the sides are greenish-white. **Foodplants:** Though nettles (*Urtica* spp.) are the only recorded foodplants, there are likely others.

OVERWINTERING STAGE: Adult.

HABITAT: Clearings and roadsides.

DISTRIBUTION AND ABUNDANCE: Largely a species of western North America, it also extends across Canada and the northeastern United States, becoming increasingly less common and more sporadic farther east. In Ontario, an uncommon resident in northern Ontario from Timiskaming District to southern James Bay westward. Farther south, it is much rarer, with records from Algonquin Park, the Ottawa area and as far south as Halton and Kingston where it can be sporadically seen; for example, about ten were seen in the Ottawa area in 2010.

GRAY COMMA *Polygonia progne*

37–50 mm

Summer form

ETYMOLOGY: *Progne* comes from the Greek mythological figure *Prokne,* daughter of King Pandion.

ADULT: Medium-sized. Wing margins are scalloped. **Upperside:** Reddish-orange with dark spots that are smaller than those of the other anglewings. The summer form is darker on the upper HW than the overwintering form. **Underside:** Heavily striated grey. FW lighter on the outer half; HW more uniform with a very thin, L-shaped silvery-white comma that is tapered at both ends.

SIMILAR SPECIES: Dorsally, the small dark spots and the row of smaller yellow spots on HW margin distinguish this from the other anglewings (although Hoary also has small yellow dots on the HW margin). Ventrally, very similar to Hoary Comma but both wings are lighter on the outer half in Hoary (only the FW is lighter in Gray) and the comma tends to be thicker in Hoary. See Plate 9.

BEHAVIOUR: Avid mudpuddler. Can be seen on the limbs and trunks of trees sipping sap. Sometimes nectars at flowers.

FLIGHT SEASON: Overwintering form individuals appear in spring and breed resulting in the summer form generation. These then breed producing another generation of overwintering form individuals in late summer/fall. There are reports of two summer broods at Point Pelee.

	Boreal/Tundra	Mixed Forest	Carolinian Zone

MAR | APR | MAY | JUN | JUL | AUG | SEP | OCT | NOV

Overwintering form

CATERPILLAR: Variable in appearance, but most often a yellow-brown with olive-brown splotches or stripes, and black or yellow spines.
Foodplants: Currants and gooseberries (*Ribes* spp.).

OVERWINTERING STAGE: Adult.

HABITAT: Openings and edges of deciduous or mixed forests.

DISTRIBUTION AND ABUNDANCE:
Widespread across North America.
In Ontario, a common resident,
though never seen in large numbers,
ranging north to southern James
Bay and Favourable Lake near the
Manitoba border. Less common in
extreme southwestern Ontario, it
may be declining in numbers at Point
Pelee as there are years when there
are no sightings reported.

NYMPHALIDAE / The Brushfoots

HOARY COMMA *Polygonia gracilis*

37–50 mm

ETYMOLOGY: Derived from the Latin *gracilis* meaning "slender".

ADULT: Medium-sized. Wing margins are highly scalloped. **Upperside:** Rust-orange with broad dark margins, the HW with a submarginal row of small orange spots. **Underside:** A two-tone appearance with the inner dark brown portion striated in pattern and contrasting strongly with the outer, pale, "hoary" part of the wings. HW with a silvery-white L-shaped comma that is tapered at each end.

SIMILAR SPECIES: Dorsally, usually distinguished from the other anglewings by a combination of its dark rust-orange colour, dark wing margins, and small yellow submarginal spots (although these are present in Gray). Ventrally, similar only to Gray Comma but Gray does not have the strong contrasting pattern on the HWs; Gray HWs are more striated. See Plate 9.

BEHAVIOUR: Often perched on the ground. More likely than other anglewings to be seen nectaring, particularly on asters and everlastings in late summer and fall.

FLIGHT SEASON: One generation per year.

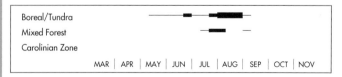

CATERPILLAR: Brownish-black with whitish patches and spines on the rear half. **Foodplants:** Gooseberries or currants (*Ribes* spp.).

OVERWINTERING STAGE: Adult.

HABITAT: Boreal forest, along woodland trails and in clearings, often close to streams and rocky areas.

DISTRIBUTION AND ABUNDANCE: Across the Boreal Forest Region of Canada from coast to coast and south through the mountains of the western United States as well as into the New England states. In Ontario, an uncommon resident throughout northern Ontario, known to occur as far south as Sudbury District.

GREEN COMMA *Polygonia faunus*

34–47 mm

ETYMOLOGY: *Faunus* was the Roman god of fields and herds.

ADULT: Medium-sized. Wing margins are the most highly scalloped of all the anglewings. **Upperside:** Reddish-orange with large dark spots. Two black, sometimes joined, spots on FW inner margin. Appears darker overall than other anglewings. **Underside:** Brownish-grey and blotchy with two submarginal rows of green spots that can be difficult to see in faded individuals. The silvery-white comma is thickened at both ends.

SIMILAR SPECIES: This species has the most irregular wing edges of Ontario's anglewings. An overall darker appearance, doubled FW spot, and underside row of green spots are distinguising features. The comma is similar in shape to that of the Eastern Comma. See Plate 9.

BEHAVIOUR: Often lands on rocky surfaces or trees to bask in the sun and to chase off any butterfly intruders. Rarely seen nectaring at flowers but often seen sipping sap from tree wounds and feeding on dung and carrion. Of the anglewings, it may be the one that most often alights on humans to sip perspiration.

FLIGHT SEASON: One generation per year.

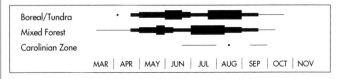

CATERPILLAR: Black with spines, orange stripes along the sides and black and orange spots. **Foodplants:** Mainly woody plants, including willows (*Salix* spp.), birches (*Betula* spp.), and alders (*Alnus* spp.), but also recorded on blueberries (*Vaccinium* spp.).

OVERWINTERING STAGE: Adult.

HABITAT: Openings and trails through coniferous and mixed forests.

DISTRIBUTION AND ABUNDANCE: Ranges across Canada and south into the mountains of the United States. In Ontario, a common resident on the Canadian Shield to James Bay and Favourable Lake. South of the Shield, it is far less common and is largely absent from southwestern Ontario.

COMMON BUCKEYE *Junonia coenia*

37–45 mm

ETYMOLOGY: *Juno* was the queen of the Roman gods; sister and wife of the god Jupiter. She was the goddess of marriage and protector of the community. *Junonia* was a city named in her honour. *Coenia* may be from the Greek word *koinos* meaning "common, commonplace".

ADULT: Medium-sized. **Upperside:** A unique pattern of six large eye-spots, one on each FW (contained within a cream-white band) and two on each HW. There is an orange submarginal band on the HW and two short orange stripes at the leading edge of the basal FW. **Underside:** Similar to upper, but much paler with smaller or even no eye-spots on the HW. Form "rosa" is rosier-coloured on both FW and HW and has a deep red line that crosses the HW.

SIMILAR SPECIES: None.

BEHAVIOUR: Males patrol open areas awaiting females. They tend to fly very close to the ground, can be very wary and use a rapid flight if alarmed. They often sit on the ground basking in sunlight.

FLIGHT SEASON: Two to three overlapping generations.

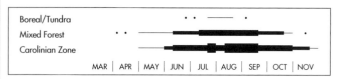

Rosa form

Eye-spot form

CATERPILLAR: Dark grey with a white pattern along the side and branching spines; blue dashes at base of spines. **Foodplants:** Low-lying plants in the Broomrape family (Orobanchaceae), such as agalinis (*Agalinis* spp.) and the Plantain family (Plantaginaceae), such as snapdragons (*Antirrhinum* spp.), and plantains (*Plantago* spp.).

OVERWINTERING STAGE: Does not overwinter in Ontario. Adults overwinter in the southern United States.

HABITAT: Open areas where the foodplants are present. Can appear anywhere during migration.

DISTRIBUTION AND ABUNDANCE: A permanent resident from southern Mexico to the southern United States, migrating northward and breeding throughout most of the United States and into southeastern Canada. In Ontario, a rare-to-uncommon breeding migrant, largely confined to southwestern Ontario. In good dispersal years, however, it can occur as far north as Thunder Bay, Manitoulin Island, Algonquin Park and Ottawa. In 2012, several individuals reached southern James Bay.

BALTIMORE CHECKERSPOT *Euphydryas phaeton*

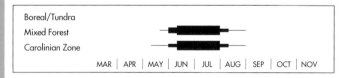

44–70 mm

ETYMOLOGY: *Euphy-* is derived from the Greek meaning "shapely, comely" and *dryas* meaning "wood nymph". In Greek, *phaeo* is the colour of the twilight sky.

ADULT: Medium-sized; however, females can be quite large for a checkerspot. **Upperside:** Wing margins have large orange spots inside of which are rows of white crescents then white spots, and the basal parts of the wings are black with large orange spots. **Underside:** Similar to upper but with more orange and cream-white spots and with cream-white crescents extending into the orange margin.

SIMILAR SPECIES: None.

BEHAVIOUR: A relatively slow flyer staying within the vicinity of the larval foodplant. Sometimes seen mudpuddling around damp spots on dirt roads near wet areas.

FLIGHT SEASON: One generation per year.

	MAR	APR	MAY	JUN	JUL	AUG	SEP	OCT	NOV
Boreal/Tundra									
Mixed Forest									
Carolinian Zone									

White turtlehead

CATERPILLAR: Newly hatched caterpillars, which are black with orange stripes and black spines, build a communal silken nest. **Foodplants:** Early instar caterpillars feed almost exclusively on white turtlehead (*Chelone glabra*). Later instar caterpillars, especially in the spring after their winter diapause, often feed on other plants including ashes (*Fraxinus* spp.) and plantains (*Plantago* spp.).

OVERWINTERING STAGE: Caterpillar.

HABITAT: Wet meadows, marshes and roadside ditches.

DISTRIBUTION AND ABUNDANCE:
Restricted to eastern North America. In Ontario, an uncommon and local resident, largely found in southern Ontario south of the Canadian Shield. Also known from Sault Ste. Marie and extreme southwestern Rainy River District.

COMMENTS: The only representative in Ontario of the mainly western North American genus *Euphydryas*.

SILVERY CHECKERSPOT *Chlosyne nycteis*

33–45 mm

ETYMOLOGY: *Chlosyne* may be derived from the Greek word *chloe* meaning "first shoots of grass in spring" and *syn* meaning "with" or "similar". From Greek, *nyct-* refers to "darkness or night".

ADULT: Small to medium-sized. **Upperside:** Orange with blackish-brown markings including wide margins. One to three of the submarginal black spots on the HW have white centres. **Underside:** HW tawny with a wide dark brown margin within which is a row of black submarginal spots (at least one of which has a white centre). There is usually a silvery median band. There is also a silvery-white crescent within the dark margin.

SIMILAR SPECIES: The Gorgone Checkerspot has the central row of silvery spots on the under HW in the shape of arrowheads, whereas Harris's Checkerspot has a brick-red base colour surrounding rows of silvery white spots. Very similar to the crescents but at least one of the black submarginal spots has a white centre in Silvery Checkerspot, visible both dorsally and ventrally. See Plate 10.

BEHAVIOUR: Often perched on the ground mudpuddling and regularly nectars at flowers. Populations tend to disappear from known localities and to re-appear randomly in subsequent years.

FLIGHT SEASON: One generation per year.

	MAR	APR	MAY	JUN	JUL	AUG	SEP	OCT	NOV
Boreal/Tundra									
Mixed Forest									
Carolinian Zone									

CATERPILLAR: Purple streaked with black, with an orange stripe on the sides and brown spines. **Foodplants:** Members of the Sunflower family (Asteraceae), including sunflowers (*Helianthus* spp.), asters (*Symphyotrichum* spp., *Oclemena* spp., and *Eurybia* spp.) and coneflowers (*Rudbeckia* spp.).

OVERWINTERING STAGE: Partly grown caterpillars.

HABITAT: Wet meadows, particularly near streams and roadside ditches.

DISTRIBUTION AND ABUNDANCE:
Most of eastern North America. In Ontario, a common resident, ranging north to southern James Bay and southern Kenora District.

COMMENTS: The Silvery Checkerspot is reported to be declining in its eastern United States range.

GORGONE CHECKERSPOT *Chlosyne gorgone*

27–38 mm

ETYMOLOGY: A reference to the mythological Greek *Gorgons*, three monstrous sisters, including Medusa.

ADULT: Small to medium-sized. **Upperside:** Similar to the orange and black pattern of most checkerspots but usually with pale-whitish markings within the dark margins. The submarginal row of spots on the HW are solid black. **Underside:** HW with a median brown-and-white zigzag (arrowhead-shaped) pattern beyond which is a row of dark spots followed by a very distinct marginal band of silvery-white, crescent-shaped markings.

SIMILAR SPECIES: Harris's and the Silvery checkerspots do not have the arrowhead-shaped markings in the band across the underside HW. The crescents are lighter-coloured and have a different underside HW pattern.

BEHAVIOUR: Stays low in the vegetation, landing often, but is capable of more rapid flight when disturbed.

FLIGHT SEASON: Two generations per year, sometimes with a partial third.

Boreal/Tundra								
Mixed Forest			—		▬▬		▬▬	
Carolinian Zone		—						
	MAR	APR	MAY	JUN	JUL	AUG	SEP	OCT	NOV

CATERPILLAR: Variable, black or with black spines, usually with pale diagonal lines and small white spots. The early instars tend to congregate in colonies on the foodplants (see page 231). **Foodplants:** Black-eyed Susan (*Rudbeckia hirta*) and occasionally asters (*Symphyotrichum* spp., *Oclemena* spp., *Doellingeria* spp. and *Eurybia* spp.). In the much larger western Canadian population, they feed on a variety of sunflowers (*Helianthus* spp.).

OVERWINTERING STAGE: Caterpillar.

HABITAT: Restricted to small areas with large numbers of black-eyed Susans in open fields with sandy soils, either fallow or planted with a mix of alfalfa (*Medicago sativa*) and clover (*Trifolium repens*).

DISTRIBUTION AND ABUNDANCE: Mainly a species of the Great Plains, extending from Texas north to the prairie provinces. In Ontario, known only from a small number of fields south of Kemptville in eastern Ontario. The populations appear to be ephemeral, appearing in some locations in some years then disappearing. There are historical records (more than 100 years old) from London, the Humber Valley in Toronto, and from Algoma District north of Lake Superior.

COMMENTS: Little is known about this butterfly in Ontario as it has been seen only sporadically over the last 100 years.

HARRIS'S CHECKERSPOT *Chlosyne harrisii*

30–41 mm

ETYMOLOGY: The species was named by W. H. Scudder for Thaddeus W. Harris, a noted American entomologist.

ADULT: Small to medium-sized. **Upperside:** Similar to the other checkerspots with an orange and black pattern but with more extensive black markings. **Underside:** Best distinguished by the orange-red colour of the HW crossed by three bands of creamy-white spots, those of the outermost band being chevron-shaped.

SIMILAR SPECIES: See Gorgone and Silvery checkerspots. The upperside is similar to the Ontario crescents, but Harris's usually has at least one white-centred black submarginal spot on the HW. The underside, however, is very different.

BEHAVIOUR: A relatively weak flyer, staying near the tops of the vegetation; nectars regularly on a variety of flowers.

FLIGHT SEASON: One generation per year.

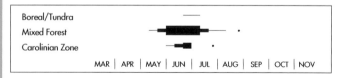

	Boreal/Tundra	Mixed Forest	Carolinian Zone
MAR	APR	MAY	JUN	JUL	AUG	SEP	OCT	NOV

Flat-topped white aster

CATERPILLAR: Orange-red and black stripes with a black dorsal stripe. The branched spines are black. **Foodplants:** Flat-topped white aster (*Doellingeria umbellata* var. *umbellata*).

OVERWINTERING STAGE: Caterpillar.

HABITAT: Wet meadows, wetland edges, roadside ditches and nearby open areas.

DISTRIBUTION AND ABUNDANCE: Southeastern Canada and northeastern United States. In Ontario, an uncommon and local resident largely concentrated in south-central Ontario but extending north to Timmins and west to Thunder Bay and Rainy River districts. Rare and even more locally distributed in southwestern Ontario.

COMMENTS: Since its numbers have been declining in some parts of its American range, this species should be carefully monitored in Ontario.

PEARL CRESCENT *Phyciodes tharos*

21–34 mm

ETYMOLOGY: The generic name likely comes from the Greek *phykos* meaning "painted". *Tharos* means "courage" in Greek.

ADULT: Small. Markings on this species can be quite variable.
Upperside: Orange with fine black markings. The orange on the upper HW is crossed by distinct black lines along the veins.
Underside: Male HW tawny with fine blackish lineation and a blackish marginal patch not extending as far as the submarginal dark spots and containing a pearly-white crescent. Females have a more mottled pattern on the HW—sometimes "calico" in appearance.

SIMILAR SPECIES: The three Ontario crescents are extremely similar and cannot always be identified in the field, especially females. The Northern Crescent male is, on average, larger than the Pearl and, in both sexes, the orange on the upper HW usually has an open patch in the centre of the wings not crossed by black lines as in the Pearl. The antennae of Northern males usually have orange tips whereas those of the Pearl are usually black-tipped. The underside HW dark patch on male Pearl is blackish (brown in Northern) and typically does not extend as far into the wing as in Northern. The lineation on the underside HW in Pearl is blackish versus orange in Northern. Also see Tawny Crescent (page 312). See Plate 10.

BEHAVIOUR: Prefers drier areas than the Northern Crescent. They will often congregate at damp patches on rural roads.

FLIGHT SEASON: Probably three generations per year in Ontario.

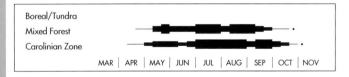

CATERPILLAR: Brown with tiny white dots, pale and brown longitudinal stripes and white-tipped brown spines. **Foodplants:** Asters (*Symphyotrichum* spp., *Oclemena* spp., *Doellingeria* spp. and *Eurybia* spp.).

OVERWINTERING STAGE: Caterpillar.

HABITAT: Open areas, such as meadows and roadsides.

DISTRIBUTION AND ABUNDANCE: Mexico north through the central and eastern United States into the prairie provinces and southern Ontario. In Ontario, a common resident south of the Canadian Shield. The northern limits of its distribution are not entirely clear, however, especially where the Northern Crescent is abundant. Adding to this uncertainty is the fact that Pearl Crescents appear to be expanding their range northward, this may be associated with climate change.

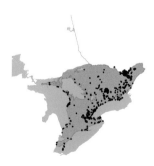

NORTHERN CRESCENT *Phyciodes cocyta*

♂

25–35 mm

ETYMOLOGY: *Cocytus* was the river of Lamentation in the Greek mythological underworld.

ADULT: Small. The antennal tips are usually orange. Females are larger and difficult to separate from other crescents. **Upperside:** Orange with extensive black markings and black borders. An open orange area in the middle of the HW with no, or limited numbers of, black lines across it. Females often have two tones of orange on FW. **Underside:** HW tawny with orange lineation and a marginal dark brown patch that extends toward and usually encompasses some of the submarginal dark spots and contains a pale-purplish to dark brown crescent. Female usually much more heavily marked on HW.

SIMILAR SPECIES: See Pearl Crescent. See Plate 10.

BEHAVIOUR: An active mudpuddler often found along trails.

FLIGHT SEASON: One to two generations in Ontario.

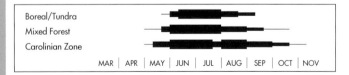

	MAR	APR	MAY	JUN	JUL	AUG	SEP	OCT	NOV
Boreal/Tundra									
Mixed Forest									
Carolinian Zone									

CATERPILLAR: Similar to that of the Pearl Crescent but with lighter brown or grey spines. **Foodplants:** Asters (*Symphyotrichum* spp., *Oclemena* spp., *Doellingeria* spp. and *Eurybia* spp.).

OVERWINTERING STAGE: Caterpillar.

HABITAT: Open areas, including old fields, forest clearings, ditches, edges of wetlands and even vacant city lots.

DISTRIBUTION AND ABUNDANCE: One of the most widespread of Canadian butterflies, it ranges south into the United States through the Rocky Mountains and the northeastern states. In Ontario, a common-to-abundant resident, ranging across the province and found pretty well anywhere asters grow.

COMMENTS: The Northern Crescent was only separated out as a species from the Pearl Crescent in the 1990s. There is some speculation that there may be another separate species that flies in southwestern Ontario in July. Further research and rearing is required.

TAWNY CRESCENT *Phyciodes batesii*

25–38 mm

ETYMOLOGY: Named after nineteenth-century entomologist and traveller, Henry Walter Bates, famous for his studies of mimicry in insects.

ADULT: Small. **Upperside:** Orange with black markings like the other crescents; it is overall darker in appearance because of more extensive black markings. **Underside:** Straw-yellow with a minimal to non-existent dark marginal patch and a pale-yellow submarginal crescent.

SIMILAR SPECIES: This species has an overall blacker appearance on the upperside than the Northern and Pearl crescents and the underside HW has little if any dark colouring, being a relatively uniform straw-yellow including the crescent and orange lineation. See Plate 10.

BEHAVIOUR: Does not stray far from its open area habitats and flies close to the ground.

FLIGHT SEASON: One generation per year.

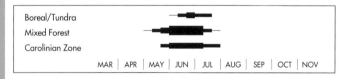

	MAR	APR	MAY	JUN	JUL	AUG	SEP	OCT	NOV
Boreal/Tundra									
Mixed Forest									
Carolinian Zone									

CATERPILLAR: Brown-tinted pink with black stripes. **Foodplants:** Asters (*Symphyotrichum* spp., *Oclemena* spp., *Doellingeria* spp. and *Eurybia* spp.).

OVERWINTERING STAGE: Caterpillar.

HABITAT: Drier, open areas, such as alvars, rock barrens, sand barrens and clearings in boreal forests.

DISTRIBUTION AND ABUNDANCE: Found from British Columbia to Quebec, into the northern United States in the northeast and some areas of the west. In Ontario, an uncommon and local resident most commonly found along the southern edge of the Canadian Shield from Ottawa to southeastern Georgian Bay, as well as on Manitoulin Island. Ranges as far north as Lake Attawapiskat and Favourable Lake near the Manitoba border. Largely absent from extreme southwestern Ontario.

COMMENTS: For many years its distribution was little known and probably overlooked because it is similar to the abundant Pearl Crescent. As it has become better known and identified, it has begun mysteriously disappearing from most of its known sites in the northeastern United States and may even be extirpated in most areas. A close eye should be kept on its known Canadian localities.

NORTHERN PEARLY-EYE *Lethe anthedon*

43–53 mm

ETYMOLOGY: In Greek mythology, *Lethe* was one of the rivers of Hades, specifically the river and spirit of forgetfulness. *Anthedon* was a town in ancient Greece.

ADULT: Medium-sized. Wing edges are somewhat scalloped.
Upperside: Dark brown and the FW has three to four black yellow-rimmed submarginal spots with five black spots on the HW.
Underside: Light brown with purplish overtones in fresh individuals. Most of the eye-spots (six on the HW) have a white pupil. All eye-spots are circled with yellowish-orange.

SIMILAR SPECIES: Generally larger and has more highly scalloped wings than the Appalachian or Eyed Brown. The second upperside FW spot is sometimes absent or reduced on the Northern Pearly-Eye, but when present is smaller than the other three spots; in other species all FW spots are of similar size. See Plate 11.

BEHAVIOUR: Tolerates high levels of shade and is most often seen alighting on tree trunks and limbs. Rarely comes to flowers, but can be seen actively sipping moisture from sap, dung and mud. This butterfly has a strong erratic flight.

FLIGHT SEASON: One generation per year.

	MAR	APR	MAY	JUN	JUL	AUG	SEP	OCT	NOV
Boreal/Tundra									
Mixed Forest									
Carolinian Zone									

CATERPILLAR: Yellowish-green caterpillars have green and yellow stripes along the body and two short, pink tails. It also has red horns on the head. **Foodplants:** Woodland grasses (Poaceae), including southern shorthusk (*Brachyelytrum erectum*).

OVERWINTERING STAGE: Caterpillar.

HABITAT: Prefers the dense understorey of deciduous and mixed woodlands and forests.

DISTRIBUTION AND ABUNDANCE:
A species of central-eastern North America, it is a locally common resident in Ontario from Windsor throughout southern Ontario and north to Lake Abitibi and west to Lake of the Woods.

EYED BROWN *Lethe eurydice*

38–48 mm

ETYMOLOGY: In Greek mythology, *Eurydice* was an oak nymph, the wife of Orpheus.

ADULT: Medium-sized. **Upperside:** Straw-brown with four or five submarginal light-rimmed dark eye-spots on the FW and six on the HW. **Underside:** The eye pattern is repeated on the under surface but the eye-spots have white pupils and are surrounded by pale-yellow and light brown concentric rings. There are several zigzag lines running the length of the underwings.

SIMILAR SPECIES: The most similar species is the Appalachian Brown which is a darker brown overall and has a relatively straight to somewhat wavy line running across the HW underside, not zigzag as in the Eyed Brown. Some individuals are intermediate and difficult, if not impossible, to identify. See also Northern Pearly-Eye and Plate 11.

BEHAVIOUR: A weak flyer that does not stray far from its chosen habitat, often landing on sedges (*Carex* spp.).

FLIGHT SEASON: One generation per year.

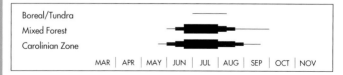

	Boreal/Tundra	Mixed Forest	Carolinian Zone

| MAR | APR | MAY | JUN | JUL | AUG | SEP | OCT | NOV |

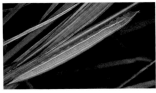

Green form

Brown form

CATERPILLAR: Brown or green with alternating dark and light green lines running along the body. It has two green tails and a green head with red horns. **Foodplants:** A number of broad-leaved sedge species (*Carex* spp.). A recent discovery in eastern Ontario has provided some evidence for the likely use of the invasive lesser lake sedge (*C. acutiformis*) as a foodplant.

OVERWINTERING STAGE: Half-grown caterpillar.

HABITAT: Wet meadows, roadside ditches and fens where sedges are common.

DISTRIBUTION AND ABUNDANCE:
Found from Nova Scotia west to Great Slave Lake in the Northwest Territories and south in the United States to Indiana. In Ontario, it is highly local to sedge patches but can be a common resident where found. Its distribution extends north to Lake Abitibi, Lake Nipigon and Lake of the Woods.

APPALACHIAN BROWN *Lethe appalachia*

39–51 mm

ETYMOLOGY: Named after the Appalachian Mountains in the eastern United States.

ADULT: Medium-sized. **Upperside:** Smoky-brown overall with four small, weakly defined spots on the FW and six larger spots on the HW. **Underside:** Lighter than upperside. There are rows of prominent, yellow-rimmed eyespots on both wings. The mid-wing dark line on the underside is relatively straight to wavy, not zigzag.

SIMILAR SPECIES: Similar to Eyed Brown but paler overall and has a relatively straight to somewhat wavy line running across the HW underside, not zigzag as in the Eyed Brown. Some individuals are intermediate and difficult, if not impossible, to identify. See Plate 11.

BEHAVIOUR: Strays farther than the Eyed Brown and can be found perched on leaves in drier parts of woods.

FLIGHT SEASON: One generation per year.

Boreal/Tundra									
Mixed Forest				▬					
Carolinian Zone				▬					
	MAR	APR	MAY	JUN	JUL	AUG	SEP	OCT	NOV

CATERPILLAR: Similar to the Eyed Brown. Green with alternating dark and light green lines running along the body. It has two green tails and a green head with red horns. Photo not available. **Foodplants:** Sedges (*Carex* spp.).

OVERWINTERING STAGE: Half-grown caterpillar.

HABITAT: Wet areas of woodlands where sedges grow.

DISTRIBUTION AND ABUNDANCE: An eastern United States species, its range extends into Canada only in southern Ontario and Quebec. In Ontario, a locally common resident as far north as Ottawa and Manitoulin Island.

COMMENTS: The two Browns were separated out as species only in 1970. Prior to that, all populations were called Eyed Brown.

319

COMMON RINGLET *Coenonympha tullia*

27–39 mm

ETYMOLOGY: *Coenonympha* is made up of the Greek words *koinos*, meaning "common" and *nymphe*, referring to the female deities of woodlands. *Tullia* was the last queen of Rome.

ADULT: One of the smallest members of the Satyrinae in Ontario. On close inspection, the body and wings appear "hairy" and suited to the species' original northern distribution. **Upperside:** Rarely seen. Variable pale to darker orange-brown with no markings, other than a forewing eye spot on some individuals, thus its subspecific name, *inornata*, meaning "unadorned" in Latin. **Underside:** Greyish-brown to olive-brown, with an orange flush on the inner FW. HW divided by an irregular pale band, the basal half typically darker. Most individuals have a small black eye-spot near the apex of the FW.

SIMILAR SPECIES: No similar species in Ontario.

BEHAVIOUR: Flits slowly, with a bouncing flight, just above or down among the grasses, often landing on grass stems.

FLIGHT SEASON: Two generations per year in Ontario.

	MAR	APR	MAY	JUN	JUL	AUG	SEP	OCT	NOV
Boreal/Tundra									
Mixed Forest									
Carolinian Zone									

Dorsal view

Dark form

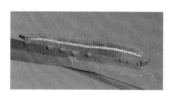

CATERPILLAR: Variable: can be green, olive or brown. They have alternating dark and light stripes along the body and two short pink tails. Head tan or green. **Foodplants:** Usually Kentucky bluegrass (*Poa pratensis*), but feeds on other grasses as well.

OVERWINTERING STAGE: Caterpillar.

HABITAT: Open grasslands, including meadows, roadsides and lawns.

DISTRIBUTION AND ABUNDANCE: Holarctic. In North America, found across Canada and into the United States through the western mountains and northeastern states. In Ontario, a common widespread resident.

COMMENTS: Formerly, did not occur in southwestern Ontario or in the northeastern United States, but during the second half of the twentieth century this species expanded its range dramatically southward. Now found throughout Ontario and as far south as West Virginia. Recent taxonomic work suggests that the North American and Eurasian species are distinct. If so, our species would be renamed *Coenonympha inornata*. However, the common name, Common Ringlet, would likely still stand as the species in Europe is commonly called Large Heath.

LITTLE WOOD-SATYR *Megisto cymela*

29–42 mm

ETYMOLOGY: *Megistos* means "greatest" in Greek. The Greek word *kyma* gives us *cym-*, which can mean "wave", or "sprout/bud", but also "swelling".

ADULT: Small with rounded wings. **Upperside:** Dull brown with eight submarginal black eye-spots, two on each wing. The eye-spots usually have two white pupils each and a pale-yellow outer ring. **Underside:** Light brown, most eye-spots are larger than those on the upperside, with metallic pupils. HW has a number of additional smaller eye-spots. There are two thin dark median lines crossing each wing.

SIMILAR SPECIES: Combination of smaller size, rounded wings and distinctive eye-spots separate this species from other Ontario satyrs.

BEHAVIOUR: Stays close to the ground with a weak, bouncing flight, but will fly into the trees if disturbed.

FLIGHT SEASON: One generation per year.

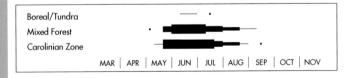

	MAR	APR	MAY	JUN	JUL	AUG	SEP	OCT	NOV
Boreal/Tundra									
Mixed Forest									
Carolinian Zone									

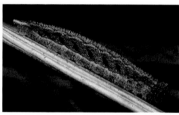

CATERPILLAR: Brown with oblique lateral lines and short tails. Head brown. **Foodplants:** A number of grasses (Poaceae), including Kentucky bluegrass (*Poa pratensis*) and orchard grass (*Dactylis glomerata*).

OVERWINTERING STAGE: Caterpillar.

HABITAT: Woodland openings, roadsides near woodland edges, rarely straying far from the trees.

DISTRIBUTION AND ABUNDANCE:
Eastern and central North America. In Canada, from Saskatchewan to Nova Scotia. In Ontario, a common resident, widespread in the southern parts of the province north to Timiskaming and southern Algoma districts. A separate population extends from south of the Great Lakes into the Rainy River/Lake of the Woods area.

323

COMMON WOOD-NYMPH *Cercyonis pegala*

38–58 mm

Dark form

ETYMOLOGY: *Cercyonis* is derived from the Greek mythological figure *Cercyon/Kerkyon* who would wrestle people to their death until he was killed by Theseus. *Pegala* is from the Greek *pege* meaning "spring or fountain" and the suffix *-al* meaning "belonging to".

ADULT: Our largest satyr, with two variable colour forms. **Upperside:** In Ontario, the "dark" form is more common and is light to dark brown with two prominent FW eye-spots with white-to-bluish pupils. The less common and more southern "light" form is similar but with a prominent yellow patch (variable in extent) surrounding the FW eye-spots. Both forms have a variable number of small eye-spots on the HW. **Underside:** Similar to upperside but with striations across the wings and with a greater number of eye-spots on the HW. The FW spots are also larger and in the dark form are surrounded by a prominent yellow ring.

SIMILAR SPECIES: The "light" form is distinctive. Dorsally, the dark form is similar to other satyrs but is larger and usually has fewer and less prominent HW spots. Ventrally, the very large FW spots and the striated pattern separate this species from other dark satyrs.

BEHAVIOUR: Far more often seen nectaring at flowers than other satyrs. Although the flight is not fast, it is difficult to follow as it is bouncy and erratic.

FLIGHT SEASON: One generation per year.

Dark form

Light form

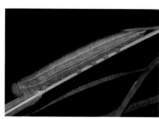

Light form

CATERPILLAR: Green with two red tails, a dark green dorsal stripe and several pale lateral stripes. **Foodplants:** A number of grasses (Poaceae).

OVERWINTERING STAGE: Newly hatched caterpillar.

HABITAT: Grassy open meadows, clearings, roadsides and along the edges of wetlands and streams.

DISTRIBUTION AND ABUNDANCE: Widespread throughout most of the United States and southern Canada. In Ontario, a common resident north to Lake Abitibi and west to the Rainy River/Lake of the Woods area.

COMMENTS: This butterfly is highly variable and forms a cline across its wide range. In Ontario, more northern individuals tend to have little or no yellow surrounding the wing eye-spots, whereas in southern areas (particularly southwestern Ontario), the yellow area can be quite prominent.

TAIGA ALPINE *Erebia mancinus*

35–43 mm

ETYMOLOGY: *Erebos* was the son of Darkness and Chaos in Greek mythology; the term also refers to the region that the dead had to pass before entering the underworld. The specific name may come from the Latin word *mancus* meaning "maimed or imperfect". Equally likely is that it is from the name of a cowardly Roman general in 137 BCE, *Gaius Hostilius Mancinus*.

ADULT: Small to medium-sized. **Upperside:** Rarely seen, but dark brown with three to five small black spots surrounded by reddish-orange. **Underside:** Similar to upperside but with some greyish dusting toward the outer edges and a small white central spot on the HW.

SIMILAR SPECIES: Red-disked Alpine lacks the spots surrounded by reddish-orange on the FW. Jutta Arctic, with which it often occurs, is a faster flyer and has a more mottled underside HW.

BEHAVIOUR: Generally a slow and weak flyer. Rarely seen visiting flowers, often mudpuddling. Commonly perches on tree trunks.

FLIGHT SEASON: One generation per year, possibly taking two years to mature in some areas.

	MAR	APR	MAY	JUN	JUL	AUG	SEP	OCT	NOV
Boreal/Tundra									
Mixed Forest									
Carolinian Zone									

Dorsal view

Semi-open spruce bog

CATERPILLAR: Early stages are undescribed. All caterpillars of known alpine species are very similar. Photo not available. **Foodplants:** Assumed to feed on grasses (Poaceae) and sedges (*Carex* spp.), as do other members of this group.

OVERWINTERING STAGE: Assumed to be as a caterpillar.

HABITAT: Spruce and tamarack bogs and especially the wet open forests around these bogs.

DISTRIBUTION AND ABUNDANCE: Holarctic. In North America, ranges from Alaska to Labrador, dipping into northern Minnesota. In Ontario, an uncommon and local resident in the north, becoming less common farther east. Recorded from Favourable Lake near the Manitoba border, and from Rainy River District, east to Lake Abitibi near the Quebec border.

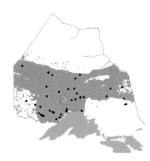

COMMENTS: This butterfly was once considered a subspecies of the Disa Alpine (*E. disa*) which is found on the Canadian and Alaskan arctic coasts. Earlier Ontario butterfly publications referred to it as *E. disa*.

RED-DISKED ALPINE *Erebia discoidalis*

35–44 mm

ETYMOLOGY: *Discoidalis* may come from the Greek *discos* meaning "disk" and the suffix *-oides* meaning "resembling".

ADULT: Small to medium-sized. **Upperside:** Rarely seen, but dark brown ground colour with no eye-spots. As referred to in its common name, there is a central orange flush through the FW. **Underside:** FW with central orange flush but paler than upperside. HW dark brown with hoary frosting on the outer half.

SIMILAR SPECIES: Similar to Taiga Alpine but Red-Disked lacks the orange band with black spots on the FW.

BEHAVIOUR: Flies weakly, low to the ground, often landing on grass stems or on the ground.

FLIGHT SEASON: One generation per year.

Boreal/Tundra									
Mixed Forest									
Carolinian Zone									
	MAR	APR	MAY	JUN	JUL	AUG	SEP	OCT	NOV

Dorsal view

Grassy peatland, Hudson Bay Lowlands

CATERPILLAR: Cream-coloured with black diagonal stripes. Photo not available. **Foodplants:** A number of sedges (*Carex* spp.) and grasses (Poaceae).

OVERWINTERING STAGE: Caterpillar.

HABITAT: In Ontario, reported from open grassy areas in jack pine forests, peatlands, clear-cuts, and along hydro corridors and railways.

DISTRIBUTION AND ABUNDANCE:
Holarctic. In North America, ranges from Alaska to Quebec and extends into some of the northern United States. In Ontario, an uncommon and local resident found from Hudson Bay (few records in the far north) south to Sudbury District.

JUTTA ARCTIC *Oeneis jutta*

35–55 mm

ETYMOLOGY: *Oeneis* was possibly the mother of *Pan*, the Greek mythological deity of flocks and shepherds. *Jutta* was probably named after the old Danish state of Jutland.

ADULT: Small to medium-sized. **Upperside:** Rarely seen, but grey-brown with a submarginal row of dull orange spots some of which have a dark centre. Male also has a dark, streak-like sex patch through the middle of the FW. **Underside:** FW has one to three orange-rimmed, black eye-spots but the FW is usually covered by the HW when perched. HW is mottled grey-and-brown with a relatively faint darker median band usually with a whitish edge on the outer side. HW fringe is checkered dark brown and white in fresh individuals.

SIMILAR SPECIES: The only Ontario arctic with orange-rimmed, black eyespots. The Taiga Alpine is darker brown, less mottled, and has a white central spot on the underside HW.

BEHAVIOUR: Sticks close to treed areas, often landing on trunks and branches. Although it flies very fast and is easily disturbed, it is territorial and often returns to its original perch.

FLIGHT SEASON: Although it takes two years to reach the adult stage, there are two cohorts in Ontario and they can be found flying every year.

	MAR	APR	MAY	JUN	JUL	AUG	SEP	OCT	NOV
Boreal/Tundra									
Mixed Forest									
Carolinian Zone									

♂

Dorsal view

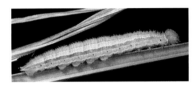

CATERPILLAR: Greenish with dark green and white stripes on the sides and red hairs. **Foodplants:** Cotton-grasses (*Eriophorum* spp.), sedges (*Carex* spp.), and rushes (*Juncus* spp.).

OVERWINTERING STAGE: Two years as a caterpillar.

HABITAT: Tamarack and spruce bogs, and wet areas in boreal forests and tundra.

DISTRIBUTION AND ABUNDANCE: Holarctic. In North America, ranges from Alaska to Newfoundland and south through the Rocky Mountains to Colorado and into the northeastern United States. In Ontario, an uncommon and local resident found from the Hudson Bay coast south to Algonquin Park with isolated populations in several bogs (Alfred Bog and the Mer Bleue) south and east of Ottawa.

COMMENTS: Recent taxonomic work suggests that the North American and Eurasian species are distinct. If so, our species would be renamed *Oeneis balderi*. The common name, Jutta Arctic, would therefore, not make sense. The common name may be changed to either Balder's Arctic or Bog Arctic.

331

MELISSA ARCTIC *Oeneis melissa*

34–50 mm

ETYMOLOGY: *Melissa* is a female name in Greek, meaning "honeybee".

ADULT: Small to medium-sized. **Upperside:** Rarely seen, but translucent, greyish-brown and usually no eye-spots in the subspecies found in Ontario. **Underside:** HW mottled black and pale-grey. A pale, indistinct, medial band may be present on the HW.

SIMILAR SPECIES: The Melissa Arctic in Ontario is most like the Polixenes Arctic (see **Additional Species to Watch for in Ontario**, page 446), but the latter is usually browner above and the band on the lower HW is darker and more contrasting.

BEHAVIOUR: This arctic can be quite territorial, chasing off other butterflies. The males perch awaiting females. Often perch on the ground, usually upon rocks, against which they are well camouflaged. Adults rarely nectar at flowers.

FLIGHT SEASON: Even though the species takes two years to mature, it can be seen flying in Ontario every year.

Boreal/Tundra			—					
Mixed Forest								
Carolinian Zone								
	MAR	APR	MAY	JUN	JUL	AUG	SEP	OCT	NOV

Dorsal view

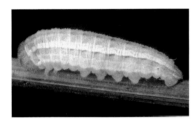

CATERPILLAR: Colour variable, from brown to green with black, brown or green stripes along the body. The head is black with six darker stripes. Pupation occurs among the rocks. **Foodplants:** Several sedges, including Bigelow's sedge (*Carex bigelowii)* and rock sedge (*Carex rupestris*). In captivity they will also eat other grasses.

OVERWINTERING STAGE: Two years as a caterpillar.

HABITAT: Mainly tundra, favouring gravelly ridges.

DISTRIBUTION AND ABUNDANCE: Although widespread across the northern and alpine parts of North America, in Ontario, it is a rare-to-uncommon resident restricted to locations along the Hudson Bay coast.

CHRYXUS ARCTIC *Oeneis chryxus*

39–54 mm

ETYMOLOGY: Named from the Greek *chryxos or chrysos* meaning "gold", for the colour of the uppersides.

ADULT: Medium-sized. **Upperside:** Not often seen, but orange-brown with two to four black submarginal spots on the FW and usually only one on the HW near the anal angle. The males have a dark diagonal sex patch on the FW. **Underside:** FW has some orange whereas lower HW is striated with dark brown and grey, usually darker on the inner half. Veins are usually lined in pale-grey, a useful identification feature. HW spot is usually visible but may be partially obscured by the striations.

SIMILAR SPECIES: Can be confused with any of the other arctics and with both Taiga and Red-disked alpines where their ranges overlap. The heavily striated pattern of the underside HW along with the prominent pale veins helps to distinguish this species.

BEHAVIOUR: Most often seen resting on lichen-covered rocks, sand or lichen with its folded wings tilted to the side leaving very little shadow. In this posture, it is well camouflaged. Once alarmed, it quickly flies off, but often returns to the same area. Males establish a territory of about 10 to 15 metres square and defend it from intruders.

FLIGHT SEASON: One generation per year.

	MAR	APR	MAY	JUN	JUL	AUG	SEP	OCT	NOV
Boreal/Tundra									
Mixed Forest									
Carolinian Zone									

CATERPILLAR: Tan-coloured and covered in reddish hairs with darker lateral stripes running along the body. The head has six brown stripes. **Foodplants:** Poverty oatgrass (*Danthonia spicata*), but also other grasses (Poaceae).

OVERWINTERING STAGE: Caterpillar.

HABITAT: Open, dry habitats including Precambrian rock barrens, alvars, openings in sandy-soiled pine forests and, in the far north, possibly bogs.

DISTRIBUTION AND ABUNDANCE: Mainly a Canadian butterfly ranging from Yukon and British Columbia east to Quebec and into Wisconsin and Michigan. The Rocky Mountain subspecies extends south through the mountains to New Mexico. In Ontario, an uncommon and local resident and the most southerly ranging of the Ontario arctics. It appears to be most common along the southern edge of the Canadian Shield but ranges north to the Hudson Bay coast.

COMMENTS: Recent taxonomic work suggests that the Rocky Mountain subspecies of Chryxus Arctic is distinct enough from the remaining North American subspecies that it may constitute a separate species. If so, the Rocky Mountain subspecies would retain the name *Oeneis chryxus* with the others being renamed *Oeneis calais*. The common name, Chryxus Arctic, would therefore remain for the mountain species and it has been proposed that the others be called either Calais Arctic or Barrens Arctic.

MACOUN'S ARCTIC *Oeneis macounii*

46–65 mm

ETYMOLOGY: *Macounii* refers to John Macoun, a noted nineteenth-century Canadian naturalist.

ADULT: The largest of the arctics found in Ontario, with a scalloped HW. **Upperside:** Orange-brown with a dark border. There are two to four dark eye-spots on the FW, the largest having white pupils, and one small eye-spot on the HW near the anal angle. **Underside:** FW is similar to the upperside whereas the HW is striated dark and light brown with two darker wavy median bands.

SIMILAR SPECIES: The only Ontario arctic with dark bordered wings dorsally. Ventrally, the striated pattern with two dark bands, helps to distinguish it from other similar species.

BEHAVIOUR: A relatively slow-flying species. If alarmed, it will fly directly into the trees and land on limbs or trunks. This is the only Ontario arctic that is commonly seen perched with wings partially open.

FLIGHT SEASON: One generation every two years. In Ontario, flies only in even-numbered years.

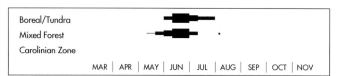

	Boreal/Tundra	Mixed Forest	Carolinian Zone
MAR	APR	MAY	JUN	JUL	AUG	SEP	OCT	NOV

Jack pines, Algonquin Provincial Park, east side

CATERPILLAR: Greenish with a grey dorsal stripe and with brown to grey-green lateral stripes. The head is yellowish-green. All known species of arctic caterpillars are very similar. Photo not available.
Foodplants: Has not been recorded in the wild, but in captivity the caterpillars eat a variety of grasses (Poaceae).

OVERWINTERING STAGE: Two years as a caterpillar.

HABITAT: Sandy, dry, jack pine forest, along roadsides or in clearings.

DISTRIBUTION AND ABUNDANCE: This is almost exclusively a Canadian butterfly, ranging from British Columbia to northern Ontario with a few locations in northern Minnesota and Michigan. There are isolated populations in western Quebec. In Ontario, a rare and local resident found from the Ontario-Manitoba border east to northern Algoma District. There is an isolated population on the eastern side of Algonquin Park. Although it has not been recorded between Algoma District and Algonquin Park, there is suitable jack pine forest in which it may be found.

Arctic Skippers

THE SKIPPERS
Family Hesperiidae

The skipper family is a large one with about 3,700 species described worldwide. More than 300 species have been recorded in North America with 51 reported from Ontario. A few of these are based on only a few sightings or collections.

The adult members of the family are mostly small, but a few range to medium-sized. They all have antennae with a club that ends in a narrow extension called an apiculus. The adult bodies are stout and they have a wide head. Most have a very rapid, buzzy flight. Of all our butterflies, the skippers are considered the most difficult to identify on the wing because of their small size, rapid flight and tendency to subtle coloration.

Males of many of our skippers regularly perch on selected sites such as exposed leaves, grasses or sedges. They buzz rapidly off their perch if a female or perceived competitor approaches. Potential competition is pursued until off site and then the males usually will resume perching, often in the same spot. A pair will regularly perform a nuptial dance sometimes high in the air. If disturbed during mating, the larger females may carry the males away.

Many skippers also have a very long proboscis compared to their body length and use it to delve deeply into flowers for nectar. Some adults will feed on bird droppings, mammal dung and other sources of nutrients.

The skipper family is grouped into six subfamilies of which three are represented in Ontario; Spread-winged Skippers (Pyrginae), Intermediate Skippers (Heteropterinae) and Grass Skippers (Hesperiinae).

SPREAD-WINGED SKIPPERS (page 344)
Subfamily: Pyrginae

Nineteen members of this subfamily have been recorded in Ontario. Most species are quite dull, being brown or brownish-grey with some pale spotting. The duskywings (*Erynnis* spp.) are one of the most difficult groups of butterflies to identify to species so we have included a general description for this genus.

DUSKYWINGS
Genus

The duskywings are dark skippers with some degree of mottling and usually a number of small whitish spots on the forewings. The hindwings usually have a diffuse row of yellowish spots along the margins. They are most often seen landing on or near the ground with wings held flat. Once disturbed, they fly very quickly and erratically. Ontario's duskywings can be broken into three main groups: 1) the species with virtually no white forewing spots—Dreamy and Sleepy; 2) the typically larger species with fairly prominent white wing spots—Juvenal's and Horace's; and 3) the species with typically smaller white wing spots—Mottled, Zarucco, Funereal, Columbine, Wild Indigo and Persius. The last three of these are particularly difficult to separate. As a result of this difficulty, many individuals have been misidentified in the past and, therefore, the maps contained within some publications are incorrect. Females are slightly to considerably larger than males.

INTERMEDIATE SKIPPERS (page 382)
Subfamily: Heteropterinae

There are about 150 species in this subfamily worldwide, but there are only five species in North America north of Mexico and only a single species in Ontario, the Arctic Skipper.

BRANDED SKIPPERS (page 384)
Subfamily: Hesperiinae

Thirty-one members of this subfamily have been recorded
in Ontario. Sizes range from the tiny Least Skipper to
the large Brazilian Skipper. When perched, the branded
skippers often hold their hindwings more open than their
forewings providing a view of both wing surfaces—often
helpful for identification. The males of most species have
a scent gland or stigma on the upper forewing and the two
sexes are usually different in their patterns and coloration.
Identification is often difficult in this group. Eggs are
rounded and laid singly. The caterpillars feed on monocots
particularly grasses (Poaceae) and sedges (Cyperaceae).
They often live in nests on the foodplants made by tying
parts of the plant together with silk. Relatively little is
known about the life histories of many of these species.

Dreamy Duskywing

Eggs

The hemispherical eggs are laid singly on the hostplants.

Arctic Skipper

Silver-spotted Skipper

Least Skipper

Tawny-edged Skipper

Northern Cloudywing

Wild Indigo Duskywing

Caterpillars

Caterpillars are smooth, tapering at both ends and are best recognized by the large head and narrow "neck". Most live in leaf nests secured by silk strands and feed at night.

Juvenal's Duskywing

Delaware Skipper

Dreamy Duskywing

Common Sootywing

Zabulon Skipper - brown form

Arctic Skipper

Chrysalides

The chrysalides are smooth and cylindrical and are usually formed in leaf litter near the hostplants.

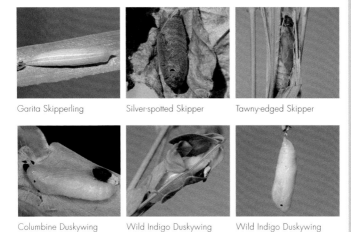

Garita Skipperling   Silver-spotted Skipper   Tawny-edged Skipper

Columbine Duskywing   Wild Indigo Duskywing   Wild Indigo Duskywing

SILVER-SPOTTED SKIPPER *Epargyreus clarus*

37–45 mm

ETYMOLOGY: *Epargyreus* means "silver-plated" in Greek. In Latin, *clarus* means "clear".

ADULT: Ontario's largest skipper. FW very pointed. **Upperside:** Brown with a yellowish-orange median band and white subapical spots. **Underside:** FW similar to upperside. HW brown with a distinctive silver median band across the middle.

SIMILAR SPECIES: The only similar species is the extremely rare Hoary Edge but its wings are more rounded with a whitish marginal band on the HW underside rather than the silver median band as in Silver-spotted Skipper.

BEHAVIOUR: A very strong flyer and avid flower visitor. Often chooses a favourite perch and returns to it regularly.

FLIGHT SEASON: One generation per year in most of its Ontario range, with a second smaller generation in the extreme southwest of the province.

CATERPILLAR: Pale green with darker green to blackish bands and orange prolegs. Head dark brown with large, orange eye-spots. Lives within a nest made of leaves of the foodplant pulled together with silk. **Foodplants:** Members of the Legume family (Fabaceae), including American hog peanut (*Amphicarpaea bracteata*), American groundnut (*Apios americana*) and showy tick-trefoil (*Desmodium canadense*). Black locust (*Robinia pseudoacacia*), native to the southern United States but widely planted in southern Ontario, may also be used in Ontario.

OVERWINTERING STAGE: The chrysalis overwinters within a nest made of leaves from the foodplant or another nearby plant. See page 343.

HABITAT: Old fields, woodland edges and gardens.

DISTRIBUTION AND ABUNDANCE:
Northern Mexico and most of the United States, north into the Canadian prairies as well as southern Ontario and Quebec. In Ontario, a common-to-uncommon resident throughout southern Ontario as well as in the Rainy River/Lake of the Woods area but rare on the Canadian Shield. Usually seen singly or in small numbers.

LONG-TAILED SKIPPER *Urbanus proteus*

37–46 mm

ETYMOLOGY: In Latin, *Urbanus* refers to "cities". In Greek mythology, *Proteus* was a sea god that could assume many forms.

ADULT: A large skipper, with long tails. **Upperside:** FW brown with large square-shaped hyaline spots. HW with long dark tails. Body and inner wing margins are iridescent blue. **Underside:** FW similar to upperside. HW brown with blackish bands and spots.

SIMILAR SPECIES: None in Ontario.

BEHAVIOUR: An extremely fast flyer; frequently hangs upside down while nectaring with wings held at 45° angles.

FLIGHT SEASON: Records from the northern part of the range are from late summer and fall.

Boreal/Tundra									
Mixed Forest									
Carolinian Zone						• •	•	•	
	MAR	APR	MAY	JUN	JUL	AUG	SEP	OCT	NOV

CATERPILLAR: Not likely to be encountered in Ontario. Mottled green with a bright yellow lateral stripe, washed orange toward the rear. Head reddish with black in the centre. **Foodplants:** Legumes (Fabaceae), especially species that grow as vines.

OVERWINTERING STAGE: Does not overwinter in Ontario.

HABITAT: Any habitat with nectar-bearing flowers.

DISTRIBUTION AND ABUNDANCE: Largely tropical and subtropical, its permanent range extends from Argentina north through Central America and the West Indies to Texas and Florida. Migrates northward in summer, breeding as far north as Connecticut. Strays periodically farther north but not known to breed. In Ontario, a very rare, non-breeding migrant that has been recorded only four times in Ontario—once at Point Pelee, once at Ojibway Prairie in Windsor, both in 1994, and most recently in Hamilton and Toronto in 2012.

HOARY EDGE *Achalarus lyciades*

40–49 mm

ETYMOLOGY: The original species epithet was *lycidas* which is the name of a goatherd in a Greek bucolic poem, *Harvest Feast*, by the Sicilian poet Theocritus (third century BCE). *Lycidas* is also the title of a poem written in 1637 by John Milton dedicated to the memory of drowned colleague Edward King.

ADULT: A large skipper. **Upperside:** Dark brown with glassy yellowish spots forming a median band. **Underside:** FW similar to the upperside. HW brown with a distinctive wide frosty-white (hoary) marginal band.

SIMILAR SPECIES: The only similar species is the Silver-spotted Skipper. Hoary Edge wings are more rounded with a whitish marginal band on the HW underside rather than the silver median band of the Silver-spotted Skipper.

BEHAVIOUR: Males watch for females from a branch 1-2 metres high along the edge of forest clearings. They fly out to chase away other insects but usually return to the same perch.

FLIGHT SEASON: One generation per year.

Boreal/Tundra								
Mixed Forest								
Carolinian Zone			———					
	MAR	APR	MAY	JUN	JUL	AUG	SEP	OCT	NOV

CATERPILLAR: Light green with a pale orange lateral stripe. Head dark.
Foodplants: Legumes (Fabaceae), including tick-trefoils (*Desmodium* spp.) and bush-clovers (*Lespedeza* spp.).

OVERWINTERING STAGE: Chrysalis.

HABITAT: Open, dry, sandy woodlands.

DISTRIBUTION AND ABUNDANCE:
Eastern and southern United States from the central New England states south to Florida and west to Iowa and central Texas. In Ontario, a very rare resident known only from intact natural habitat within the city of Windsor in the extreme southwestern part of the province.

SOUTHERN CLOUDYWING *Thorybes bathyllus*

32–38 mm

ETYMOLOGY: *Thorybes* is derived from the Greek word *thorybos* meaning "noise of crowded assembly, cheers, applause, uproar". In the old city of Megalopolis in Greece, *Bathyllus* was a spring that flowed into the Helisson river. *Bathy* is "deep" in Greek.

ADULT: Medium-sized to large skipper with a pale face. **Upperside:** Uniform brown with prominent glassy-white diagonal markings on the FW forming a median band with another elongated subapical spot. **Underside:** FW markings similar to upperside. HW dark brown with two mottled bands and often with whitish frosting toward the margin.

SIMILAR SPECIES: Most similar to Northern Cloudywing but the white wing markings are usually much less prominent in Northern and are arranged in a less regular pattern. Also, Southern has a pale face while Northern has a dark face.

BEHAVIOUR: Males are very territorial, guarding their territory from a single low perch. Commonly seen nectaring.

FLIGHT SEASON: Typically only one generation in Ontario, occasionally a smaller second generation.

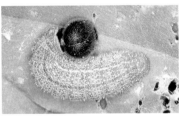

CATERPILLAR: Pale green to brown with minute cream-to-yellowish spots, a thin brownish mid-dorsal line and yellowish lateral lines. Head and collar dark brown to black. Cannot be distinguished from the caterpillar of Northern Cloudywing. **Foodplants:** Various legumes (Fabaceae).

OVERWINTERING STAGE: Mature caterpillar within a leaf nest.

HABITAT: Open areas, especially dry ones.

DISTRIBUTION AND ABUNDANCE: Most of the eastern United States. In Ontario, a rare resident largely restricted to the southwest but with some records in the greater Toronto area.

NORTHERN CLOUDYWING *Thorybes pylades*

28–38 mm

ETYMOLOGY: *Pylades* means "faithful friend" in Greek; in Greek mythology, Pylades was the close friend of Orestes.

ADULT: Medium-sized to large skipper with a dark face. **Upperside:** Uniform brown with small glassy white spots arranged in an irregular fashion on the FW. **Underside:** FW markings similar to upperside. HW dark brown with two mottled bands and usually with prominent whitish frosting toward the margin.

SIMILAR SPECIES: Most similar to Southern Cloudywing but the white wing markings are usually much less prominent in Northern and are arranged in a less regular pattern. Also, Southern has a pale face, whereas Northern has a dark face.

BEHAVIOUR: Males defend a territory from a perch on or near the ground. Commonly seen nectaring.

FLIGHT SEASON: One generation throughout most of Ontario with a smaller second generation in extreme southwestern Ontario.

	Boreal/Tundra								
	Mixed Forest								
	Carolinian Zone								
	MAR	APR	MAY	JUN	JUL	AUG	SEP	OCT	NOV

CATERPILLAR: Pale green to brown with minute cream-to-yellowish spots, a thin brownish mid-dorsal line and yellowish lateral lines. Head and collar dark brown to black. Cannot be distinguished from the caterpillar of Southern Cloudywing. **Foodplants:** Various legumes (Fabaceae).

OVERWINTERING STAGE: Mature caterpillar within a leaf nest.

HABITAT: Dry to medium-dry open or semi-open areas.

DISTRIBUTION AND ABUNDANCE:
Mexico north through most of the United States and Canada south of the Territories. In Ontario, a relatively common and widespread resident across southern Ontario as well as in the Rainy River area. Less common in northern Ontario where it ranges as far north as Moosonee and to Favourable Lake near the Manitoba border.

353

HAYHURST'S SCALLOPWING *Staphylus hayhurstii*

`19–24 mm`

ETYMOLOGY: In Greek mythology, *Staphylus* was an Argonaut, the son of Dionysus and Ariadne. This species is named for Dr. L.K. Hayhurst, an American physician who provided W. H. Edwards with much information about western butterflies.

ADULT: Very small. **Upperside:** Dark wings with even darker concentric bands. FW with two small white subapical spots and a small median white spot. HW margin scalloped. **Underside:** Rarely seen, but similar in pattern to the upperside.

SIMILAR SPECIES: No other dark skippers have a scalloped HW margin.

BEHAVIOUR: Usually perches low, often on foliage, with wings horizontally flattened. Rapid, darting flight, especially when disturbed.

FLIGHT SEASON: Two overlapping generations.

Boreal/Tundra									
Mixed Forest									
Carolinian Zone				————					
	MAR	APR	MAY	JUN	JUL	AUG	SEP	OCT	NOV

West beach, Fish Point Nature Reserve, Pelee Island. Last known Ontario resident colony.

CATERPILLAR: Dark green with many white-to-yellowish spots and a faint white subdorsal stripe. Sometimes the body becomes purplish toward the rear. Head black, collar brown. **Foodplants:** In Ontario, common lamb's-quarters (*Chenopodium album*).

OVERWINTERING STAGE: Mature caterpillar within a dead-leaf nest.

HABITAT: Open areas.

DISTRIBUTION AND ABUNDANCE: Eastern United States west to Nebraska. In Ontario, had been a very rare resident with the only extant population occurring at several sites on Pelee Island. However, the species has not been seen on the island in several years. Very rarely, individuals stray to Point Pelee National Park, where there was formerly a second resident population.

COMMENTS: Although this is the only scallopwing in most of North America, this genus contains several dozen species in the tropics. It is unknown why this particular species has expanded northward, feeding on a non-native plant species.

COMMON SOOTYWING *Pholisora catullus*

21–28 mm

ETYMOLOGY: *Pholis* is "scaly" in Greek; *ora* means "mouth" in Latin. *Gaius Valerius Catullus* was a Roman poet of the first century BCE.

ADULT: Very small. **Upperside:** FW dark sooty-black with many round white spots in the submarginal area and a single spot in the median. HW all dark. Worn individuals can appear brown with reduced white wing spots. **Underside:** Uniform dark brown with few submarginal white spots on the FW.

SIMILAR SPECIES: Duskywings are superficially similar but lack the very uniform dark wings of Common Sootywing and have far fewer white wing spots.

BEHAVIOUR: A very skittish species, almost always on the move. When perched, their wings are most often held flat—sometimes raised.

FLIGHT SEASON: Two generations per year.

Worn individual

CATERPILLAR: Pale green with many white or pale yellow spots. Head black. Collar black, broken in the middle and bordered with white.
Foodplants: Usually common lamb's-quarters (*Chenopodium album*), but also members of the Amaranth family (Amaranthaceae), including redroot amaranth (*Amaranthus retroflexus*).

OVERWINTERING STAGE: Mature caterpillar in silken nest.

HABITAT: Open habitats, mostly disturbed areas.

DISTRIBUTION AND ABUNDANCE:
Central Mexico north through most of the United States and into southern Canada. In Ontario, an uncommon resident, most common in southwestern Ontario, with records from Toronto and as far north as Haliburton and the Ottawa area (the latter in the early 1960s, but not seen since).

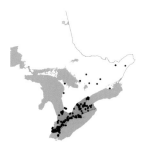

DREAMY DUSKYWING *Erynnis icelus*

23–30 mm

ETYMOLOGY: In Greek mythology, the *Erinyes*, or furies, were netherworld goddesses who avenged crimes against the natural order, particularly homicides; the god *Icelus* was believed to shape the dreams of men.

ADULT: Small. FW with no prominent white spots and head with long labial palps. Due to the similarity with Sleepy Duskywing, most of the description is contained below.

SIMILAR SPECIES: Extremely similar to Sleepy Duskywing—both species have similar wing patterns and no prominent white spots on the upper FW. Where their ranges overlap, best separated by these characters: 1) FW outer dark band is less defined near the leading edge in Dreamy; 2) FW inner dark band typically more distinct in Sleepy; 3) FW subcostal patch of Dreamy more prominent and silvery, especially in males; 4) labial palps longer in Dreamy, especially in males; 5) when perched, Dreamy tends to hold the wings farther forward; 6) Sleepy tends to be found only in dry oak woods, whereas Dreamy is found in a variety of habitats; and 7) Dreamy has a white spot, although very small, on the FW leading edge—such a spot is never present in Sleepy. See Plate 12.

BEHAVIOUR: Most often seen perched on the ground in sandy or muddy areas, less often seen nectaring on flowers. Flies low but fast.

FLIGHT SEASON: One generation.

	MAR	APR	MAY	JUN	JUL	AUG	SEP	OCT	NOV
Boreal/Tundra									
Mixed Forest									
Carolinian Zone									

CATERPILLAR: Pale green with many small white dots, a dark green mid-dorsal stripe and white lateral stripes. Head pale brown without the orange spots found in many other duskywing caterpillars. **Foodplants:** Aspens and poplars (*Populus* spp.), willows (*Salix* spp.) and birches (*Betula* spp.).

OVERWINTERING STAGE: Mature caterpillar within a silken nest.

HABITAT: Open areas, usually near forests and woodlands.

DISTRIBUTION AND ABUNDANCE: Much of Canada and south through the western mountains to New Mexico as well as through the eastern United States to Georgia. In Ontario, a common and widespread resident as far north as Favourable Lake and southern James Bay. Far less common and more locally distributed in southwestern Ontario.

SLEEPY DUSKYWING *Erynnis brizo*

28–35 mm

ETYMOLOGY: In Greek, *brizo* means "to nod" or "sleep".

ADULT: Small to medium-sized skipper. FW with no white markings. Due to the similarity with Dreamy Duskywing, most of the description is contained below in the Similar Species section.

SIMILAR SPECIES: Extremely similar to Dreamy Duskywing—both species have similar wing patterns and no prominent white spots on the upper FW. Where their ranges overlap, best separated by these characters: 1) FW outer dark band is less defined near the leading edge in Dreamy; 2) FW inner dark band typically more distinct in Sleepy; 3) FW subcostal patch of Dreamy more prominent and silvery, especially in males; 4) labial palps longer in Dreamy, especially in males; 5) when perched, Dreamy tends to hold the wings farther forward; 6) Sleepy tends to be found only in dry oak woods, whereas Dreamy is found in a variety of habitats; and 7) Dreamy has a white spot, although very small, on the FW leading edge—such a spot is never present in Sleepy Duskywing. See Plate 12.

BEHAVIOUR: Often seen perching on or near the ground or nectaring on flowers in oak woodlands. Flies low and fast, often quite skittish.

FLIGHT SEASON: One generation.

	Boreal/Tundra								
	Mixed Forest								
	Carolinian Zone								
MAR	APR	MAY	JUN	JUL	AUG	SEP	OCT	NOV

CATERPILLAR: Pale green with many small white dots, a dark green mid-dorsal stripe and white lateral stripes. Head pale orange-brown with three orange spots on each side, although often with only the lowermost spots. **Foodplants:** Oaks (*Quercus* spp.).

OVERWINTERING STAGE: Mature caterpillar within a leaf nest.

HABITAT: Dry oak woodlands.

DISTRIBUTION AND ABUNDANCE: Central Mexico and the southern United States north through the eastern United States to southern Canada, ranging from eastern Saskatchewan to southern Ontario. In Ontario, a rare and local resident restricted to a few locations in southwestern Ontario.

COMMENTS: Records in the literature from north of the above range are very likely misidentified Dreamy Duskywings.

JUVENAL'S DUSKYWING *Erynnis juvenalis*

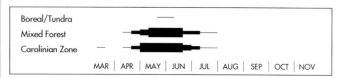

30–37 mm

ETYMOLOGY: *Juvenal* or *Decimus Iunius Iuvenalis* was a Roman poet and author in the first century AD.

ADULT: Medium-sized to large skipper. **Upperside:** Dark brown and black mottled FW with a slightly frosted appearance when fresh. White wing spots large with a prominent spot in the centre of the wing and a chain of spots toward the tips. Females much more mottled than males, and they can be very brown, especially when worn. **Underside:** White spots on the upperside FW are visible from below. The most useful feature is the two pale white spots toward the leading edge of the HW, but some individuals lack these spots.

SIMILAR SPECIES: Most similar to Horace's and Zarucco duskywings (both rare migrants) but the white wing spots in males are typically much smaller than those of Juvenal's. Wild Indigo Duskywing is also similar but has smaller white wing spots (especially in males). The two ventral HW spots in Juvenal's, when present, are normally diagnostic, but some Horace's Duskywings have similar spots. Face often whitish in Horace's, darker in Juvenal's but this can be variable.

BEHAVIOUR: Most often seen perched on the ground with flattened wings, often mudpuddling. Very wary and difficult to approach, darting off with fast, erratic flight when disturbed.

FLIGHT SEASON: One generation per year.

	MAR	APR	MAY	JUN	JUL	AUG	SEP	OCT	NOV
Boreal/Tundra									
Mixed Forest									
Carolinian Zone									

362

CATERPILLAR: Pale to medium-green with many small white dots, a dark green mid-dorsal stripe and pale yellow lateral stripes. Head light to dark orange-brown rimmed on either side with three bright orange spots. **Foodplants:** Oaks (*Quercus* spp.)

OVERWINTERING STAGE: Mature caterpillar.

HABITAT: Open areas near oak woodlands.

DISTRIBUTION AND ABUNDANCE: Occurs throughout the eastern United States. In Canada, found from southeastern Saskatchewan to southern Quebec, as well as in Nova Scotia. In Ontario, a common and widespread resident found throughout most of southern Ontario north to the Sudbury area and west across the north shore of Lake Superior to the Rainy River area, essentially coinciding with the distribution of oaks.

HORACE'S DUSKYWING *Erynnis horatius*

♀

28–39 mm

ETYMOLOGY: *Quintus Horatius Flaccus* was a leading Roman poet in the first century BCE.

ADULT: Medium-sized to large skipper. Face often whitish. **Upperside:** Male FW dark blackish-brown with small white subapical spots and very little to no whitish frosting. Male HW dark blackish-brown. Female FW very mottled with very large glassy spots. Female HW pale brown with darker submarginal spots. **Underside:** White spots on FW same as upperside. Female HW with large dark submarginal spots. Rarely, this duskywing has two white spots near the leading edge of the HW similar to Juvenal's.

SIMILAR SPECIES: See Juvenal's Duskywing. Zarucco Duskywing is very similar but has more pointed FW and a brown or yellow-brown HW fringe (rather than dark as in Horace's). Also, the HW underside in Zarucco is dark with few to no pale dots, unlike the heavily dotted HW of Horace's. Females can be very similar to female Wild Indigo Duskywing but the underside HW of Horace's has large dark submarginal spots, whereas Wild Indigo has small pale spots.

BEHAVIOUR: Most often seen perched on or near the ground in the typical duskywing posture with wings held flat.

FLIGHT SEASON: All individuals in Ontario are thought to be migrants. Most likely to be seen in late summer.

Boreal/Tundra								
Mixed Forest								
Carolinian Zone		·	·			━━		
MAR	APR	MAY	JUN	JUL	AUG	SEP	OCT	NOV

CATERPILLAR: Not likely to be encountered in Ontario, but similar in appearance to Juvenal's. **Foodplants:** Oaks (*Quercus* spp.).

OVERWINTERING STAGE: Mature caterpillar, but not known to overwinter in Ontario.

HABITAT: Open areas, usually near oaks, but any open area is possible.

DISTRIBUTION AND ABUNDANCE:
Widespread through the central and eastern United States. A rare, non-breeding migrant to extreme southwestern Ontario as well as a single record from Toronto (August 7, 2011). Ovipositing has been observed at Point Pelee; afterwards small caterpillars were found but it is not known if these grew to maturity.

MOTTLED DUSKYWING *Erynnis martialis*

♂

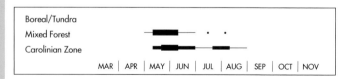

25–29 mm

ETYMOLOGY: *Marcus Valerius Martialis* was a satirical Latin poet from Hispania in the first century AD. He is considered the creator of the modern epigram.

ADULT: Small. **Upperside:** FW brown with irregularly placed black patches and whitish markings and a purplish gloss (especially in fresh individuals). This pattern creates a very mottled, almost checkerboard pattern. HW also mottled in appearance, although not to the same degree as the FW. **Underside:** FW and HW are darker and less mottled.

SIMILAR SPECIES: No other duskywing has such a heavily mottled appearance on both the FW and HW. See Plate 12.

BEHAVIOUR: Often seen nectaring on flowers or mudpuddling. Fast erratic flight and easily disturbed.

FLIGHT SEASON: One to two generations per year.

	MAR	APR	MAY	JUN	JUL	AUG	SEP	OCT	NOV
Boreal/Tundra									
Mixed Forest									
Carolinian Zone									

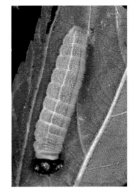

♀

CATERPILLAR: Pale green with many small white dots, a dark green mid-dorsal stripe and pale yellow lateral stripes. Head dark **Foodplants:** New Jersey tea (*Ceanothus americanus*) and narrow-leaved New Jersey tea (*Ceanothus herbaceus*).

OVERWINTERING STAGE: Mature caterpillar.

HABITAT: Restricted to dry, open habitats such as alvars and sandy areas.

DISTRIBUTION AND ABUNDANCE: Eastern United States north into southern Ontario and southeastern Manitoba. In Ontario, a rare and very local resident with widely scattered populations throughout southern Ontario as far north as Manitoulin Island and the Ottawa area (where it has not been seen for several years).

COMMENTS: This species is declining throughout its North American range, including Ontario, as its localized distribution and low dispersal capability make it subject to local extirpation. Designated Endangered by COSEWIC in 2012; and, in 2013, listed as Endangered under Ontario's *Species at Risk Act.*

ZARUCCO DUSKYWING *Erynnis zarucco*

♀

32–38 mm

ETYMOLOGY: Named for the Cuban town *Jaruco;* the type specimen is from Cuba.

ADULT: Large skipper. FW relatively narrow and pointed. **Upperside:** Inner half of FW in males very dark with little patterning. White FW spots very small, especially in males. Both sexes have a prominent reddish-brown FW subcostal patch. HW with a pale brown fringe. **Underside:** Dark with few to no dots on the HW.

SIMILAR SPECIES: Similar to Horace's Duskywing but Zarucco has more pointed FW and a brown or yellow-brown HW fringe (rather than dark as in Horace's). Also the HW underside in Zarucco is dark with few to no pale dots, unlike the heavily dotted HW of Horace's. Similar to Juvenal's Duskywing but the white wing spots in males are typically much smaller than those of Juvenal's. See Plate 13.

BEHAVIOUR: Most often seen perched on or near the ground in the typical duskywing posture with wings held flat.

FLIGHT SEASON: Most likely to occur in late summer or fall but has occurred as early as June.

Boreal/Tundra								
Mixed Forest								
Carolinian Zone			•		•			
	MAR	APR	MAY	JUN	JUL	AUG	SEP	OCT	NOV

CATERPILLAR: Not likely to be encountered in Ontario. Pale green with many small white dots, a dark green mid-dorsal stripe and pale yellow lateral stripes. Head tan or brown rimmed on either side with three orange patches. **Foodplants:** Mostly woody members of the Legume family (Fabaceae), including black locust (*Robinia pseudoacacia*).

OVERWINTERING STAGE: Mature caterpillar, but not known to overwinter in Ontario.

HABITAT: Open areas, usually near caterpillar foodplant.

DISTRIBUTION AND ABUNDANCE: The southeastern United States, as well as Cuba and Hispaniola, occasionally straying northward. In Ontario, an extremely rare, non-breeding migrant known from only one record: a specimen in the Canadian National Collection of Insects, Arachnids and Nematodes in Ottawa collected from the Rouge River, Toronto, on June 20, 1935.

COMMENTS: Some authorities consider Zarucco and Funereal Duskywing to be the same species.

FUNEREAL DUSKYWING *Erynnis funeralis*

33–45 mm

ETYMOLOGY: *Funeralis* may be a derivative of the Latin *funus* for "funeral".

ADULT: Large skipper. **Upperside:** FW dark and very pointed with small white subapical spots and a pale reddish-brown subcostal patch. HW dark with a bright white fringe. **Underside:** Dark with few to no dots on the HW.

SIMILAR SPECIES: Most similar to Zarucco Duskywing but note the bright white HW fringe in Funereal. See Plate 13.

BEHAVIOUR: Most often seen perched on or near the ground in the typical duskywing posture with wings held flat.

FLIGHT SEASON: In Ontario, a very rare migrant most likely to occur in late summer and fall.

	MAR	APR	MAY	JUN	JUL	AUG	SEP	OCT	NOV
Boreal/Tundra									
Mixed Forest						•			
Carolinian Zone						———			

CATERPILLAR: Not likely to be encountered in Ontario but similar in appearance to Zarucco. **Foodplants:** Legumes (Fabaceae).

OVERWINTERING STAGE: Mature caterpillar, but not known to overwinter in Ontario.

HABITAT: Open areas.

DISTRIBUTION AND ABUNDANCE: Largely a tropical and subtropical species ranging from Argentina north through central America to the southern United States, occasionally straying northward. In Ontario, a very rare, non-breeding migrant. Most often recorded at Point Pelee but there are also several records from Toronto, a single record from Milton (October 8, 2010) and one from the Hamilton area (August 15, 2012).

WILD INDIGO DUSKYWING *Erynnis baptisiae*

♂

29–34 mm

ETYMOLOGY: *Baptisia* is the genus of plants that includes yellow wild indigo (*Baptisia tinctoria*).

ADULT: Medium-sized skipper. **Upperside:** Male FW usually oily black basally with very small whitish subapical spots and an indistinct pale subcostal patch. Female similar but more mottled. **Underside:** Largely dark with two rows of pale dots along the HW margin.

SIMILAR SPECIES: Variable; intermediate in size and appearance compared to other duskywings. May be confused with Juvenal's and Columbine duskywings; females are also very similar to female Horace's Duskywing (see Similar Species under those species). See Plate 13.

BEHAVIOUR: Most often seen perched on or near the ground with wings held flat.

FLIGHT SEASON: Two to three generations per year.

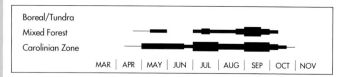

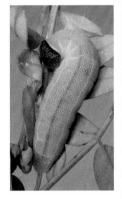

CATERPILLAR: Pale green with many small white dots, a dark green mid-dorsal stripe and pale yellow lateral stripes. Head black, mottled with orange spots. **Foodplants:** Historically, mostly yellow wild indigo (*Baptisia tinctoria* and other *Baptisia* spp.) but most populations currently feed on purple crown-vetch (*Securigera varia,* formerly *Coronilla varia*), an exotic species planted along road verges and hydro and railway rights-of-way to stabilize banks.

OVERWINTERING STAGE: Mature caterpillar.

HABITAT: Formerly restricted to dry sandy areas supporting populations of the provincially rare yellow wild indigo. Now occurs in many open areas where purple crown-vetch grows.

DISTRIBUTION AND ABUNDANCE: Widespread in the eastern half of the United States. In Ontario, originally a rare and very local resident restricted to a few locations in southwestern Ontario. Currently, it is much more common, although in Ontario still locally distributed, with records as far north as Simcoe County and Ottawa. This species appears poised to become common across much of southern Ontario, and should be sought wherever purple crown-vetch occurs.

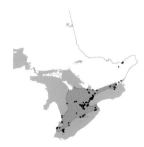

COLUMBINE DUSKYWING *Erynnis lucilius*

21–29 mm

ETYMOLOGY: *Gaius Lucilius* was the earliest known Roman satirist, from the second century BCE.

ADULT: Small. **Upperside:** Male FW dark basally, paler on the outer half with small white subapical spots and a silvery-grey subcostal patch. Female FW similar to male but with additional brown in the silvery-grey patch. **Underside:** Largely dark with two rows of pale dots along the HW margin.

SIMILAR SPECIES: Wild Indigo Duskywing is extremely similar in appearance to, but typically larger than, Columbine. Also, the white subapical spots tend to be in more of a zigzag pattern in Wild Indigo, straighter in Columbine. Habitat and hostplant presence should be taken into account in identification. See also Persius Duskywing, and Plate 13.

BEHAVIOUR: More often observed nectaring on flowers than other duskywings. Very skittish and difficult to approach.

FLIGHT SEASON: Two generations per year; the second generation may be more numerous than the first.

	MAR	APR	MAY	JUN	JUL	AUG	SEP	OCT	NOV
Boreal/Tundra									
Mixed Forest									
Carolinian Zone									

Red columbine

CATERPILLAR: Pale green with many small white dots, a dark green mid-dorsal stripe and pale yellow lateral stripes. Head black with no pale spots. **Foodplants:** Columbines (*Aquilegia* spp.), mostly red columbine (*Aquilegia canadensis*). Not attracted to hybrid garden columbines.

OVERWINTERING STAGE: Mature caterpillar within leaf litter.

HABITAT: Open areas, including rocky outcrops, alvars and areas with sandy soils.

DISTRIBUTION AND ABUNDANCE: Found throughout the northeastern United States and southern Canada from eastern Manitoba to southern Quebec. In Ontario, a common resident within suitable habitat, most commonly found along the southern edge of the Canadian Shield but also found locally as far south as Windsor and as far north as Sudbury and southern Algoma District. Also found in the Rainy River/Lake of the Woods area.

375

"BOREAL" PERSIUS DUSKYWING *Erynnis persius borealis*
"EASTERN" PERSIUS DUSKYWING *Erynnis persius persius*

24–31 mm

Subspecies *borealis*

ETYMOLOGY: *Aulus Persius Flaccus* was a Roman poet and satirist of the first century AD. *Borealis*, from Greek *boreas*, means "northern", a reference to the northern boreal forest where this species is found.

ADULT: Small. **Upperside:** Mottled FW with the four small white subapical spots aligned in a tight row perpendicular to the leading edge of the wing. FW also has raised white hairs but these are difficult to see in the field. **Underside:** FW similar to upperside. HW mostly dark brown with two rows of white spots.

SIMILAR SPECIES: Range alone distinguishes "Boreal" Persius Duskywing as it is the only duskywing with white wing spots in Ontario's far north. In the south, "Eastern" Persius is most similar to Wild Indigo and Columbine. In Persius, the white subapical spots are arranged in a very straight line, whereas in Wild Indigo they are zigzagged and in Columbine they are intermediate between the other two species. See Plate 13.

BEHAVIOUR: Adults will feed on nectar from a variety of flowers. Often seen perched on or near the ground with wings held flat.

FLIGHT SEASON: One generation per year.

	MAR	APR	MAY	JUN	JUL	AUG	SEP	OCT	NOV
Boreal/Tundra				———					
Mixed Forest									
Carolinian Zone			———						

HESPERIIDAE / The Skippers

Subspecies *persius*

Subspecies *borealis*

CATERPILLAR: Pale green with many small white dots, a dark green mid-dorsal stripe and pale yellow lateral stripes. Head black, mottled with tan or dark brown. **Foodplants:** Subspecies *persius* feeds on sundial lupine (*Lupinus perennis*). Although subspecies *borealis* is reported to feed on poplars (*Populus* spp.) and willows (*Salix* spp.), it likely rather feeds on legumes, including locoweed (*Oxytropis* spp.) and possibly *Astragalus* spp., which occur along, gravelly river shores.

OVERWINTERING STAGE: Mature caterpillar.

HABITAT: Subspecies *persius* restricted to areas of sandy soil where sundial lupine grows. Subspecies *borealis* is found in open and semi-open areas within the northern Boreal Forest Region/Tundra.

DISTRIBUTION AND ABUNDANCE: *E. p. persius* is found in the northeastern United States, while *E. p. borealis* is widespread in the western United States and Canada. In Ontario, *E. p. persius* was only known from Pinery Provincial Park and St. Williams, Norfolk County but it is now considered extirpated. Subspecies *borealis* is a rarely recorded resident currently known from coastal or near-coastal sites within the Hudson Bay Lowlands from Moosonee in the south to Fort Severn in the northwest.

377

GRIZZLED SKIPPER *Pyrgus centaureae*

22–28 mm

ETYMOLOGY: *Pyrgus* may be a derivative of the Greek word *pyrgos* meaning "tower" or a reference to the Greek city of Pyrgos. *Centaureae* may be derived from the Latin *centaureum,* or the Greek *kentaurion*, a plant of the Sunflower family (Asteraceae).

ADULT: Small. **Upperside:** Dark grey with white, squarish, irregularly placed FW spots and smaller rounded HW spots. Both FW and HW have a strongly checkered fringe. **Underside:** FW similar to upperside but paler grey. HW also paler grey and brown but with larger, more prominent white spots.

SIMILAR SPECIES: Common Checkered Skipper is superficially very similar but has a less checkered fringe, more evenly patterned white markings on the FW and more extensive white patches on the HW upper- and undersides.

BEHAVIOUR: Although the flight is not fast, individuals are difficult to follow as they have a low, winding flight pattern. Often mistaken for a moth.

FLIGHT SEASON: One generation per year.

	MAR	APR	MAY	JUN	JUL	AUG	SEP	OCT	NOV
Boreal/Tundra									
Mixed Forest									
Carolinian Zone									

CATERPILLAR: Grey-to-pinkish covered with fine white hairs. Head dark and collar reddish. **Foodplants:** Members of the Rose family (Rosaceae) including cloudberry (*Rubus chamaemorus*) and wild strawberry (*Fragaria virginiana*).

OVERWINTERING STAGE: Chrysalis.

HABITAT: Coastal tundra along Hudson Bay, taiga, spruce bogs, semi-open jack pine forests and clear-cuts in boreal forests.

DISTRIBUTION AND ABUNDANCE: Holarctic. In North America, ranges from Alaska through most of northern Canada to Newfoundland and south through the Rocky Mountains to New Mexico. An isolated population also occurs in the Appalachian Mountains of the United States. In Ontario, an uncommon resident found throughout northern Ontario from the Chapleau area in the south to the coast of Hudson Bay in the north.

COMMON CHECKERED SKIPPER *Pyrgus communis*

♂

23–29 mm

ETYMOLOGY: *Communis* is a Latin word meaning "common".

ADULT: Small. **Upperside:** Male bluish-grey with many large white squares and spots on both the FW and HW. Female similar but brownish-grey with less white. **Underside:** FW similar but paler grey. HW also a paler grey but with very large whitish patches forming two bands.

SIMILAR SPECIES: Grizzled Skipper is superficially similar but has a more checkered fringe, less evenly patterned white markings on the FW and less extensive white patches on the HW both above and below.

BEHAVIOUR: Low, erratic flight pattern. Appears very moth-like in flight.

FLIGHT SEASON: Many individuals in Ontario are migrants from farther south, but individuals can establish temporary breeding colonies, producing one to two generations.

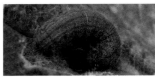
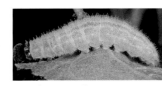

Brown form caterpillar   Green form caterpillar

CATERPILLAR: Pale green or brown covered with fine white hairs. Head black and collar reddish. **Foodplants:** Various members of the Mallow family (Malvaceae) including velvetleaf (*Abutilon theophrasti*) and dwarf mallow (*Malva neglecta*).

OVERWINTERING STAGE: Mature caterpillar which probably cannot survive Ontario's winters.

HABITAT: Open areas, disturbed sites.

DISTRIBUTION AND ABUNDANCE: A permanent resident from southern Mexico north through the United States to about 40° N latitude. Migrates northward to temporarily colonize areas as far north as the Canadian prairies and southern Ontario. In Ontario, a rare breeding migrant and temporary resident mostly in southern Ontario. In 2007, a temporary population established itself in Thunder Bay. Since 2008, migrants are becoming more regular and arriving earlier in the season establishing temporary colonies with at least two generations.

ARCTIC SKIPPER *Carterocephalus palaemon*

19–32 mm

ETYMOLOGY: *Karteros* in Greek means "strong"; *kephalos* is Greek for "head". *Palaemon* was a god of the sea in Greek mythology.

ADULT: Small. **Upperside:** Blackish-brown with many square-shaped orange spots on the FW and fewer, mostly rounded orange spots on the HW. **Underside:** FW mirrors the upperside but in reverse. HW is orange and brown with many whitish oval spots.

SIMILAR SPECIES: None in Ontario.

BEHAVIOUR: Flight weak and low to the ground. When perched on vegetation or basking on the ground, the wings are usually held flat or half-way open. When actively feeding on flowers or when mudpuddling, the wings are usually closed.

FLIGHT SEASON: One generation per year.

CATERPILLAR: Pale green with white lateral stripes. Head green and round. **Foodplants:** Grasses (Poaceae), including reedgrass (*Calamagrostis* spp.) and brome (*Bromus* spp.).

OVERWINTERING STAGE: Mature caterpillar.

HABITAT: Open, often damp areas with grasses.

DISTRIBUTION AND ABUNDANCE: Holarctic. In North America ranging from Alaska through most of Canada to Newfoundland and into the northeastern United States. Also south through the western mountains to California and Wyoming. In Ontario, a common and widespread resident as far north as about 50° N latitude. Largely absent from extreme southwestern Ontario south of the Waterloo area.

COMMENTS: Some authorities have recently included the Intermediate Skippers, the subfamily containing the Arctic Skipper, with the Branded Skippers. The Arctic Skipper has been considered Holarctic, but recent taxonomic work suggests that the Eurasian and North American populations are distinct with the latter possibly made up of several species. If they are split, the butterfly found in Ontario would likely be called *Carterocephalus mandan*.

LEAST SKIPPER *Ancyloxypha numitor*

♂

17–26 mm

ETYMOLOGY: *Ancyloxypha* is from the Greek *anklylos* meaning "curved or hooked", and *xiphos* meaning "sword". *Numitor* was the mythical king of Alba, grandfather of Romulus and Remus.

ADULT: Ontario's smallest butterfly with a very slender abdomen that projects beyond the base of the folded wings, most obvious in males. **Upperside:** FW dark brown, sometimes with some orange. HW orange with a wide, dark brown border. **Underside:** FW black with an orange border. HW solid bright golden-orange colour.

SIMILAR SPECIES: The introduced European Skipper is larger, is almost completely orange on both the FW and HW, and has a wider abdomen. See Plate 16.

BEHAVIOUR: A weak, low flyer that flits among the grasses, often alighting on them.

FLIGHT SEASON: Two generations per year.

	MAR	APR	MAY	JUN	JUL	AUG	SEP	OCT	NOV
Boreal/Tundra									
Mixed Forest									
Carolinian Zone									

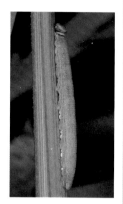

CATERPILLAR: Small and green with white spots and lines. Head dark.
Foodplants: Many different grasses (Poaceae), including bluegrass
(*Poa* spp.) and rice cutgrass (*Leersia oryzoides*).

OVERWINTERING STAGE: Mature caterpillar.

HABITAT: Restricted to wet, grassy areas including roadside ditches,
wet meadows, and the edges of wetlands, streams and lakes.

DISTRIBUTION AND ABUNDANCE: Ranges from northeastern Mexico
north throughout the eastern and central United States and into
Canada from Saskatchewan to Nova Scotia. In Ontario, a common
but local resident in wet, grassy areas from southern Ontario north
to Lake Abitibi and Lake of the Woods. Could be expected farther
north.

GARITA SKIPPERLING *Oarisma garita*

20–25 mm

ETYMOLOGY: *Oarisma* and *garita* are from Greek meaning, respectively, "loving conversation" and "to chatter".

ADULT: Very small skipper. **Upperside:** Orange-brown above with no distinct markings. **Underside:** FW orange. HW greyish-brown with an orange inner margin and whitish veins.

SIMILAR SPECIES: In Ontario, the European Skipper could be mistaken for the Garita Skipperling, but the former is bright orange on the FW. The Least Skipper is similar but has a large orange patch on the upperside HW.

BEHAVIOUR: Restricted to grassland areas where disturbed individuals tend to fly low over the grasses and alight in the undergrowth.

FLIGHT SEASON: One generation per year.

	MAR	APR	MAY	JUN	JUL	AUG	SEP	OCT	NOV
Boreal/Tundra									
Mixed Forest				• ——					
Carolinian Zone									

CATERPILLAR: Light green with white lines along the sides. Unusual among the grass-feeding skippers in not making silk nests.
Foodplants: Many different grasses (Poaceae).

OVERWINTERING STAGE: Partially grown caterpillar.

HABITAT: Usually prairies but the only known Ontario population was recorded from an alvar. This alvar, however, has many prairie-affinity grasses suggesting that the Garita Skipperling occurs on Manitoulin Island as a prairie relict and not as a transitory breeding immigrant as has been suggested in some texts.

DISTRIBUTION AND ABUNDANCE: Restricted to prairie grasslands from Mexico to the Peace River region in Alberta and British Columbia. In Ontario, a very rare and local resident, known only from an isolated population on Great Cloche Island, north of Manitoulin Island, hundreds of kilometres from the nearest Canadian populations in Manitoba.

COMMENTS: The single, known colony in Ontario was discovered in 1976 in an alvar habitat along Highway 6, which crosses Grand Cloche Island, along with other prairie plants, insects and birds. The current status of the population is not known as most of the area is privately owned and has not been surveyed in recent years.

387

HESPERIIDAE / The Skippers

EUROPEAN SKIPPER *Thymelicus lineola*

♂

19–26 mm

ETYMOLOGY: *Thymelicus* is possibly from the Greek word *thymelikos* meaning "theatrical musician". *Lineola* is derived from the Latin for "a small line", which likely refers to the male's narrow, black stigma.

ADULT: Very small skipper. **Upperside:** Wings are bright orange with a thin, dark brown border along the outer edges. Male has a very thin black stigma on FW. **Underside:** Paler orange to greyish-orange with no markings.

SIMILAR SPECIES: See Least Skipper and Garita Skipperling. The Delaware Skipper is brighter orange, larger, and has a much more rapid flight. See Plate 16.

BEHAVIOUR: Relatively slow-flying; stays down in grasses, rarely flying more than several feet above them.

FLIGHT SEASON: One generation per year.

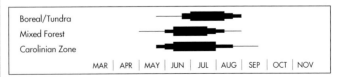

	MAR	APR	MAY	JUN	JUL	AUG	SEP	OCT	NOV
Boreal/Tundra									
Mixed Forest									
Carolinian Zone									

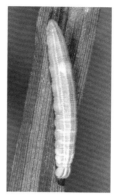

CATERPILLAR: Green with a dark stripe down the back and several white stripes along the sides. Head has several red and white bars. **Foodplants:** Many grasses (Poaceae), but common timothy (*Phleum pratense*) is preferred.

OVERWINTERING STAGE: Egg.

HABITAT: Grassy open areas. Abundant in agricultural areas where common timothy is grown.

DISTRIBUTION AND ABUNDANCE: Native to temperate Eurasia and northwestern Africa and introduced to North America. Now resident across most of the northeast but still localized in the west. In Ontario, a common-to-abundant resident found north to James Bay and west to Lake of the Woods. Can often be found in the thousands in, and close to, planted fields of common timothy.

COMMENTS: Much is known about the original introduction of this species to North America. Eggs arrived in Canada in 1910 at London, Ontario on timothy grass seeds imported from Europe. Continues to disperse in all directions, possibly on common timothy (*Phleum pratense*) seeds contaminated with eggs.

BRAZILIAN SKIPPER *Calpodes ethlius*

39–53 mm

ETYMOLOGY: Unknown.

ADULT: Very large skipper, with long pointed FW. **Upperside:** Brown with clear white patches on both the FW and HW. **Underside:** Lighter brownish-red, the upperside FW patches are also visible on the underside HW.

SIMILAR SPECIES: Ocola Skipper is somewhat similar but has fewer FW spots and lacks spots on the HW.

BEHAVIOUR: A highly migratory species. An active flower visitor, it prefers larger flowers where its long proboscis aids in reaching deep nectar sources.

FLIGHT SEASON: Non-breeding migrants may appear in late summer and fall.

Boreal/Tundra								
Mixed Forest								
Carolinian Zone								
MAR	APR	MAY	JUN	JUL	AUG	SEP	OCT	NOV

CATERPILLAR: Not likely to be encountered in Ontario. Green with white spots near the rear and a subdorsal white line. **Foodplants:** Canna lilies (Cannaceae).

OVERWINTERING STAGE: Does not overwinter in Canada.

HABITAT: Migrants could occur in any habitat with nectar-bearing flowers. In the southern United States, often found in gardens where the larval foodplant is grown widely as an ornamental.

DISTRIBUTION AND ABUNDANCE: Largely tropical and subtropical. Its permanent range extends from Argentina north through Central America and the West Indies to Florida and California. Migrates northward in the late summer, breeding as far north as southern Virginia. Strays periodically farther north but not known to breed. In Ontario, an extremely rare, non-breeding migrant known from only a single record— September 21, 1991 at Point Pelee National Park.

OCOLA SKIPPER *Panoquina ocola*

29–33 mm

ETYMOLOGY: *Panoquin* was a Native American chief, also known as Quanopin. *Ocola* is likely a derivation of *Osceola*, a Seminole war chief of mixed parentage who lived in the early 1800s.

ADULT: Large skipper, with unusually elongated forewings. **Upperside:** Dark brown with several white patches on the FW, the most notable being arrowhead-shaped. HW dark brown and unmarked. **Underside:** Brown with pale veins.

SIMILAR SPECIES: Similar to Brazilian Skipper but Ocola has fewer FW spots and lacks spots on the HW.

BEHAVIOUR: A highly migratory species that moves north out of its permanent range, always in the fall. A rapid flyer that regularly visits flowers, most noticeably in gardens.

FLIGHT SEASON: Non-breeding migrants show up in the north in the fall. All the Ontario records have occurred in September and October.

Boreal/Tundra									
Mixed Forest									
Carolinian Zone							• • ———		
	MAR	APR	MAY	JUN	JUL	AUG	SEP	OCT	NOV

CATERPILLAR: Not likely to be encountered in Ontario. Grey-green with lateral white stripes and a dorsal stripe. Head green. **Foodplants:** Many different grasses (Poaceae), including sugarcane (*Saccharum officinarum*) and rice (*Oryza sativa*) in the southern United States.

OVERWINTERING STAGE: Does not overwinter in Canada.

HABITAT: Migrants could occur in any habitat with nectar-bearing flowers.

DISTRIBUTION AND ABUNDANCE: Largely tropical and subtropical. Its permanent range extends from Argentina north through Central America and the West Indies to Texas and Florida. Migrates northward in the late summer, breeding as far north as Virginia. Strays periodically farther north (in some years major incursions occur). In Ontario, a rare, non-breeding migrant with the majority of records from Point Pelee National Park, but has also been recorded in Hamilton (September 9, 1991, Ontario's first record) and in Toronto (September 23–24, 2012).

PEPPER AND SALT SKIPPER *Amblyscirtes hegon*

18–22 mm

ETYMOLOGY: *Amblyscirtes* could be from *amblys*, Greek for "blunt" and *skirtao* meaning "to leap", possibly referring to the flight pattern. The name *hegon* is probably a contraction of *Mohegan*, a tribe of Native Americans living in Connecticut. The word *Mohegan* translates as "people of the wolf".

ADULT: Very small skipper. **Upperside:** FW dark brown with several small white median spots and a row of white subapical spots. HW dark brown. Fringes are checkered brown-and-whitish. **Underside:** Both wings flecked with greyish-green when fresh, creating the "pepper and salt" effect. With age, the flecking wears away and the wings become more uniform dark brown. Both wings also have numerous whitish spots, those on the HW forming a semicircle.

SIMILAR SPECIES: The Common Roadside Skipper is also small and dark, but usually lacks dorsal median spots on the FW and has a dark, unmarked HW underside.

BEHAVIOUR: Regularly nectars at flowers, including honeysuckle. An avid mudpuddler.

FLIGHT SEASON: One generation per year.

Boreal/Tundra			·						
Mixed Forest			▬▬▬						
Carolinian Zone			──						
	MAR	APR	MAY	JUN	JUL	AUG	SEP	OCT	NOV

CATERPILLAR: Pale green with a dark green stripe down the back and lighter lateral stripes. Head dark brown with paler stripes. **Foodplants:** Grasses (Poaceae), including Kentucky bluegrass (*Poa pratensis*) and yellow Indiangrass (*Sorghastrum nutans*).

OVERWINTERING STAGE: Caterpillar.

HABITAT: Deciduous and mixed forest clearings and roadsides, especially in wet areas.

DISTRIBUTION AND ABUNDANCE: An eastern North American species found from the southeastern United States north to central Manitoba and Nova Scotia. In Ontario, an uncommon resident found largely in central Ontario from the Carden Plain and Ottawa north to Timiskaming; with scattered records across the southern portions of northern Ontario to the Lake of the Woods area. Extremely local in southern Ontario with records from Windsor, Norfolk County and a 1944 record from Kitchener.

COMMENTS: Small populations of this species can appear for a year or two in some locations then seem to disappear. May have been affected by woodland spraying for Gypsy Moths.

COMMON ROADSIDE SKIPPER *Amblyscirtes vialis*

18–25 mm

ETYMOLOGY: *Vialis* is possibly from the Latin *via* meaning highway.

ADULT: Very small skipper. **Upperside:** Dark brown with three small subapical white spots on the FW. Fringes checkered dark brown and tan. **Underside:** Similar to upperside with a slight purplish-white frosting to outer wings (more extensive in the HW)—such frosting wears away in older individuals.

SIMILAR SPECIES: See Pepper and Salt Skipper. Female Zabulon and the female "pocahontas"-form Hobomok skippers are superficially similar but are larger, and have more white spots on the FW and a subtle pattern can usually be seen on the ventral HW. Dusted Skipper is also superficially similar but is larger, with longer wings and a prominent white stripe above the eyes.

BEHAVIOUR: A small, rapid-flying skipper most often seen perched on dirt roads. Easily overlooked as it is so small and dark. Rarely seen at flowers.

FLIGHT SEASON: One generation per year.

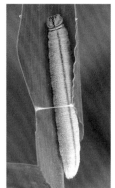

CATERPILLAR: Pale green with a lighter yellow toward the rear. Head white with red stripes. **Food plants:** Cultivated oats (*Avena sativa*) and grasses (Poaceae), including Kentucky bluegrass (*Poa pratensis*) and bentgrass (*Agrostis* spp.).

OVERWINTERING STAGE: Caterpillar.

HABITAT: Woodland roads and dry, sandy clearings.

DISTRIBUTION AND ABUNDANCE: Widespread throughout the temperate United States and Canada as far north as northern Alberta. In Ontario, an uncommon-to-common resident throughout most of the province as far north as southern James Bay and Attawapiskat and the Red Lake area in southern Kenora District.

CLOUDED SKIPPER *Lerema accius*

♀

26–40 mm

ETYMOLOGY: *Lerem* is "idle talk" in Greek. *Lucius Accius* was a Roman tragic poet and writer from the second century BCE.

ADULT: Large skipper, with antennal clubs that are unusually long and pointed. **Upperside:** FW dark brown with one or two small median white spots and three small subapical white spots. HW dark brown and unmarked. **Underside:** Similar to uppersides, but with some purplish-grey frosting along the margins and in the middle of the HW.

SIMILAR SPECIES: Dusted Skipper has a prominent white eyebrow stripe. Female Zabulon Skipper has large glassy spots on the dorsal FW and a distinctive white costal edge on the HW. Female "pocahontas"-form Hobomok Skippers are also similar but the distinctive pale patch on the underside HW is usually visible. Common Roadside Skipper is considerably smaller.

BEHAVIOUR: A highly migratory species. Males sit on leaves awaiting females.

FLIGHT SEASON: Non-breeding migrants show up in the north in late summer and fall.

Boreal/Tundra									
Mixed Forest									
Carolinian Zone						•			
	MAR	APR	MAY	JUN	JUL	AUG	SEP	OCT	NOV

CATERPILLAR: Not likely to be encountered in Ontario. White mottled with black. **Foodplants:** Many different grasses (Poaceae).

OVERWINTERING STAGE: Does not overwinter in Canada.

HABITAT: Migrants could occur in any open habitat.

DISTRIBUTION AND ABUNDANCE: Largely tropical and subtropical. Its permanent range extends from Venezuela and Colombia into southern Texas and Florida. Migrates in the summer and fall, breeding as far north as Virginia. Periodically strays farther north where it is not known to breed. In Ontario, an extremely rare, non-breeding migrant known from only a single record at Point Pelee National Park on October 30, 2000.

FIERY SKIPPER *Hylephila phyleus*

♂

22–33 mm

ETYMOLOGY: *Hyle* in Greek refers to "wood", *phila* is "love or loving". In Greek mythology, *Phyleus* was a son of King Augeias of Elis and supporter of Heracles.

ADULT: Medium-sized skipper, with very short antennae and pointed forewing. **Upperside:** Male wings orange with dark borders, the orange extending into the dark borders with tooth-like projections. FW with a prominent dark stigma and an additional dark dash between the stigma and apex. Female brown with an irregular band of orange markings on the FW and an orange patch that is often arrow-shaped on the HW. **Underside:** Male light orange with a row of small submarginal brown spots. Female greyish-brown with a crescent of light marks on the HW bordered on either end by dark spots.

SIMILAR SPECIES: Male is most similar to the Whirlabout which is smaller and less distinctly marked on the upperside but has larger dark spots on the underside HW. Female is similar to many other female skippers, especially the Sachem, but Sachem has a large transparent patch in the upper FW. See Plate 16.

BEHAVIOUR: An active and rapid-flying skipper.

FLIGHT SEASON: Migrants typically arrive in mid-to-late summer but have appeared as early as May. Two to three overlapping generations.

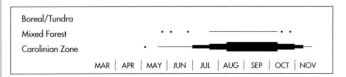

Boreal/Tundra									
Mixed Forest									
Carolinian Zone									
	MAR	APR	MAY	JUN	JUL	AUG	SEP	OCT	NOV

CATERPILLAR: Shades of brown and green with brown lateral lines.
Foodplants: A selection of grasses (Poaceae), including lawn grasses.

OVERWINTERING STAGE: Does not overwinter in Canada.

HABITAT: Most open habitats, including fields, meadows and roadsides.

DISTRIBUTION AND ABUNDANCE: Its permanent range extends from Argentina north through Central America and the West Indies to the southeastern United States but is slowly expanding northward. Migrates northward each year and establishes temporary breeding colonies as far north as northern California, southern Ontario and southern New England. In Ontario, a rare-to-uncommon breeding migrant that is gradually becoming more common as its range expands northward.

COMMENTS: Prior to the early 1990s, this was a fairly rare migrant to Ontario with most records occurring in the fall and restricted to southwestern Ontario. Since then it has gradually been extending its range in the province and typically arrives earlier in the season. In 2012, several localized colonies were observed in Prince Edward County and Ottawa.

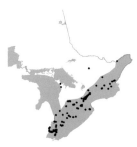

COMMON BRANDED SKIPPER *Hesperia comma*

22–30 mm

ETYMOLOGY: *Hesperia* was the daughter of river god Kebren in Greek mythology. *Comma* is likely a reference to the comma-shaped stigma on the FW of the male.

ADULT: Medium-sized skipper. **Upperside:** Male orange-brown with dark brown borders. FW with an elongate comma-shaped stigma and several squarish orange spots between the stigma and apex. Females mostly brown on the upperside with orange spots. **Underside:** Olive-brown with distinct white spots, the ones closest to the body often in a loose "C" shape.

SIMILAR SPECIES: Leonard's Skipper is similar but the underside HW is usually a dark chestnut-brown and there is only a single white spot toward the HW base, rather than two or more as in Common Branded. See Plate 14.

BEHAVIOUR: A very swift flyer that regularly nectars on flowers.

FLIGHT SEASON: One generation per year.

	MAR	APR	MAY	JUN	JUL	AUG	SEP	OCT	NOV
Boreal/Tundra									
Mixed Forest									
Carolinian Zone									

CATERPILLAR: Olive-green. Head dark. **Foodplants:** Many different grasses (Poaceae).

OVERWINTERING STAGE: Caterpillar.

HABITAT: Mainly a coniferous forest species; also occurs in grassy meadows in mixed forests south of the Boreal Forest Region.

DISTRIBUTION AND ABUNDANCE: Previously, considered a holarctic species found around the northern parts of the globe, including all of northern Canada north to the tundra. In Ontario, a common resident and the most northerly of the three *Hesperia* species, with records extending from Algonquin Park north to Hudson Bay and west to Manitoba.

COMMENTS: Recent reviews of the status of this species have determined that the Old World populations are a different species from those of North America. Several former subspecies in North America have already been given status as their own species. The most recent evidence suggests that the subspecies found in Ontario (*H. comma laurentina*) is part of a North American species that will likely be called *Hesperia manitoba*.

LEONARD'S SKIPPER *Hesperia leonardus*

28–34 mm

ETYMOLOGY: *Leonardus* is named after the Reverend L. W. Leonard of Dublin, New Hampshire, who had provided Thaddeus Harris, the species' author, with his first specimen.

ADULT: Medium-sized to large skipper. **Upperside:** Male is a dark orange with a heavy brown border and a stigma on the FW. Female is mostly brown with orange patches. **Underside:** Dark chestnut with a distinct row of silver-white rectangles crossing the HW and a single spot closer to the base.

SIMILAR SPECIES: Common Branded Skipper is similar but the underside HW is usually olive-brown and there are two or more white spots toward the base of HW rather than one as in Leonard's. See Plate 14.

BEHAVIOUR: A very fast and strong-flying skipper that is wary and easily disturbed. Often nectars on the late blooming New England aster (*Symphyotrichum novae-angliae*).

FLIGHT SEASON: One generation per year.

CATERPILLAR: Brown mottled with a reddish tinge. **Foodplants:** A large selection of grasses, including little bluestem (*Schizachyrium scoparium* var. *scoparium*) and blue grama (*Bouteloua gracilis*).

OVERWINTERING STAGE: Early instar caterpillar.

HABITAT: Grassy meadows and woodland clearings.

DISTRIBUTION AND ABUNDANCE: Occurs from southeastern Saskatchewan east to Nova Scotia and south to Colorado and northeastern Georgia. In Ontario, an uncommon resident found throughout the southern parts of the province north to Manitoulin Island and Algonquin Park. There are isolated records north of Sault Ste. Marie; also occurs at Thunder Bay and in the Rainy River/Lake of the Woods area.

405

INDIAN SKIPPER *Hesperia sassacus*

♀

25–30 mm

ETYMOLOGY: *Sassacus* was the last chief and sachem (spiritual leader) of the Native American Pequot tribe.

ADULT: Medium-sized skipper. **Upperside:** Male and female are similar, having orange uppersides with a broad dark border, and the orange extends into the border along the veins. Male has a dark stigma on the FW. **Underside:** Yellow-orange with a sharply L-shaped band of lighter rectangles across the HW. FW with two pale spots near the wing margin below the pale subapical spots.

SIMILAR SPECIES: Most similar to the Long Dash Skipper with which it overlaps in the southern part of the province. The Long Dash male has a larger black stigma and a row of lighter rectangles arranged in a crescent shape on the underside HW, not the L-shape of the Indian Skipper. In addition, any FW underside spots below the subapical spots in Long Dash are not as close to the wing margin as those in Indian Skipper. See Plate 14.

BEHAVIOUR: A very fast-flying skipper that nectars regularly at a variety of flowers.

FLIGHT SEASON: One generation per year.

	MAR	APR	MAY	JUN	JUL	AUG	SEP	OCT	NOV
Boreal/Tundra									
Mixed Forest									
Carolinian Zone									

CATERPILLAR: Brown with dark brown spots and a black and white collar. Head black. Photo not available but similar to other *Hesperia* skippers.. **Foodplants:** Many different grasses, including little bluestem (*Schizachyrium scoparium* var. *scoparium*), poverty oatgrass (*Danthonia spicata*) and panicgrasses (*Panicum* spp.).

OVERWINTERING STAGE: Caterpillar.

HABITAT: Dry and wet open meadows and fields, woodland clearings and grassy roadsides.

DISTRIBUTION AND ABUNDANCE:
The Great Lakes region east to Nova Scotia and south through the Appalachians to northeast Georgia. In Ontario, an uncommon resident found mostly along the southern edge of the Canadian Shield and Manitoulin Island. Less common and more local north of this region. Much less common and more locally distributed in southwestern Ontario.

PECK'S SKIPPER *Polites peckius*

19–27 mm

ETYMOLOGY: *Polites* may refer to the son of Priam and Hecuba of Troy in Greek mythology. *Peckius* was named after W. D. Peck, an early North American entomologist.

ADULT: Very small skipper. **Upperside:** Male FW brown with orange on the leading edge below which is a prominent dark stigma. Male HW brown with a central row of elongated spots. Female similar to male but lacking the stigma and with several median orange spots on the FW. **Underside:** The key diagnostic feature of this species is the large, irregular-shaped yellow patch filling most of the HW.

SIMILAR SPECIES: Hobomok Skipper also has a large yellowish patch on the HW underside but it does not extend toward the base. Hobomok is also larger and has more orange on the upperside. From above, males are similar to Tawny-edged Skipper but the HW upper- and underside in Tawny-edged is unpatterned. See Plate 14.

BEHAVIOUR: Commonly nectars at flowers, especially members of the Legume family (Fabaceae).

FLIGHT SEASON: One generation per year.

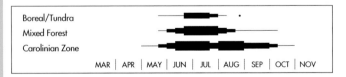

	MAR	APR	MAY	JUN	JUL	AUG	SEP	OCT	NOV
Boreal/Tundra									
Mixed Forest									
Carolinian Zone									

♂

♀

CATERPILLAR: Maroon-coloured with brown mottling. Head black with white streaks. **Foodplants:** Grasses (Poaceae), including Kentucky bluegrass (*Poa pratensis*) and little bluestem (*Schizachyrium scoparium* var. *scoparium*).

OVERWINTERING STAGE: Partly grown caterpillar.

HABITAT: Open grassy habitats, including meadows, roadsides, urban parks and clearings in forested areas.

DISTRIBUTION AND ABUNDANCE:
Ranges from British Columbia to Newfoundland, and south to Oregon and northern Georgia. In Ontario, a common resident widespread from the extreme southwest north to southern James Bay and the north shore of Lake Nipigon.

TAWNY-EDGED SKIPPER *Polites themistocles*

♂

19–28 mm

ETYMOLOGY: *Themistocles* was an Athenian statesman in Greece.

ADULT: Very small skipper. **Upperside:** Male FW brown with a bright orange patch along the leading edge (thus tawny-edged), below which is a black stigma. HW is orange-brown and unpatterned. Female FW with limited to no orange along the leading edge, several pale median spots and three pale subapical spots. **Underside:** Tawny edge on FW also visible from below and contrasts with the plain brown of the HW. HW with a crescent of small pale spots in some individuals.

SIMILAR SPECIES: Crossline Skipper can be confusingly close in appearance but is larger, does not have a tawny edge on the underside FW, and usually has two to three orange spots on the inner side of the stigma, absent in Tawny-edged. See also Peck's Skipper.

BEHAVIOUR: Flies rapidly from flower to flower (most often plants in the Legume family) nectaring. Also, a regular mudpuddler, sometimes in the dozens, on dirt roads close to meadows.

FLIGHT SEASON: One generation per year in most of Ontario, with a smaller second generation in the southern parts of the province.

	MAR	APR	MAY	JUN	JUL	AUG	SEP	OCT	NOV
Boreal/Tundra									
Mixed Forest									
Carolinian Zone									

♀

CATERPILLAR: Small and brownish with dark lines along the sides and back. Head black with white spots and lines. **Foodplants:** Many different grasses (Poaceae), especially panicgrasses (*Panicum* spp.), crabgrasses (*Digitaria* spp.) and bluegrasses (*Poa* spp.).

OVERWINTERING STAGE: Chrysalis.

HABITAT: Open grassy habitats, usually those that are moist.

DISTRIBUTION AND ABUNDANCE:
Ranges from southern British Columbia across southern Canada to Nova Scotia and south through most of the United States. In Ontario, a common resident north to the Albany River on James Bay, west to Red Lake.

COMMENTS: A second generation appeared in eastern Ontario for the first time in the late 1990s.

411

CROSSLINE SKIPPER *Polites origenes*

♂

23–30 mm

ETYMOLOGY: *Origen* was a third-century AD theologian from Alexandria in Greece.

ADULT: Medium-sized skipper. **Upperside:** Male FW dark brown with an orange leading edge and a black straight stigma beyond which are two or three orange spots. Male HW brown. Female FW with two or three prominent squarish median spots, three pale subapical spots and sometimes with orange along the leading edge. Female HW brown, sometimes with a faint central orange patch. **Underside:** Both wings uniform pale brown usually with a submarginal crescent of small pale dots on the HW.

SIMILAR SPECIES: Tawny-edged Skipper can be confusingly close in appearance but is smaller, has a tawny edge on the underside FW and lacks the two to three orange spots on the inner side of the stigma. Two-spotted Skipper is also similar but Crossline is duller below and lacks the prominent white ray along the bottom of the HW. See Plate 16.

BEHAVIOUR: A rapid-flying skipper that tends to be seen on its own.

FLIGHT SEASON: One generation per year.

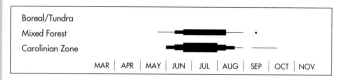

	Boreal/Tundra								
Mixed Forest									
Carolinian Zone									
	MAR	APR	MAY	JUN	JUL	AUG	SEP	OCT	NOV

♀

CATERPILLAR: Brown with grey mottling. Head black. **Foodplants:** Grasses (Poaceae), including little bluestem (*Schizachyrium scoparium* var. *scoparium*).

OVERWINTERING STAGE: Mature caterpillar.

HABITAT: Dry meadows and rocky or sandy clearings.

DISTRIBUTION AND ABUNDANCE: Most of the eastern United States north into Ontario and southern Quebec. In Ontario, an uncommon and local resident largely found south of the Canadian Shield north to Ottawa and Algonquin Park and west to southern Algoma District where it appears to be much rarer.

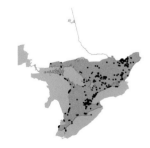

COMMENTS: Due to its similarity to the more common Tawny-edged Skipper, this species may be overlooked, especially in the northern portions of its range where it is scarcer.

LONG DASH SKIPPER *Polites mystic*

23–29 mm

ETYMOLOGY: *Mystic* is from the Greek *mystikos* for "mysterious".

ADULT: Medium-sized skipper. **Upperside:** Male FW orange with a broad dark brown border and a thick dark brown stigma that extends into a second dark brown dash (hence "long dash"). Female similar, but with less orange. HW in both sexes brown with a central orange patch. **Underside:** Male yellow-orange, the HW with a crescent-shaped band of submarginal yellow spots and single central spot. Female similarly patterned but a darker orange-red or reddish-brown.

SIMILAR SPECIES: Most similar to Indian Skipper which has a smaller black stigma and an L-shaped row of lighter rectangles on the underside HW. See Plate 14.

BEHAVIOUR: Darts about from flower to flower, nectaring or sitting on vegetation. Establishes a territory which it defends against intruders.

FLIGHT SEASON: One generation per year with a possible second one in the more southerly parts of the province.

	MAR	APR	MAY	JUN	JUL	AUG	SEP	OCT	NOV
Boreal/Tundra									
Mixed Forest									
Carolinian Zone									

♂

♀

CATERPILLAR: Brown-to-green with whitish mottling and a dark stripe down the back. **Foodplants:** Grasses (Poaceae), including common species such as quackgrass (*Elymus repens*) and common timothy (*Phleum pratense*).

OVERWINTERING STAGE: Partially grown caterpillar.

HABITAT: Grassy habitats including moist meadows, roadsides, and disturbed areas.

DISTRIBUTION AND ABUNDANCE: Found across the northern United States and southern Canada from eastern British Columbia and Oregon to the Atlantic coast. In Ontario, a common and widespread resident north to James Bay and west to Manitoba.

415

WHIRLABOUT *Polites vibex*

♂

26–30 mm

ETYMOLOGY: In Latin, *vibex* is "line, streak". This may refer to the streak-like stigma.

ADULT: Medium-sized skipper. **Upperside:** Male FW orange with a ragged-edged brown border and a prominent black stigma with another brown spot at its end. Male HW orange with a broad brown border. Female FW dark brown with small white median spots and three small subapical spots. **Underside:** Male pale orange with large smudgy brown spots. Female greyish with paler banding.

SIMILAR SPECIES: Male could be mistaken for a Fiery Skipper. However, the latter has smaller, neater spots on the underside HW. Female most similar to a worn male Sachem from the underside but the two differ significantly on the upperside (a male Sachem is mostly orange and possesses a prominent dark stigma). See Plate 16.

BEHAVIOUR: Has been recorded migrating northward, but not as commonly as many other migratory species. Tends to whirl about flowery meadows in a smaller circular trajectory than other similar skippers—hence its common name.

FLIGHT SEASON: Non-breeding migrants have been known to appear in late summer and fall.

Boreal/Tundra								
Mixed Forest								
Carolinian Zone				•				
	MAR	APR	MAY	JUN	JUL	AUG	SEP	OCT	NOV

CATERPILLAR: Not likely to be encountered in Ontario. Pale green with dark stripes. Head black with white lines and spots. **Foodplants:** Grasses (Poaceae).

OVERWINTERING STAGE: Does not overwinter in Canada.

HABITAT: Migrants could occur in any open habitat.

DISTRIBUTION AND ABUNDANCE:
Its permanent range extends from Argentina through Central America and the West Indies to the southeastern United States. Migrants have been recorded in West Virginia, Iowa and Ontario. In Ontario, an extremely rare, non-breeding migrant known from a single individual collected at Toronto before 1910 and a well documented sight record from Scarborough on July 25, 2008.

NORTHERN BROKEN-DASH *Wallengrenia egeremet*

♂

24–29 mm

ETYMOLOGY: Hans Daniel Johan Wallengren was a Swedish entomologist (1823–1894). Native American Chief *Egeremet* fought against English settlers between 1688 and 1692.

ADULT: Medium-sized skipper. **Upperside:** Male brown with some purplish overtones when fresh. The stigma is broken in two giving this butterfly its common name. There are usually some orange spots around the stigma and the leading edge of the FW is often tawny. HW has a flush of orange in the centre. Female similar but lacks the stigma and usually has larger orange-yellow FW spots. **Underside:** HW brown with purplish overtones when fresh and with a faint crescent of pale spots, the middle two being somewhat larger than the others creating a vague "backward 3" shape.

SIMILAR SPECIES: Dun Skipper male has an unbroken stigma and usually lacks the row of pale spots on the underside HW. Females of the two species are difficult to distinguish from one another. However, when present, the pale spots on the FW of the Dun Skipper are smaller and the spots forming the crescent on the HW underside are more even-sized. See Plate 15.

BEHAVIOUR: Often visits flowers with the similar Dun Skipper, but the Northern Broken-Dash is almost always in fewer numbers.

FLIGHT SEASON: One generation per year.

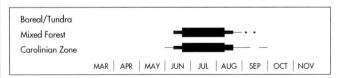

	MAR	APR	MAY	JUN	JUL	AUG	SEP	OCT	NOV
Boreal/Tundra									
Mixed Forest									
Carolinian Zone									

CATERPILLAR: Pale mottled brown with faint yellow stripes on the sides and a green stripe down the back. Head dark with several light vertical stripes. **Foodplants:** Grasses (Poaceae), particularly hairy crabgrass (*Digitaria sanguinalis*) and panicgrasses (*Panicum* spp.).

OVERWINTERING STAGE: Caterpillar.

HABITAT: Grassy meadows and clearings, often near woodlands and forests.

DISTRIBUTION AND ABUNDANCE: Eastern North America from Texas and Florida to North Dakota and southern Quebec. In Ontario, a common resident south of the Canadian Shield. On the Shield it is much rarer and probably does not occur much farther north than a band extending from Muskoka to Renfrew County.

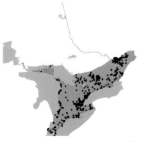

COMMENTS: This species is probably often overlooked due to its similarity to the much more common Dun Skipper.

419

LITTLE GLASSYWING *Pompeius verna*

♀

24–33 mm

ETYMOLOGY: *Pompeius* was the name of an important Roman family with many famous members who lived during the Roman Republic and the Roman Empire. *Verna* is a Latin term for a person born into slavery.

ADULT: Medium-sized skipper. Pale spot on antennae just below the club. **Upperside:** Dark brown with distinct translucent patches in the FW, particularly large and squared off in the female. **Underside:** Dark brown with similar clear spots visible on the FW and a row of faint spots on the HW.

SIMILAR SPECIES: Very similar to Northern Broken-Dash and Dun Skipper but the FW spots on both are smaller and opaque, not clear like those of Little Glassywing. The three species are often referred to as the "Three Witches". Sachem females also have clear FW spots, but have a more distinct row of light spots on the under FW.

BEHAVIOUR: Often visits flowers, particularly milkweeds (*Asclepias* spp.). An avid mudpuddler.

FLIGHT SEASON: One generation per year.

420

CATERPILLAR: Yellowish-green to brown with small dark bumps and dark lines running along the body. Head dark. **Foodplants:** Grasses (Poaceae).

OVERWINTERING STAGE: Caterpillar.

HABITAT: Wet meadows and grasslands, as well as roadsides, often near wetlands and forest edges.

DISTRIBUTION AND ABUNDANCE: Eastern North America from Texas and Florida north into southern Ontario and extreme southern Quebec. In Ontario, an uncommon and local resident traditionally found in the Carolinian Zone, north to the southeastern shore of Lake Huron and the Carden Plain east of Lake Simcoe. Has been moving northeast in recent years and is now regularly seen in colonies in Kingston and the Rideau Lakes area.

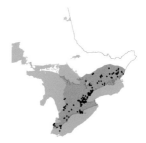

SACHEM *Atalopedes campestris*

♂

23–30 mm

ETYMOLOGY: In Greek, *pedes* refers to children; *Atalo* or *Attalus* was the name of a series of Pergamon kings. The genus may refer to the four sons of the first *Atalo*. *Campestris* is derived from Latin meaning "associated with fields".

ADULT: Medium-sized skipper. **Upperside:** Male FW very pointed and bright orange with a large, rectangular stigma and a dark trailing edge. HW orange with a dark border. Female FW dark brown with a streaky orange leading edge and several translucent spots. **Underside:** Male HW yellowish-brown with vague irregular-shaped paler patches. Female olive-brown with a V-shaped band of cream-coloured spots on the HW. The translucent spots on the female FW can also be seen from below.

SIMILAR SPECIES: See Little Glassywing and Fiery Skipper. See Plate 16.

BEHAVIOUR: A generalist skipper of open areas. Migrates north in most years in the summer.

FLIGHT SEASON: Up to three generations per year in the northern parts of its resident range in the United States. In Ontario, recorded from late May to mid-November.

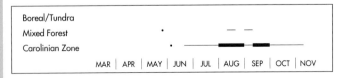

CATERPILLAR: Olive-green with dark lines and bumps. Head black.
Foodplants: Many species of grass (Poaceae), including crabgrasses (*Digitaria* spp.).

OVERWINTERING STAGE: Does not overwinter in Ontario. Caterpillars are incapable of overwintering in areas that experience extended periods below about -4°C.

HABITAT: Open, disturbed areas with low grass cover, including lawns, fields, roadsides, gardens, and abandoned lots.

DISTRIBUTION AND ABUNDANCE: Permanent range from Brazil north through Central America to California and southern Virginia but expanding northward due to warmer winters. Migrates north each summer and establishes temporary breeding colonies. In Ontario, a very rare, usually non-breeding migrant, but in some years, such as 1988 and 2012, arrived in large numbers with subsequent breeding. Most migrants are recorded in extreme southwestern Ontario but they have also been recorded in Toronto and Kingston.

HOBOMOK SKIPPER *Poanes hobomok*

24–32 mm

ETYMOLOGY: In Greek, *poa* refers to grass. *Hobomok* was a Native American who served as a guide, interpreter and aide to the Pilgrims of Plymouth, Massachusetts; it is also the name of a mischievous Algonquin spirit.

ADULT: Medium-sized skipper. **Upperside:** Orange-yellow with broad, dark irregular-shaped borders that are wider in females. Male has a dark dash at end of FW cell. There is a fairly common all-blackish-brown to purplish female form ("pocahontas") that has some white spots in FW, usually including a spot at the end of the FW cell. **Underside:** HW brown with a large, solid, median yellow patch. Both wings have brown margins frosted with purplish-white. Female "pocahontas" similarly patterned, but appear as if they have been covered in a layer of brownish-purple ash.

SIMILAR SPECIES: Similar to rare Zabulon Skipper. Male Zabulon has a more pointed FW; is brighter yellow-orange; and underside HW has small rust-coloured spots within the yellow patch and a smaller yellow patch along the leading edge of the HW base. See also Peck's Skipper.

BEHAVIOUR: Nectars on a variety of flowers. Males fly rapidly along woodland edges, often perching on leaves awaiting females.

FLIGHT SEASON: One generation per year.

Pocahontas form

Pocahontas form

CATERPILLAR: Tan to orange-brown with short, white fine hairs. Head brown with white hairs. **Foodplants:** Grasses (Poaceae), including panicgrasses (*Panicum* spp.) and bluegrasses (*Poa* spp.).

OVERWINTERING STAGE: Caterpillar.

HABITAT: Deciduous and mixed-forest edges, including roadsides and clearings.

DISTRIBUTION AND ABUNDANCE:
Eastern North America from
Oklahoma and Georgia north to
Saskatchewan and Nova Scotia. In
Ontario, a common resident found
north to southern James Bay.

ZABULON SKIPPER *Poanes zabulon*

♂

25–32 mm

ETYMOLOGY: This species may have been named after *Zebulun*, the sixth son of Jacob and Leah in the Bible.

ADULT: Medium-sized skipper, with pointed FW. **Upperside:** Bright orange-yellow with somewhat narrow dark border in male. Females are dark brown with large white patches in the central FW but with no white marks in FW cell (unlike most "pocahontas"-form Hobomok females). **Underside:** Male with broad yellow patch on HW dotted with some rust-coloured spots. Female rich dark brown with some purplish frosting along the margins and a distinctive white line along HW costa.

SIMILAR SPECIES: See Hobomok Skipper and Plate 14.

BEHAVIOUR: Males perch on leaves awaiting females that often perch lower in the greenery, usually in the shade. Regularly nectar from a variety of flowers.

FLIGHT SEASON: One or two generations per year.

Boreal/Tundra									
Mixed Forest									
Carolinian Zone				•		• •			
	MAR	APR	MAY	JUN	JUL	AUG	SEP	OCT	NOV

Green form caterpillar

CATERPILLAR: Similar to Hobomok Skipper. Green-to-brown with short, white fine hairs. See page 342 for brown form. Head is brown with white hairs. **Foodplants:** In the United States, grasses (Poaceae). Unknown in Canada.

OVERWINTERING STAGE: Unreported, but likely caterpillar.

HABITAT: Second-growth, woodland clearings and roadsides, but also parks and gardens.

DISTRIBUTION AND ABUNDANCE: Panama north through the central and eastern United States to Kansas, southern Michigan and Massachusetts. In Ontario, it appears to be a very rare, breeding resident only on Pelee Island. Also reported twice at Ojibway Prairie in Windsor where it may have strayed from nearby Michigan.

MULBERRY WING *Poanes massasoit*

♂

22–29 mm

ETYMOLOGY: *Massasoit* (Ousamequin), meaning "Great Sachem", was the leader of the Wampanoag Confederacy who helped the early Plymouth Colony settlers.

ADULT: Medium-sized skipper, with rounded wings. **Upperside:** Male variable: FW rich dark brown and either unmarked or with a few small orange central spots and subapical spots; sometimes also with a rusty-brown leading edge. HW dark brown with a median band of small orange spots. Female similar but larger, with larger and typically paler spots on the FW and a broader band of orange spots on the HW. **Underside:** HW orange-brown with a distinctive yellow arrow-shaped patch.

SIMILAR SPECIES: The bright, arrow-shaped mark on the underside HW separates this from most other sedge skippers with the exception of some strongly marked Broad-winged Skippers. Viewed from above, Broad-winged has a larger orange HW patch. See Plate 14.

BEHAVIOUR: Both sexes of this skipper seldom leave their sedge patch habitat, usually flying slowly, down among the narrow-leaved sedges, and nectaring on flowers such as swamp milkweed (*Asclepias incarnata*). May stray to nectar on flowers in drier upland habitat.

FLIGHT SEASON: One generation per year.

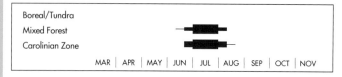

Boreal/Tundra								
Mixed Forest								
Carolinian Zone								
MAR	APR	MAY	JUN	JUL	AUG	SEP	OCT	NOV

CATERPILLAR: Tan with mid-dorsal and lateral stripes and covered in fine hairs. Head brown. **Foodplants:** Narrow-leaved sedges (*Carex* spp.) including tussock sedge (*Carex stricta*). A recent discovery in eastern Ontario provides some evidence for the likely use of the invasive lesser pond sedge (*C. acutiformis*) as a foodplant.

OVERWINTERING STAGE: Unreported, but likely caterpillar.

HABITAT: Restricted entirely to narrow-leaved sedge patches, often along roadsides.

DISTRIBUTION AND ABUNDANCE: Has a very narrow two-part range: 1) from North Dakota across the Great Lakes states into southern Ontario and extreme southwestern Quebec; and 2) the United States Atlantic coast from southern Vermont and New Hampshire to Maryland. In Ontario, an uncommon and local resident found across southern Ontario, north to the southern edge of the Canadian Shield.

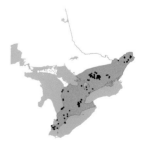

BROAD-WINGED SKIPPER *Poanes viator*

27–34 mm

ETYMOLOGY: *Marcus Calventius Viator* was a Roman soldier and commander of Emperor Hadrian's horse guards in the early second century AD.

ADULT: Medium-large skipper, females larger than males. **Upperside:** Male FW brown with several squarish orange patches and no stigma. Male HW orange with scalloped brown border. Female similar but the FW patches are smaller and cream-coloured and the HW orange patch is smaller. **Underside**: The pale-brown HW has a long tawny streak through the centre, sometimes flanked by a band of spots towards its end, usually more prominent in females. Some individuals are pale along the HW anal margin.

SIMILAR SPECIES: Large size and the patchy nature of the squarish spots on upper FW separate this from other sedge skippers. The Dion Skipper is most similar, but it has a very rapid flight and perches on sedge tips. Ventrally, can be confused with Dion Skipper but the wings of Broad-winged males are more rounded and usually have some orange spots flanking the sides of the middle HW streak. In females, the HW is more elongate in Broad-winged than in Dion.

BEHAVIOUR: Both sexes keep to their sedge patch habitat, mostly flying slowly, down among the broad-leaved sedges. Sometimes stray out of the sedges to nectar on flowers.

FLIGHT SEASON: One generation per year.

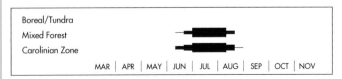

Boreal/Tundra									
Mixed Forest									
Carolinian Zone									
	MAR	APR	MAY	JUN	JUL	AUG	SEP	OCT	NOV

CATERPILLAR: Tan with faint whitish lateral stripes; head pale with a black vertical dash. **Foodplants:** Broad-leaved sedges (*Carex* spp.), including lake sedge (*Carex lacustris*) and northern beaked sedge (*Carex utriculata*). A recent discovery in eastern Ontario provides some evidence for the likely use of the invasive lesser pond sedge (*C. acutiformis*) as a foodplant.

OVERWINTERING STAGE: Caterpillar.

HABITAT: Restricted largely to broad-leaved sedge patches, often along roadsides but also along the edges of rivers, fens and other wetlands.

DISTRIBUTION AND ABUNDANCE: Distributed in two main bands: 1) across northeastern North America from the eastern Dakotas through the Great Lakes region, including southern Ontario and extreme southern Quebec to New York; and 2), an Atlantic coastal band extending from Massachusetts to the Gulf coast of Texas. In Ontario, an uncommon and local resident throughout southern Ontario south of the Canadian Shield. It can be numerous in its isolated sedge patches.

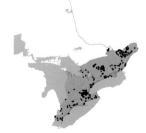

DELAWARE SKIPPER *Anatrytone logan*

♂

26–30 mm

ETYMOLOGY: *Atrytone* (its original genus name) refers to the Greek name for the Roman goddess Minerva. *Logan* the Orator (ca. 1723–1780) was a Native American war leader born in the Iroquois Confederacy.

ADULT: Medium-sized skipper. **Upperside:** Male FW bright golden-orange with a black border and darkening along the veins near the apex. There is a black hook-shaped mark at the end of the cell. Female similar but with thick dark veins and a thick black patch nearer the body. **Underside:** Bright golden-orange lacking black markings except for a darker FW fringe.

SIMILAR SPECIES: The European Skipper looks like a smaller version of the Delaware Skipper but has less pointed wings. See Plate 16.

BEHAVIOUR: A very fast-flying skipper that often chases other skippers from its chosen territory. Often seen perched on the ground.

FLIGHT SEASON: One generation per year.

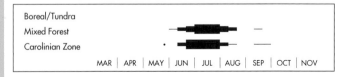

| | MAR | APR | MAY | JUN | JUL | AUG | SEP | OCT | NOV |

Boreal/Tundra
Mixed Forest
Carolinian Zone

CATERPILLAR: Bluish with small dark bumps and a black band near its rear. Head white with black stripes. **Foodplants:** A number of grass species (Poaceae), including big bluestem (*Andropogon gerardii*) and old switch panicgrass (*Panicum virgatum*).

OVERWINTERING STAGE: Caterpillar or chrysalis.

HABITAT: A wide variety of open habitats.

DISTRIBUTION AND ABUNDANCE: El Salvador north through Mexico and across eastern and central North America to the Canadian prairies and southern Ontario. In Ontario, formerly an uncommon-to-rare resident restricted to the southwest as far north as Toronto. The first record for the Delaware Skipper in eastern Ontario was in 1998, near Burritt's Rapids. In more recent years, this species has been expanding north and east and is now considered an uncommon resident throughout southern Ontario south of the Canadian Shield. It continues to expand its range, being recorded in Algonquin Park in 2005 and in southern Algoma District, east of Sault Ste. Marie, in 2012.

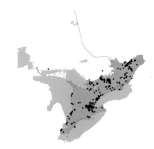

BLACK DASH *Euphyes conspicua*

♂

26–32 mm

ETYMOLOGY: *Euphyes* is derived from the Greek word *euphues* meaning "graceful, witty". Derived from Latin, *conspicua* means "outstanding".

ADULT: Medium-sized skipper. **Upperside:** Male FW orange with a broad dark blackish-brown margin and a long dark stigma. HW dark brown with a small orange patch in the centre. Female differs in being mostly dark blackish-brown with several pale creamy-orange spots on the FW and three small, similarly coloured spots near the FW apex. **Underside:** Rusty-brown with a row of paler orange spots past the centre of the HW, the spots in the centre being the thickest.

SIMILAR SPECIES: Dorsally, quite similar to Long Dash but the stigma is usually thicker, especially toward the apex, in Long Dash which also has a larger, crescent-shaped patch of pale spots on the HW. See Dion Skipper and Plate 15.

BEHAVIOUR: Often easily approachable, found in or near sedge patches, nectaring on flowers including milkweeds (*Asclepias* spp.) and thistles (*Cirsium* spp. and *Carduus* spp.). Males perch on low vegetation in search of females.

FLIGHT SEASON: One generation per year.

Boreal/Tundra									
Mixed Forest									
Carolinian Zone									
	MAR	APR	MAY	JUN	JUL	AUG	SEP	OCT	NOV

CATERPILLAR: Bluish-green with a dark green mid-dorsal line and covered with many small white spots. Head whitish (with some amount of brown through the centre), bordered with a brown stripe and with a black oval spot near the top. Essentially indistinguishable from other members of this genus. **Foodplants:** Tussock sedge (*Carex stricta*) and possibly other sedges (*Carex* spp.).

OVERWINTERING STAGE: Early instar caterpillar.

HABITAT: Sedge meadows.

DISTRIBUTION AND ABUNDANCE: Two main populations exist: 1) an Atlantic population from New Hampshire south to southern Virginia; and 2) a Midwest United States/Great Lakes population extending from eastern Nebraska to Ohio in the south, north to Minnesota, Wisconsin, Michigan and into southern Ontario. In Ontario, a rare and local resident largely restricted to southwestern Ontario northeast to Toronto and Durham Region.

COMMENTS: This species may be expanding its range northward as the records from Toronto and Durham Region are all relatively recent and may represent newly established colonies.

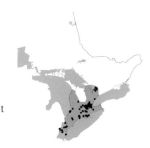

435

DION SKIPPER *Euphyes dion*

29–35 mm

ETYMOLOGY: In Greek mythology, *Dione* was a titan beloved by *Zeus* and the mother of *Aphrodite*.

ADULT: A relatively large skipper. **Upperside:** Male FW orange with a broad, dark-brown margin, and a long, dark stigma that is hooked at the apex. HW dark brown with a central long, orange rectangular stripe beside which there are often one or two fainter, shorter stripes. Female mostly dark brown with four to seven pale-cream spots on the FW and usually only a single rectangular stripe on the HW. **Underside:** Dark orange-brown with two pale orange streaks on the HW, one through the centre of the wing, the other along the anal margin.

SIMILAR SPECIES: Dorsally, very similar to Black Dash but the orange patch on the HW of Dion is long and rectangular versus a series of short spots as in Black Dash. Ventrally, quite similar to Dukes' Skipper but Dion HW has two orange streaks rather than just one. Ventrally, can also be confused with Broad-winged Skipper, but the wings of Broad-winged males are more rounded and usually have some orange spots flanking the sides of the middle HW streak. In females, the HW is more elongate in Broad-winged. See Plate 15.

BEHAVIOUR: Very fast and wary. Perches on top of sedges and nectars on milkweeds, thistles, common buttonbush and other flowers.

FLIGHT SEASON: One generation per year.

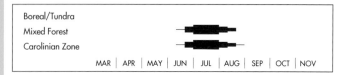

Boreal/Tundra								
Mixed Forest								
Carolinian Zone								
	MAR	APR	MAY	JUN	JUL	AUG	SEP	OCT	NOV

CATERPILLAR: Bluish-green with a dark green mid-dorsal line and covered with many small white spots. Head whitish (with some amount of brown through the centre), bordered with a brown stripe and with a black oval spot near the top. Essentially indistinguishable from other members of this genus. **Foodplants:** Sedges, including lake sedge (*Carex lacustris*), shoreline sedge (*C. hyalinolepis*) and tussock sedge (*C. stricta*). A recent discovery in eastern Ontario provides some evidence for the likely use of the invasive lesser pond sedge (*C. acutiformis*) as a foodplant.

OVERWINTERING STAGE: Partially grown caterpillar.

HABITAT: Marshes, calcareous fens and roadside ditches dominated by sedges.

DISTRIBUTION AND ABUNDANCE:
Eastern North America from Texas and Florida north into southern Ontario and extreme southern Quebec. In Ontario, an uncommon and local resident found within its restricted habitat throughout the area south of the Canadian Shield.

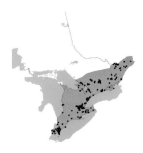

DUKES' SKIPPER *Euphyes dukesi*

31–37 mm

ETYMOLOGY: Named after the collector of the type specimens, Mr. W. C. Dukes of Mobile, Alabama.

ADULT: A relatively large skipper. **Upperside:** Male FW and HW sooty-black sometimes with some orange on the leading edge of the FW and in the centre of the HW. Females are similar to males but are dark brown sometimes with one to two pale-orange spots in the centre of the FW. **Underside:** Both sexes are rich orange-brown below with a paler orange-to-yellowish streak running through the centre of the HW.

SIMILAR SPECIES: See Dion Skipper and Plate 15.

BEHAVIOUR: Slow-flying, they can be found within sedge patches, or in nearby areas, nectaring on a variety of flowers including milkweeds (*Asclepias* spp.). Males actively patrol for females.

FLIGHT SEASON: Usually only one generation per year, although two generations have been recorded at Point Pelee.

| | Boreal/Tundra |
| Mixed Forest |
| Carolinian Zone |

| MAR | APR | MAY | JUN | JUL | AUG | SEP | OCT | NOV |

CATERPILLAR: Bluish-green with a dark-green mid-dorsal line and covered with many small, white spots. Head whitish (with some amount of brown through the centre), bordered with a brown stripe and a black oval spot near the top. Essentially indistinguishable from other members of this genus. **Foodplants:** Sedges (*Carex* spp.), including lake sedge (*Carex lacustris*) and probably more important in Ontario, shoreline sedge (*Carex hyalinolepis*).

OVERWINTERING STAGE: Caterpillar.

HABITAT: Sedge patches in shaded or partially shaded areas including woodland clearings, forest edges, ditches, and along riverbanks.

DISTRIBUTION AND ABUNDANCE: A fairly rare and highly localized skipper throughout its range which includes three main populations: 1) an Atlantic population from southern Virginia to northern Florida; 2) a lower Mississippi River valley population from southern Illinois to the Gulf Coast; and 3) a southern Great Lakes population that includes Ontario. In Ontario, a rare and local resident restricted to extreme southwestern Ontario: largely Essex County with some records from bordering areas of Chatham-Kent to the east and Lambton to the north.

TWO-SPOTTED SKIPPER *Euphyes bimacula*

25–30 mm

ETYMOLOGY: *Bimacula* is Latin, meaning "two-spotted".

ADULT: Medium-sized skipper. **Upperside:** Male dark brown with a little orange bordering each side of the stigma on the FW. Female dark brown with two to three pale-orange spots in the middle of the FW and two to three small spots near the FW apex. **Underside:** Uniform orange-brown with a prominent white streak along the anal margin. Often, the HW veins are also white.

SIMILAR SPECIES: No other skipper has a prominent white streak along the bottom margin of the HW. See Plate 15.

BEHAVIOUR: Often described as rare and difficult to find, but can be located by searching the bases of harlequin blue flag (*Iris versicolor*) flowers where they are often found nectaring. Also found outside of wetland habitats nectaring on a variety of flowers including milkweeds (*Asclepias* spp.).

FLIGHT SEASON: One generation per year.

	MAR	APR	MAY	JUN	JUL	AUG	SEP	OCT	NOV
Boreal/Tundra									
Mixed Forest									
Carolinian Zone									

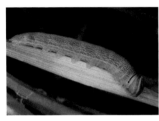

CATERPILLAR: Bluish-green with a dark green mid-dorsal line and covered with many small white spots. Head whitish (with some amount of brown through the centre), bordered with a brown stripe and with a black oval spot near the top. Essentially indistinguishable from other members of this genus. **Foodplants:** Sedges (*Carex* spp.), including tussock sedge (*Carex stricta*) and hairy-fruited sedge (*C. trichocarpa*).

OVERWINTERING STAGE: Caterpillar.

HABITAT: Open wetlands including wet meadows, fens, marshes and roadside ditches.

DISTRIBUTION AND ABUNDANCE: Largely restricted to northeastern North America and west across the north central plains of the United States to northeastern Colorado. In Ontario, an uncommon and local resident throughout southern and central Ontario as far north as the Sudbury and North Bay areas.

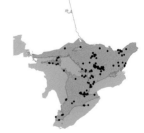

DUN SKIPPER *Euphyes vestris*

♂

23–27 mm

ETYMOLOGY: *Vestris* appears to be derived from Latin *vestire*, meaning "to cover, dress, clothe".

ADULT: A medium-sized skipper, with a characteristically bronzy-coloured head and upper thorax. **Upperside:** Male dark brown with a purplish sheen when fresh and no other prominent markings with the exception of the somewhat darker stigma. Female similar but with two whitish central spots on the FW and also sometimes smaller whitish spots toward the apex. **Underside:** Male uniform dull brown to bronzy. Female similar but with the same whitish spots visible on the FW above, also visible below. Females also often show a faint crescent of small, pale spots across the middle of the HW.

SIMILAR SPECIES: See Northern Broken-Dash and Little Glassywing, and Plate 15.

BEHAVIOUR: Males often perch on low vegetation looking for mates and can be regularly seen mudpuddling. Both sexes nectar on a variety of flowers.

FLIGHT SEASON: One generation per year in most of Ontario with a rare second generation at Point Pelee.

	MAR	APR	MAY	JUN	JUL	AUG	SEP	OCT	NOV
Boreal/Tundra									
Mixed Forest									
Carolinian Zone									

CATERPILLAR: Similar to Dion Skipper but the brown patch in the centre of the head is more extensive and is the same dark colour as the border. **Foodplants:** Many different sedges (Cyperaceae).

OVERWINTERING STAGE: Caterpillar.

HABITAT: Open habitats with a preference for wet areas.

DISTRIBUTION AND ABUNDANCE: Found from northeastern Mexico north throughout the central and eastern United States and into Canada where it ranges from the Alberta-Saskatchewan border east to Nova Scotia. There is also a Pacific coast population ranging from California north to southern British Columbia. In Ontario, a common and widespread resident found at least as far north as Nakina and Wabakimi Provincial Park.

DUSTED SKIPPER *Atrytonopsis hianna*

♀

25–33 mm

ETYMOLOGY: *Atrytone* "the unwearying" is another name for the Greek goddess Athena. *Opsis* is from Greek, meaning "likeness or appearance". Thus, "looks a bit like Athena". *Hianna* was a Native American also known as the sachem Yanno who lived in the 1600s.

ADULT: A medium-large skipper, with pointed wings. There is a prominent half-circle of white above the eye. **Upperside:** Male dingy-brown with a few small, weak white FW spots; its stigma is inconspicuous. Female similar but white spots on FW conspicuous. **Underside:** Darker-brown with heavy grey frosting toward the outer edges of all wings and with three white subapical FW spots and a white basal spot.

SIMILAR SPECIES: Northern and Southern cloudywings have two sets of white spots above that touch the leading edge of the FW and lack the grey frosting below; the wings are also rounder. Clouded Skipper has frosting in the middle of the HW.

BEHAVIOUR: Flies rapidly like a *Hesperia* skipper. Tends to sit in short grasses and flies up when disturbed.

FLIGHT SEASON: One generation per year.

Boreal/Tundra								
Mixed Forest								
Carolinian Zone								
MAR	APR	MAY	JUN	JUL	AUG	SEP	OCT	NOV

CATERPILLAR: Dull green to tan sometimes with a pinkish hue. Lives in silk nest at the base of the foodplant. **Foodplants:** Several grasses (Poaceae), including big bluestem (*Andropogon gerardii*) and shore bluestem (*Schizachyrium littorale*).

OVERWINTERING STAGE: Mature caterpillar.

HABITAT: Restricted to dry, sandy areas with short grasses.

DISTRIBUTION AND ABUNDANCE: Found locally throughout much of the eastern and central United States, north into southern Canada, ranging through southeastern Saskatchewan and southern Manitoba. In Ontario, a rare resident restricted to the sandy dunes in the vicinity of Pinery Provincial Park on Lake Huron north of Sarnia where the species is regularly observed. There is also a specimen in the University of Guelph collection taken from the St. Williams area in 1987.

COMMENTS: Occurs in southeastern Manitoba and should be looked for in grassy, dry areas of northwestern Ontario.

ADDITIONAL SPECIES TO WATCH FOR IN ONTARIO

There are a number of butterfly species that have not yet been recorded in Ontario but could occur. These are either resident species in areas bordering the province (e.g., Quebec, Manitoba, or northern states) that may stray into Ontario or are migratory and may appear in years of strong butterfly migrations northward from the United States. Some of the northern species may already occur in Ontario but have not been found due to the difficulty of access to their habitats.

SWARTHY SKIPPER *Nastra lherminier*

This is a small, nondescript skipper with a plain, brown upper surface (occasionally with small pale FW spots) and a yellowish underside. The veins of the underside HW are pale. Can be confused with the female Two-spotted Skipper which has somewhat more prominent dorsal FW spots and a white anal margin on the ventral HW. The Swarthy Skipper favours dry, grassy areas and has been found as far north as the southern shore of Lake Erie. In some years, this species' population explodes expanding its distribution. Not considered cold-hardy, the Swarthy Skipper may expand its range north into Ontario if the province experiences warmer winters.

COBWEB SKIPPER *Hesperia metea*

A mid-sized branded skipper; the uppersides of males and females are similar to other members of the group. The ventral HW resembles both Common Branded Skipper and female Sachem. The Cobweb Skipper's white leading-edge of the FW and the additional white scaling along the veins of the ventral HW, giving it a "cobweb" look, distinguishes it from these two butterflies. A species of dry, open, grassy sand dunes, it is found in northern and western Michigan and strays could be encountered in western parts of southern or central Ontario. There is the possibility that a resident population occurs in the largely inaccessible sand dunes of Long Point on Lake Erie.

LARGE ORANGE SULPHUR *Phoebis agarithe*

A large, tropical sulphur similar to the Cloudless Sulphur but is uniform bright orange above, not yellow. Unlike the Orange Sulphur, the Large Orange Sulphur does not have wide black borders on the uppersides. This species is common in Florida, but strays far to the north and has reached New York State. This butterfly cannot tolerate cold, so even if it did reach Ontario as a migrant, it could not survive the winter.

LABRADOR SULPHUR *Colias nastes*

This species is more greenish than yellow and has considerable dark scaling. There is also a smudge of red around the silver spot on the ventral HW. Favours dry, rocky areas across northern Canada and into the Rocky Mountains and is resident on the southeast shore of James Bay in Quebec and along the Manitoba coast of Hudson Bay. Rocky areas of Ontario's Hudson Bay and James Bay coasts may provide habitat for this species.

LYSIDE SULPHUR *Kricogonia lyside*

Looks like a small, pale version of the Cloudless Sulphur. The male has a small black bar on the leading edge of the upperside HW that usually shows through on the underside when the wings are closed. A breeding resident in southern Texas and in some years of heavy rains will move north in late summer/early fall into the mid-states in large numbers; during these periods it could occur in Ontario. On April 4, 2011, a dead, battered, headless specimen was picked up from the ground near the University of Guelph campus— its origin is open to speculation.

RED-BANDED HAIRSTREAK *Calycopis cecrops*

If seen in Ontario, this striking hairstreak would be easily recognized by the combination of the dorsal blue colour and the ventral reddish-orange postmedial band. A resident of the eastern United States, strays have been found into Pennsylvania, with one reaching even as far as Saskatchewan, the only Canadian record to date. This species should be looked for in late summer in years when migrants are common in Ontario.

EUROPEAN COMMON BLUE *Polyommatus icarus*

In 2005, a largish blue was discovered near the Mirabel Airport in western Quebec. Images sent several years later to the CNC in Ottawa were identified as this species. This is a common butterfly in Europe and is presumed to have arrived in an airplane at Mirabel. Now a common resident around Mirabel, producing three generations from May to October. By 2011, this butterfly was approaching the Ottawa River and is anticipated to show up soon in Ontario. Feeds mainly on garden bird's-foot trefoil (*Lotus corniculatus*), an introduced plant which is widespread in Ontario. See Plate 5.

REAKIRT'S BLUE *Echinargus isola*

A small, common blue of the American southwest. The black mark along the ventral margins of the HW and the median band of white-ringed black spots on the ventral HW help distinguish it from other blues. Although resident only as far north as South Dakota, this species strays farther to the north and east to Manitoba and Michigan where it sometimes establishes temporary colonies. Caterpillars feed on a variety of legumes. It should be looked for in dry, open habitats in the southwest and northwest parts of Ontario.

CRANBERRY BLUE *Plebejus optilete*

A small blue of western North America, this butterfly is a dark violet blue above with no black borders in the male and wide dark borders in the female. The grey underside has a postmedian band of white-ringed black spots and a unique-for-the-blues single orange spot above the HW marginal spot band. This butterfly flies weakly around open bogs in taiga and tundra where the larval foodplants blueberries and cranberries grow. The Cranberry Blue could be found in the northwestern part of Ontario, particularly along the Hudson Bay coast near the Manitoba border. It flies in northern Manitoba in July.

PEACOCK *Inachus io*

This very striking, medium-sized brushfoot is not native to North America but it is very common and widespread in Europe. Only the Common Buckeye has similar large eyespots dorsally, but the Peacock is unique with its deep, lustrous purple colour dorsally and irregular wing edges. This species was noticed in 1997 in Montreal near the shipping docks, and has since been seen in the Montreal area several times, suggesting a breeding population exists. In 2012, an individual was photographed at Trois-Rivières on the St. Lawrence River considerably east of Montreal. Because it feeds on nettles, the Peacock could easily wander and find appropriate foodplants in eastern Ontario.

POLIXENES ARCTIC *Oeneis polixenes*

A medium-sized butterfly similar to the other arctics but with the ventral HW appearing mottled with an irregular dark median band edged in white, especially along the outer side. There are no eyespots. It is a weak flyer that tends to make short flights across the dry, rocky tundra often landing on small rocks. The Polixenes Arctic ranges from Alaska through northern Canada to Labrador and south through the Rocky Mountains to northern New Mexico. It has been found on the Hudson Bay coast in Manitoba and the coast of James Bay in Quebec and has been reported from Ontario but no specimen evidence exists. It surely occurs and it will only be a matter of time before its presence is confirmed.

WHITE-VEINED ARCTIC *Oeneis borc*

This mid-sized, brown butterfly is similar to other arctics but is best distinguished by the white lining along the ventral HW veins on most individuals. Males have a dark sex patch on the FW. A holarctic species that is found across northern Canada in tundra areas, mostly in wet, hummocky locales but also on nearby gravel ridges. This species has been found on the Hudson Bay coast of northern Manitoba and could be expected on the adjacent Ontario coastline. In Manitoba, the White-veined Arctic flies from June into July in even-numbered years.

A PARTIAL LIST OF PLANTS FOR USE IN BUTTERFLY GARDENS

This list includes plants, both native and cultivated, that can be grown in Ontario to attract butterflies. While not meant to be exhaustive, it includes a mix of species that provide food for caterpillars and nectar for butterflies, and that bloom from spring to fall. Species are arranged in three sections based on the plants' place in the garden. For details on which plants attract which species of butterfly, refer to the species accounts.

The inclusion of native plants in gardens is beneficial to butterflies and other wildlife. Native plants should never be dug up in the wild; rather, they should be purchased as seeds or plants from a reputable grower. Some species sold by large commercial growers as native plants are in fact not native to Ontario. The Ontario Chapter of the Society for Ecological Restoration publishes a Native Plant Resource Guide that is helpful in locating reliable suppliers throughout the Province (see www.serontario.org/publications.htm).

When planting cultivated species, gardeners should avoid planting any species that can be invasive. Invasive plants are introduced species that survive without human assistance, reproduce aggressively, and take over to the exclusion of other plants. The Ontario Invasive Plant Council publishes useful information on actual and potentially invasive species, and native alternatives for gardens (see www.ontarioinvasiveplants.ca/index.php/publications).

LEGEND FOR PLANT LIST

Status

N   **Native** plants that grew in Ontario before the arrival of Europeans.

E   **Extirpated** no longer found in the wild in Ontario but found in the wild elsewhere

I   **Introduced** plants that have been brought to Ontario, intentionally or unintentionally. When such species are able to survive in the wild without human assistance, they are considered to have naturalized.

C   **Cultivated** plants, native or introduced, that have been bred and that require human assistance to grow and persist.

Species

spp. indicates more than one species
ssp. indicates subspecies

Used By = life stage(s) that use the plant

)(Nectar Plant for Adult Butterflies

🐛 Caterpillar Foodplant

Season = flowering season of the plant

🌷 Spring (March–early June)
❋ Summer (June–August)
🍂 Fall (September–October)
E Early
L Late

Span = life span of the plant

A   Annual: a plant that completes its life cycle in one year
P   Perennial: a plant that lives for more than two years
B   Biennial: a plant that takes two years to complete its life cycle

WOODY TREES, SHRUBS AND VINES

STATUS	SPECIES (BY FAMILY)	USED BY	SEASON	SPAN
	Betulaceae (Birch family)			
N	paper birch, *Betula papyrifera*	🐛	🌷	P
	Cannabaceae (Hemp family)			
N	common hackberry, *Celtis occidentalis*	🐛	🌷	P
	Cornaceae (Dogwood family)			
N C	dogwoods, *Cornus spp.*	🐛	🌷	P
	Ericaceae (Heath family)			
N C	azaleas, rhododendrons, Laborador tea, *Rhododendron spp.*	🦋 🐛	🌷	P
N C	blueberries, *Vaccinium spp.*	🐛	🌷	P
	Fabaceae (Pea family)			
I C X	eastern redbud, *Cercis canadensis*	🐛	L🌷 E☀	P
	Fagaceae (Oak family)			
N I C	oaks, *Quercus spp.*	🐛	🌷	P
	Juglandaceae (Walnut family)			
N C	hickories, *Carya spp.*	🐛	🌷	P
	Lauraceae (Laurel family)			
N	northern spicebush, *Lindera benzoin*	🐛	🌷	P
	Magnoliaceae (Magnolia family)			
N	tulip tree, *Liriodendron tulipifera*	🐛	L🌷 E☀	P
	Oleaceae (Olive family)			
I C	lilacs, *Syringa spp.*	🦋 🐛	L🌷 E☀	P
	Pinaceae (Pine family)			
N	eastern red cedar, *Juniperus virginiana*	🐛		P
N	eastern white pine, *Pinus strobus*	🐛		P
N	jack pine, *Pinus banksiana*	🐛		P
	Ranunculaceae (Buttercup family)			
N	Virginia clematis, *Clematis virginiana*	🦋	☀	P
	Rhamnaceae (Buckthorn family)			
N	New Jersey tea, *Ceanothus americanus*	🦋 🐛	🌷 ☀	P
	Rosaceae (Rose family)			
N I C	hawthorns, *Crataegus spp.*	🦋 🐛	🌷	P
N	pin cherry, *Prunus pensylvanica*	🦋 🐛	🌷	P

STATUS	SPECIES (BY FAMILY)	USED BY	SEASON	SPAN
	Rosaceae (Rose family)			
N	black cherry, *Prunus serotina*	🦋 🐛	❀	P
N C	choke cherry, *Prunus virginiana*	🦋 🐛	❀	P
N I C	blackberries & raspberries, *Rubus* spp.	🦋 🐛	❀ ☀	P
N I C	meadowsweets, *Spiraea* spp.	🦋 🐛	❀ ☀	P
	Rubiaceae (Bedstraw family)			
N	common buttonbush, *Cephalanthus occidentalis*	🦋 🐛	L❀ E☀	P
	Salicaceae (Willow family)			
N I C	poplars & aspens, *Populus* spp.	🐛	❀	P
N I C	willows, *Salix* spp.	🐛	❀	P
	Saxifragaceae (Saxifrage family)			
N I C	gooseberries & currants, *Ribes* spp.	🐛	❀	P
	Scrophulariaceae (Figwort family)			
I C	orange-eye butterflybush, *Buddleja davidii*	🦋	☀ ❦	P
	Thymelaeaceae (Daphne family)			
I C	daphnes, *Daphne* spp.	🦋	❀	P
	Ulmaceae (Elm family)			
N	white elm, *Ulmus americana*	🐛	❀	P

HERBACEOUS FLOWERING PLANTS

STATUS	SPECIES (BY FAMILY)	USED BY	SEASON	SPAN
	Apiaceae (Carrot family)			
N	golden alexanders, *Zizia aurea*	🦋 🐛	❀ ☀	P
	Apocynaceae (Milkweed family)			
N	spreading dogbane, *Apocynum androsaemifolium*	🦋 🐛	☀	P
N	hemp dogbane, *Apocynum cannabinum*	🦋 🐛	☀	P
N	swamp milkweed, *Asclepias incarnata*	🦋 🐛	☀	P
N	butterfly milkweed, *Asclepias tuberosa*	🦋 🐛	☀	P
N	poke milkweed, *Asclepias exaltata*	🦋 🐛	☀	P
N	common milkweed, *Asclepias syriaca*	🦋 🐛	☀	P

HERBACEOUS FLOWERING PLANTS (continued)

STATUS	SPECIES (BY FAMILY)	USED BY	SEASON	SPAN
	Asteraceae (Sunflower family)			
I C	common yarrow, *Achillea millefolium*	🦋	✳	P
C	ageratum, *Ageratum houstonianum*	🦋	🌷 ✳	A
N	pearly everlasting, *Anaphalis margaritacea*	🐛	🌷	P
N	field pussytoes, *Antennaria neglecta*	🐛	🌷	P
I C	bachelor's button, *Centaurea cyanus*	🦋	🌷 🍃	A
N I C	tickseed, *Coreopsis* spp.	🦋	✳	P
I C	cosmos, *Cosmos* spp.	🦋	✳	A
I C	eastern purple coneflower, *Echinacea purpurea*	🦋	✳	P
I C	globe-thistles, *Echinops* spp.	🦋 🐛	✳	P
N	common boneset, *Eupatorium perfoliatum*	🦋	L ✳ 🍃	P
N	spotted Joe Pye weed, *Eutrochium maculatum* var. *maculatum*	🦋	L ✳ 🍃	P
I C	blanketflowers, *Gaillardia* spp.	🦋	✳	A P
N	common sneezeweed, *Helenium autumnale*	🦋	L ✳ 🍃	P
N I C	sunflowers, *Helianthus* spp.	🦋	✳ 🍃	A P
I	oxeye daisy, *Leucanthemum vulgare*	🦋	✳	A
C	shasta daisy, *Leucanthemum x superbum*	🦋	E ✳	P
N C	blazing-stars, *Liatris* spp.	🦋	✳	P
N I C	grey-headed coneflowers, *Ratibida* spp.	🦋	✳	P
N	black-eyed Susan, *Rudbeckia hirta*	🦋 🐛	✳ 🍃	P
N	brown-eyed Susan, *Rudbeckia triloba*	🦋 🐛	✳ 🍃	P
N	compass plant, *Silphium laciniatum*	🦋	✳	P
N	cup plant, *Silphium perfoliatum*	🦋	L ✳ 🍃	P
N	goldenrods, *Solidago* spp.	🦋	L ✳ 🍃	P
N	New England aster, *Symphyotrichum novae-angliae*	🦋 🐛	🍃	P
N I C	asters, *Symphyotrichum* spp.	🦋 🐛	🍃	P
C	marigolds, *Tagetes* spp.	🦋	✳	A
N C	ironweeds, *Vernonia* spp.	🦋	✳	P
C	zinnias, *Zinnia* spp.	🦋	✳ 🍃	A

STATUS	SPECIES (BY FAMILY)	USED BY	SEASON	SPAN
	Balsaminaceae (Balsam family)			
N	spotted jewelweed, *Impatiens capensis*	butterfly	sun	A
N	pale jewelweed, *Impatiens pallida*	butterfly	sun	A
	Brassicaceae (Mustard family)			
N I	toothworts, *Cardamine* spp.	butterfly, caterpillar	flower	P
I C	candytufts, *Iberis* spp.	butterfly	flower	P
I C	sweet alyssum, *Lobularia maritima*	butterfly	flower	P
	Caprifoliaceae (Honeysuckle family)			
C	scabiosas, *Scabiosa* spp.	butterfly	sun	P
	Cornaceae (Dogwood family)			
N	bunchberry, *Cornus canadensis*	butterfly, caterpillar	flower	P
	Cyperaceae (Sedge family)			
N I	sedges, *Carex* spp.	caterpillar	flower sun	P
	Ericaceae (Heath family)			
N I C	common bearberry, *Arctostaphylos uva-ursi*	butterfly, caterpillar	flower	P
	Fabaceae (Pea family)			
I	blue wild indigo, *Baptisia australis*	butterfly, caterpillar	E sun	P
C	showy partridge pea, *Chamaecrista fasciculata*	butterfly, caterpillar	sun	P
N I C	lupines, *Lupinus* spp.	butterfly, caterpillar	E sun	P
	Hemerocallidaceae (Day Lily family)			
I C	daylilies, *Hemerocallis* spp.	butterfly	sun	P
	Iridaceae (Iris family)			
N I C	irises, *Iris* spp.	butterfly	L flower E sun	P
	Lamiaceae (Mint family)			
N	blue giant hyssop, *Agastache foeniculum*	butterfly	sun	P
N C	scarlet beebalm, *Monarda didyma*	butterfly	sun	P
N	wild bergamot, *Monarda fistulosa*	butterfly	sun	P
I C	catnip, *Nepeta cataria*	butterfly	sun	P
C	sages, *Salvia* spp.	butterfly	sun	A
	Liliaceae (Lily family)			
N	Michigan lily, *Lilium michiganense*	butterfly	sun	P

459

HERBACEOUS FLOWERING PLANTS (continued)

STATUS	SPECIES (BY FAMILY)	USED BY	SEASON	SPAN
	Linaceae (Flax family)			
I C	wild blue flax, *Linum lewisii*	🦋	❀ ✹	P
	Lobeliaceae (Lobelia family)			
N C	cardinal flower, *Lobelia cardinalis*	🦋	L ✹	P
N C	lobelias, *Lobelia* spp.	🦋	❀ ✹	A P
	Malvaceae (Mallow family)			
I C	hollyhocks, *Alcea* spp.	🐛	✹	P
	Phrymaceae (Lopseed family)			
N C	monkeyflowers, *Mimulus* spp.	🦋	✹	A P
	Plantaginaceae (Plantain family)			
C	snapdragons, *Antirrhinum* spp.	🦋	✹	A
N	white turtlehead, *Chelone glabra*	🦋 🐛	L ✹	P
	Poaceae (Grass family)			
N	big bluestem, *Andropogon gerardii*	🐛	L ✹	P
N I	grama, *Bouteloua* spp.	🐛	L ✹	P
N I C	panicgrasses, *Panicum* spp.	🐛	L ✹	P
	Polemoniaceae (Phlox family)			
N I C	phloxes, *Phlox* spp.	🦋	❀ ✹	P
	Ranunculaceae (Buttercup family)			
N	red columbine, *Aquilegia canadensis*	🐛	❀	P
N I C	buttercups, *Ranunculus* spp.	🦋	❀ ✹	P
N	sharp-lobed hepatica, *Anemone acutiloba*	🦋	❀	P
	Rosaceae (Rose family)			
N	prairie smoke, *Geum triflorum*	🦋	❀	P
N	wild strawberry, *Fragaria virginiana*	🦋	❀	P
N I C	cinquefoils, *Potentilla* spp.	🦋 🐛	✹	P
	Rutaceae (Citrus family)			
C	gas plant, *Dictamnus albus*	🦋 🐛	✹	P
	Solanaceae (Potato family)			
I C	tobacco, *Nicotiana* spp.	🦋	✹	A
	Valerianaceae (Valerian family)			
C	red valerian, *Centranthus ruber*	🦋	✹ 🍂	P

STATUS	SPECIES (BY FAMILY)	USED BY	SEASON	SPAN
	Verbenaceae (Vervain family)			
C	lantanas, *Lantana* spp.	[butterfly]	[summer] [fall]	A
N	blue vervain, *Verbena hastata*	[butterfly]	[summer] [fall]	P
N	hoary vervain, *Verbena stricta*	[butterfly]	[summer] [fall]	P
	Violaceae (Violet family)			
N I C	violets, *Viola* spp.	[butterfly] [larva]	[spring]	P
C	pansy, *Viola x wittrockiana*	[butterfly]	[spring] [summer]	A

CULINARY HERBS AND VEGETABLES

STATUS	SPECIES (BY FAMILY)	USED BY	SEASON	SPAN
	Amaryllidaceae (Amaryllis family)			
N C	wild chives, *Allium schoenoprasum*	[butterfly]	[spring]	P
	Apiaceae (Parsley family)			
C	dill, *Anethum graveolens*	[larva]	[summer]	P
C	sweet fennel, *Foeniculum vulgare*	[butterfly]	[summer]	A
C	garden parsley, *Petroselinum crispum*	[larva]	[summer]	B
C	domestic carrot, *Daucus carota* ssp. *sativa*	[larva]	[summer]	B
	Brassicaceae (Mustard family)			
C	broccoli, *Brassica oleracea*	[larva]	[summer]	A
C	cabbage, *Brassica oleracea*	[larva]	[summer]	A
C	cauliflower, *Brassica oleracea*	[larva]	[summer]	A
C	Brussels sprout, *Brassica oleracea*	[larva]	[summer]	A
C	wild radish, *Raphanus raphanistrum*	[larva]	[spring]	P
	Lamiaceae (Mint family)			
I C	mints, *Mentha* spp.	[butterfly]	[summer]	P
C	kitchen sage, *Salvia officinalis*	[butterfly]	[summer]	A
I C	thyme, *Thymus* spp.	[butterfly]	[spring]	A

While space does not permit an exhaustive listing of the books, articles and websites available to the butterfly enthusiast, we have included here a listing of those that we most recommend as well as those that were most consulted in the preparation of this book (some of which are cited throughout the text).

BOOKS AND ARTICLES

Allen, T. J., J. P. Brock and J. Glassberg. 2005. *Caterpillars in the Field and Garden: A Field Guide to Caterpillars of North America*. Oxford University Press, New York, NY.

Brock, J. P. and K. Kaufman. 2006. *Kaufman Field Guide to Butterflies of North America.* Houghton Mifflin Harcourt, New York, NY.

Carmichael, I. and A. Vance. 2003. *Photo Field Guide to the Butterflies of Southern Ontario*. St. Thomas Field Naturalist Club Inc., St. Thomas, ON.

Cassie, B., J. Glassberg, A. Swengel and G. Tudor. 2005. *North American Butterfly Association (NABA) Checklist and English Names of North American Butterflies*. North American Butterfly Association, Morristown, NJ.

Cech, R., and G. Tudor. 2005. *Butterflies of the East Coast: An observer's guide* Princeton University Press, Princeton, NJ.

City of Toronto. 2011. *Butterflies of Toronto: A guide to their remarkable world.* City of Toronto Biodiversity Series, Toronto, ON.

Dickinson, T., D. Metsger, J. Bull and R. Dickinson. 2004. *The ROM Field Guide to Wildflowers of Ontario*. Royal Ontario Museum and McClelland & Stewart Limited, Toronto, ON.

Dole, C. H. (ed.). 2003. *The Butterfly Gardener's Guide* (No. 175). Brooklyn Botanic Garden, New York, NY.

Douglas, M. M. and J. M. Douglas. 2005. *Butterflies of the Great Lakes Region*. The University of Michigan Press, Ann Arbor, MI.

Emmel, T. C. 1997. *Butterfly Gardening: Creating a Butterfly Haven in Your Garden*. Cavendish Books, Vancouver, BC.

Folsom, W. 2009. *Butterfly Photographer's Handbook: A Comprehensive Reference for Nature Photographers*. Amherst Media, Inc., Buffalo, NY.

Glassberg, J. 1999. *Butterflies through Binoculars: The East*. Oxford University Press, New York, NY.

Gurr, M. 2000. *Butterflies of Presqu'ile and Southern Ontario*. Friends of Presqu'ile, Guelph, ON.

Hall, P. W. 2009. *Sentinels on the Wing: The Status and Conservation of Butterflies in Canada*. NatureServe Canada, Ottawa, ON.

Harrison, Barry. 2007. *The Butterflies of the Toronto Region: 140 Years of History*. Toronto Entomologists' Association, Toronto, ON. <www.ontarioinsects.org/chklst.htm>.

Hébert Allard, S. 2013. *Manitoba Butterflies: A Field Guide*. Turnstone Press, Winnipeg, MB.

Holmes, A. M., R. R. Tasker, Q. F. Hess and A. J. Hanks. 1991. *The Ontario Butterfly Atlas*. Toronto Entomologists' Association, Toronto, ON.

Johnson, L. 2001. *The New Ontario Naturalized Garden*. Whitecap Books, Toronto, ON.

Johnson, L. 2005. *100 Easy-To-Grow Native Plants For Canadian Gardens*. Whitecap Books, Toronto, ON.

Jones, C. D. 2012. *Checklist of Ontario Butterflies*. Hamilton Naturalists' Club, Hamilton, ON.

Jones, C. D. 2003. *Checklist and Seasonal Status of the Butterflies of Algonquin Provincial Park*. Friends of Algonquin Park, Whitney, ON.

Laplante, J.-P. 2004. *Papillons et chenilles du Québec et de l'est du Canada*. HOMME, Montreal, QC.

Layberry, R. A., P. W. Hall, and J. D. Lafontaine. 1998. *The Butterflies of Canada*. University of Toronto Press, Toronto, ON.

Layberry, R. A. 2007. Butterflies of the Ottawa District: 103 species...and counting. *Trail and Landscape* (1): 16-36. [Ottawa Field-Naturalists' Club]

Leboeuf, M. and S. Le Tirant. 2012. *Papillons et Chenilles du Québec et des Maritimes*. Éditions Michel Quintin, Waterloo, QC.

Lewis, A. (ed.) and S. Buchanan. 2007. *Butterfly Gardens: Luring Nature's Loveliest Pollinators to Your Yard*. Brooklyn Botanic Garden, Brooklyn, NY.

Oberhauser, K. S. and M. J. Solensky (eds.). 2004. *Monarch Butterfly: Biology and Conservation*. Cornell University Press, Ithaca, NY.

Opler, P. A. and V. Malikul. 1998. *A Field Guide to Eastern Butterflies (Peterson Field Guide)*. Houghton Mifflin, New York, NY.

Otis, G. W. and C. D. Jones. 2013. *Butterflies of Algonquin Provincial Park*. The Friends of Algonquin Park, Whitney, ON.

Pelham. J. P. 2011. *A Catalogue of the Butterflies of the United States and Canada with a Complete Bibliography of the Descriptive and Systematic Literature*. <www.butterfliesofamerica.com/US-Can-Cat.htm>

Pyle, R. M. 1992. *Handbook for Butterfly Watchers*. Houghton Mifflin, New York, NY.

Schappert, P. J. 2005. *A World for Butterflies: Their Lives, Behaviour and Future*. Firefly Books, Toronto, ON.

Scott, J. A. 1992. *The Butterflies of North America: A Natural History and Field Guide*. Stanford University Press, Stanford, CA.

Tallamy, D. W. 2009. *Bringing Nature Home: How You Can Sustain Wildlife with Native Plants*. Timber Press, Portland, OR.

Wagner, D. L. 2010. *Caterpillars of Eastern North America: A Guide to Identification and Natural History*. Princeton University Press, Princeton, NJ.

Weber, L. 2006. *Butterflies of the North Woods: Minnesota, Wisconsin & Michigan*. Kollath-Stensaas Publishers, Duluth, MN.

Wormington, A. 2001. *Butterflies of Point Pelee National Park, Including Southern Ontario*. Friends of Point Pelee, Leamington, ON

Wright, A. B. 1998. *Peterson First Guide to Caterpillars of North America*. Houghton Mifflin Co., Boston, MA.

JOURNALS/PERIODICALS

American Butterflies is published quarterly by the North American Butterfly Association: <www.naba.org>

Journal of the Lepidopterists' Society and *News of the Lepidopterists' Society* are published quarterly by The Lepidopterists' Society: <www.lepsoc.org>

Journal of Research on the Lepidoptera is published by The Lepidoptera Research Foundation, Inc: <lepidopteraresearchfoundation.org>

Ontario Lepidoptera is published annually by the Toronto Entomologists' Association: <www.ontarioinsects.org>

WEBSITES

Butterflies and Moths of North America: <www.butterfliesandmoths.org>
    Contains species profiles, maps and photographs as well as a way of submitting records.

Butterflies of America: <butterfliesofamerica.com>
    Essentially an interactive taxonomic list with photos of specimens housed in institutional collections, all life stages, habitats as well as information on general distribution across the Americas.

Butterflies of Canada: <www.cbif.gc.ca/spp_pages/butterflies/index_e.php>
    An electronic version of the published book.

eButterfly: <e-butterfly.org>
    A real-time, online checklist and photo storage program, eButterfly provides a way for the butterfly community to report, organize and access information about butterflies in North America.

HOSTS - a Database of the World's Lepidopteran Hostplants
<www.nhm.ac.uk/research-curation/research/projects/hostplants/>
    An interactive online database for known hostplants of a particular species and for all species that are known to feed on a particular hostplant.

Native Plant Resource Guide, 6th Edition. Society for Ecological Restoration, Ontario Chapter, 2014 <www.serontario.org/publications.htm>

Ontario Butterfly Atlas Online: <ontarioinsects.org/atlas_online.htm>
    An interactive atlas displaying maps for each of Ontario's species with flight periods. All species reported from 10x10 km squares also included.

Ontario Butterflies: <groups.google.com/forum/#!forum/onbutterflies>
    A Google Groups forum for sharing observations and information on Ontario's butterflies.

Monarch Joint Venture: <www.monarchjointventure.org/>
    Information on the conservation of this migratory species, including links to many other online resources.

Raising Butterflies: <www.raisingbutterflies.org>
    Extensive information on how to rear butterflies from egg to adult.

GLOSSARY

abdomen – the posterior division of an insect body

alvar – a flat area of limestone with patchy vegetation where sparse soil has accumulated in cracks

anal margin – the edge of the hindwing closest to the body

androconial scales – scales on the wing that produce scent used in courtship and mating; often visible as a black or grey spot on the male

antenna/antennae – the paired, segmented sensory organs found on the head. Clubbed (expanded on the tip) on butterflies

anterior – in front or nearer to the head

apex – the part of the wing farthest from the attachment point

apiculus – in the Hesperiidae, an extension of the terminal end of a butterfly's antennae that ends in a hook-shaped club

basal – at the base or point of attachment with the body

bog – an acidic wetland that receives water and nutrients solely from the atmosphere. Accumulates peat; dominated by sphagnum moss.

boreal forest – forest region dominated by conifer trees that extends around the globe between 45° and 65° North latitudes.

cell – area of the wing enclosed by veins

chrysalis/chrysalides – the stage of a butterfly between the caterpillar and adult; the pupa; it has a hard outer case

costa – the thicker, anterior margin or edge of a wing

cremaster – the hook or spine at the end of the chrysalis; used for attachment

diapause – a state of rest in which an insect stops developing; often used in overwintering

disjunct – refers to the range of a species separated geographically into different populations

dorsal – the upper surface

endemic – native or confined to a particular area

extinct – no living individuals of a species exists

extirpated – no individuals of a species currently exist in an area where they formerly occurred

family – a taxonomic grouping; a division or classification containing genera with similar characteristics that are apparently descended from a common ancestor

fen – a wetland dominated by mosses and accumulated peat. Fed by nutrient-rich ground water. Usually dominated by grasses, sedges, rushes, shrubs and brown mosses

forest – a densely treed area; more than 65 percent tree cover

forewing/FW – one of the two forward wings

genitalia – the sex organs of an insect; claspers on male, ovipositor on female

genus/genera – a taxonomic grouping; a division or classification containing species with similar characteristics that are apparently descended from a common ancestor The first name in the binomial scientific name of a species

gynandromorph – a butterfly with characteristics of both sexes

haustellum – the portion of an insect's proboscis that is adapted for sucking

hilltopper – a butterfly that seeks the highest point in an area and patrols it awaiting a mate

hindwing/HW – one of the two rear wings

Holarctic – the biogeographic region of the northern hemisphere that includes the Nearctic (North American) and Palearctic (Eurasian) regions

inner margin – the hind edge of a forewing

instar – the period or stage between moults in an insect larva

introduced – a species not native to an area in which it occurs

labial palps/palpi – a pair of segmented, sensory structures covered in hairs for detecting/tasting food

larva/larvae – the immature stage of an insect that undergoes complete metamorphosis; also called caterpillars in butterflies

Lepidoptera – the order of insects with scales on their wings; includes butterflies and moths

local – a species that may be found in a small colony or restricted to a very specific habitat

lunule – a crescent-shaped marking on the wings

marginal – the outer edge of the wings

marsh – an open, treeless wetland with emergent vegetation (grasses, rushes and/or sedges)

meadow – a grassland than can be wet or dry, may be an old field

median – the middle portion of a butterfly's wing

melanic – a dark or blackish form

metamorphosis – the series of changes through which an insect passes in its growth from egg to adult

migrant – an insect that flies a distance from its place of origin to find food, overwinter or for other purposes

moult – in insects, to cast off the outgrown exoskeleton; occurs when a caterpillar develops from one instar to the next

mudpuddler – butterflies, usually males, that regularly sip moisture from the ground; it is believed that the moisture contains salts and nutrients, particularly sodium and nitrogen, which aid in sexual maturation.

Nearctic – the terrestrial ecozone that includes North America (including northern Mexico) and Greenland.

nectar – the sugar-rich liquid produced by plants

osmeterium – the fleshy, tubular, organs found on swallowtail caterpillars; they produce a strong odour

oviposit – to lay eggs

patrolling – male butterflies flying in a specific territory to find mates or drive away rival males

peatlands – wetlands with layers of accumulated peat; includes bogs and fens

polymorphic – occurring in several forms; may be gender- or geography-based

posterior – hindmost, at the rear

postmedial – the area of the wing between the medial and submarginal bands

proboscis – an extended mouth structure; a coiled feeding tube of Lepidoptera; a haustellum

pupa /pupae – the resting, inactive stage during which physical transformation occurs; the chrysalis in butterflies

riparian – the areas bordering on streams, rivers and wetlands linking land to water

rock barren – an area of exposed bedrock often interspersed with stunted trees and shrubs

savanna – open grassland with scattered widely-spaced trees

scales – the tiny, modified hairs covering the wings of Lepidoptera;

their colour or structure creates the wing pattern

setae – long, sensory hairs

species – the primary biological unit; an aggregation of individuals alike in appearance and structure, mating freely and producing viable offspring. spp. - indicates more than one species

spiracles – breathing pores found on insects

stigma – specialized scent scales on the forewings of some skippers and hairstreaks

subapical – the part of the forewing inward from the tip

subdorsal – the location on a caterpillar, between its dorsal surface and sides

submarginal – near to the wing margin

subspecies (ssp.) – a subdivision of a species with geographical or hostplant variation which may be marked by differences in morphological characteristics; different subspecies may breed with one another

swamp – a nutrient-rich wooded wetland with deciduous or coniferous trees or shrubs; often with seasonal pools that form in the spring but dry up as the season progresses

tallgrass prairie – an ecosystem native to central North America that is dominated by tall perennial grasses and has rich loess (wind-blown silt) soils, moderate rainfall and is maintained by frequent fires

tarsal claws – the claw or claws at the end of the tarsus

tarsus/tarsi – the foot of an insect; may have 1-5 segments or joints

thicket – a shrub-dominated plant community with scattered trees

thorax – the intermediate region of the insect body to which wings and legs are attached

translucent – transmits light but is not transparent

tubercle – a bump on a caterpillar's body

ultraviolet light – electromagnetic radiation with a short wavelength, not visible to humans but visible to a number of insects and birds

venation – the vein pattern on an insect wing

ventral – the lower or under surface

wetland – area covered by shallow water for some or all of the year, or an area where the ground water is at or very close to the surface

woodland – an open forest, less than 65 percent tree cover

ACRONYMS

CDC – Conservation Data Centre

CNC – Canadian National Collection of Insects, Arachnids and Nematodes

COSEWIC – Committee on the Status of Endangered Wildlife in Canada

ESA 2007 – Ontario *Endangered Species Act*

ESO – Entomological Society of Ontario

FW – forewing

HW – hindwing

NCC – Nature Conservancy of Canada

NGS – National General Status of Species in Canada

NHIC – Natural Heritage Information Centre

OMNR – Ontario Ministry of Natural Resources

ROM – Royal Ontario Museum

SARA – *Species at Risk Act*

TEA – Toronto Entomologists' Association

CHECKLIST OF ONTARIO BUTTERFLIES

The authors have chosen to follow the butterfly systematic order and species names (scientific and common) from *Butterflies of Canada* (1998) except where compelling biological, molecular, and/or morphological evidence published since 1998 dictates that changes should be made. These will be reflected in the checklist and noted in the text. Foremost is that the Papilionidae (swallowtails) have been shown to have diverged from all the other butterflies early on in the evolutionary process, and as such are listed first. In addition, the Hesperiidae (skippers) are placed at the end of the five Ontario families. As well, we have altered the order in which certain subfamilies and genera of butterflies appear from that in *Butterflies of Canada* to reflect some recent publications. In particular, we have re-ordered the subfamilies and certain genera of sulphurs and whites in the family Pieridae and some groups of Nymphalidae (brushfoots) to coincide with recent changes published in the *Catalogue of the Butterflies of the United States and Canada* by Jon Pelham (2011). As well, the choice and spelling of certain scientific names reflects changes appearing in Pelham.

We have also tried to use butterfly names that are as consistent as possible with other Canadian and international butterfly publications and online information and monitoring sources. These include *eButterfly* and the *Ontario Butterfly Atlas Online*, to which many Ontarians contribute their observations, and the North American Butterfly Association. In a few cases, where recent research is showing the likely need to alter names in the near future, this will be explained, usually in the comments section at the end of the species account. In essence we have chosen largely to go with a more conservative approach to butterfly names for consistency of usage and to avoid confusion unless more compelling evidence has been published.

Gorgone Checkerspot

SWALLOWTAILS: FAMILY PAPILIONIDAE
- ❏ Pipevine Swallowtail — *Battus philenor*
- ❏ Zebra Swallowtail — *Eurytides marcellus*
- ❏ Old World Swallowtail — *Papilio machaon*
- ❏ Black Swallowtail — *Papilio polyxenes*
- ❏ Giant Swallowtail — *Papilio cresphontes*
- ❏ Canadian Tiger Swallowtail — *Papilio canadensis*
- ❏ Eastern Tiger Swallowtail — *Papilio glaucus*
- ❏ Spicebush Swallowtail — *Papilio troilus*

SULPHURS AND WHITES: FAMILY PIERIDAE
- ❏ Dainty Sulphur — *Nathalis iole*
- ❏ Mexican Yellow — *Eurema mexicana*
- ❏ Little Yellow — *Pyrisitia lisa*
- ❏ Sleepy Orange — *Abaeis nicippe*
- ❏ Clouded Sulphur — *Colias philodice*
- ❏ Orange Sulphur — *Colias eurytheme*
- ❏ Giant Sulphur — *Colias gigantea*
- ❏ Pelidne Sulphur — *Colias pelidne*
- ❏ Pink-edged Sulphur — *Colias interior*
- ❏ Palaeno Sulphur — *Colias palaeno*
- ❏ Southern Dogface — *Zerene cesonia*
- ❏ Cloudless Sulphur — *Phoebis sennae*
- ❏ Orange-barred Sulphur — *Phoebis philea*
- ❏ Large Marble — *Euchloe ausonides*
- ❏ Olympia Marble — *Euchloe olympia*
- ❏ Mustard White — *Pieris oleracea*
- ❏ West Virginia White — *Pieris virginiensis*
- ❏ Cabbage White — *Pieris rapae*
- ❏ Checkered White — *Pontia protodice*
- ❏ Western White — *Pontia occidentalis*
- ❏ Great Southern White — *Ascia monuste*

GOSSAMER-WINGS: FAMILY LYCAENIDAE
- ❏ Harvester — *Feniseca tarquinius*
- ❏ American Copper — *Lycaena phlaeas*
- ❏ Gray Copper — *Lycaena dione*
- ❏ Bronze Copper — *Lycaena hyllus*
- ❏ Bog Copper — *Lycaena epixanthe*
- ❏ Dorcas Copper — *Lycaena dorcas*
- ❏ Purplish Copper — *Lycaena helloides*
- ❏ Acadian Hairstreak — *Satyrium acadica*
- ❏ Coral Hairstreak — *Satyrium titus*
- ❏ Edwards' Hairstreak — *Satyrium edwardsii*
- ❏ Banded Hairstreak — *Satyrium calanus*
- ❏ Hickory Hairstreak — *Satyrium caryaevorus*
- ❏ Striped Hairstreak — *Satyrium liparops*

GOSSAMER-WINGS: FAMILY LYCAENIDAE (continued)

- ❏ Oak Hairstreak — *Satyrium favonius*
- ❏ Juniper Hairstreak — *Callophrys gryneus*
- ❏ Brown Elfin — *Callophrys augustinus*
- ❏ Hoary Elfin — *Callophrys polios*
- ❏ Frosted Elfin — *Callophrys irus*
- ❏ Henry's Elfin — *Callophrys henrici*
- ❏ Bog Elfin — *Callophrys lanoraieensis*
- ❏ Eastern Pine Elfin — *Callophrys niphon*
- ❏ Western Pine Elfin — *Callophrys eryphon*
- ❏ Gray Hairstreak — *Strymon melinus*
- ❏ White-M Hairstreak — *Parrhasius m-album*
- ❏ Early Hairstreak — *Erora laeta*
- ❏ Marine Blue — *Leptotes marina*
- ❏ Eastern Tailed Blue — *Cupido comyntas*
- ❏ Western Tailed Blue — *Cupido amyntula*
- ❏ Spring Azure — *Celastrina lucia*
- ❏ Cherry Gall Azure — *Celastrina serotina*
- ❏ Summer Azure — *Celastrina neglecta*
- ❏ Silvery Blue — *Glaucopsyche lygdamus*
- ❏ Northern Blue — *Plebejus idas*
- ❏ Karner Blue — *Plebejus samuelis*
- ❏ Greenish Blue — *Plebejus saepiolus*
- ❏ Arctic Blue — *Plebejus glandon*

BRUSHFOOTED BUTTERFLIES: FAMILY NYMPHALIDAE

- ❏ American Snout — *Libytheana carinenta*
- ❏ Monarch — *Danaus plexippus*
- ❏ White Admiral — *Limenitis arthemis arthemis*
- ❏ Red-spotted Purple — *Limenitis arthemis astyanax*
- ❏ Weidemeyer's Admiral — *Limenitis weidemeyerii*
- ❏ Viceroy — *Limenitis archippus*
- ❏ Gulf Fritillary — *Agraulis vanillae*
- ❏ Variegated Fritillary — *Euptoieta claudia*
- ❏ Bog Fritillary — *Boloria eunomia*
- ❏ Silver-bordered Fritillary — *Boloria selene*
- ❏ Meadow Fritillary — *Boloria bellona*
- ❏ Frigga Fritillary — *Boloria frigga*
- ❏ Freija Fritillary — *Boloria freija*
- ❏ Arctic Fritillary — *Boloria chariclea*
- ❏ Great Spangled Fritillary — *Speyeria cybele*
- ❏ Aphrodite Fritillary — *Speyeria aphrodite*
- ❏ Regal Fritillary — *Speyeria idalia*
- ❏ Atlantis Fritillary — *Speyeria atlantis*
- ❏ Hackberry Emperor — *Asterocampa celtis*
- ❏ Tawny Emperor — *Asterocampa clyton*
- ❏ American Lady — *Vanessa virginiensis*

❏ Painted Lady	*Vanessa cardui*
❏ Red Admiral	*Vanessa atalanta*
❏ Milbert's Tortoiseshell	*Aglais milberti*
❏ Compton Tortoiseshell	*Nymphalis l-album*
❏ Mourning Cloak	*Nymphalis antiopa*
❏ Question Mark	*Polygonia interrogationis*
❏ Eastern Comma	*Polygonia comma*
❏ Satyr Comma	*Polygonia satyrus*
❏ Gray Comma	*Polygonia progne*
❏ Hoary Comma	*Polygonia gracilis*
❏ Green Comma	*Polygonia faunus*
❏ Common Buckeye	*Junonia coenia*
❏ Baltimore Checkerspot	*Euphydryas phaeton*
❏ Silvery Checkerspot	*Chlosyne nycteis*
❏ Gorgone Checkerspot	*Chlosyne gorgone*
❏ Harris's Checkerspot	*Chlosyne harrisii*
❏ Pearl Crescent	*Phyciodes tharos*
❏ Northern Crescent	*Phyciodes cocyta*
❏ Tawny Crescent	*Phyciodes batesii*
❏ Northern Pearly-Eye	*Lethe anthedon*
❏ Eyed Brown	*Lethe eurydice*
❏ Appalachian Brown	*Lethe appalachia*
❏ Common Ringlet	*Coenonympha tullia*
❏ Little Wood-Satyr	*Megisto cymela*
❏ Common Wood-Nymph	*Cercyonis pegala*
❏ Taiga Alpine	*Erebia mancinus*
❏ Red-disked Alpine	*Erebia discoidalis*
❏ Jutta Arctic	*Oeneis jutta*
❏ Melissa Arctic	*Oeneis melissa*
❏ Chryxus Arctic	*Oeneis chryxus*
❏ Macoun's Artic	*Oeneis macounii*

SKIPPERS: FAMILY HESPERIIDAE

❏ Silver-spotted Skipper	*Epargyreus clarus*
❏ Long-tailed Skipper	*Urbanus proteus*
❏ Hoary Edge	*Achalarus lyciades*
❏ Southern Cloudywing	*Thorybes bathyllus*
❏ Northern Cloudywing	*Thorybes pylades*
❏ Hayhurst's Scallopwing	*Staphylus hayhurstii*
❏ Common Sootywing	*Pholisora catullus*
❏ Dreamy Duskywing	*Erynnis icelus*
❏ Sleepy Duskywing	*Erynnis brizo*
❏ Juvenal's Duskywing	*Erynnis juvenalis*
❏ Horace's Duskywing	*Erynnis horatius*
❏ Mottled Duskywing	*Erynnis martialis*
❏ Zarucco Duskywing	*Erynnis zarucco*
❏ Funereal Duskywing	*Erynnis funeralis*

- ❏ Wild Indigo Duskywing — *Erynnis baptisiae*
- ❏ Columbine Duskywing — *Erynnis lucilius*
- ❏ "Boreal" Persius Duskywing — *Erynnis persius borealis*
- ❏ "Eastern" Persius Duskywing — *Erynnis persius persius*
- ❏ Grizzled Skipper — *Pyrgus centaureae*
- ❏ Common Checkered Skipper — *Pyrgus communis*
- ❏ Arctic Skipper — *Carterocephalus palaemon*
- ❏ Least Skipper — *Ancyloxypha numitor*
- ❏ Garita Skipperling — *Oarisma garita*
- ❏ European Skipper — *Thymelicus lineola*
- ❏ Brazilian Skipper — *Calpodes ethlius*
- ❏ Ocola Skipper — *Panoquina ocola*
- ❏ Pepper and Salt Skipper — *Amblyscirtes hegon*
- ❏ Common Roadside Skipper — *Amblyscirtes vialis*
- ❏ Clouded Skipper — *Lerema accius*
- ❏ Fiery Skipper — *Hylephila phyleus*
- ❏ Common Branded Skipper — *Hesperia comma*
- ❏ Leonard's Skipper — *Hesperia leonardus*
- ❏ Indian Skipper — *Hesperia sassacus*
- ❏ Peck's Skipper — *Polites peckius*
- ❏ Tawny-edged Skipper — *Polites themistocles*
- ❏ Crossline Skipper — *Polites origenes*
- ❏ Long Dash Skipper — *Polites mystic*
- ❏ Whirlabout — *Polites vibex*
- ❏ Northern Broken-Dash — *Wallengrenia egeremet*
- ❏ Little Glassywing — *Pompeius verna*
- ❏ Sachem — *Atalopedes campestris*
- ❏ Hobomok Skipper — *Poanes hobomok*
- ❏ Zabulon Skipper — *Poanes zabulon*
- ❏ Mulberry Wing — *Poanes massasoit*
- ❏ Broad-winged Skipper — *Poanes viator*
- ❏ Delaware Skipper — *Anatrytone logan*
- ❏ Black Dash — *Euphyes conspicua*
- ❏ Dion Skipper — *Euphyes dion*
- ❏ Dukes' Skipper — *Euphyes dukesi*
- ❏ Two-spotted Skipper — *Euphyes bimacula*
- ❏ Dun Skipper — *Euphyes vestris*
- ❏ Dusted Skipper — *Atrytonopsis hianna*

Page numbers for species accounts are in **bold**.

All plants named in the introductory sections and species accounts appear in this index. For plants that could be grown in a butterfly garden, but not included in this index, see **A Partial List of Plants for Use in Butterfly Gardens**, page 455.

PHOTOGRAPHERS

Lowercase letters adjacent to each page number refer to the position of the photograph on the page (a-d, top to bottom). After the dash, l=left, c=centre and r=right. Most photos in comparative plates taken by Brian Boyle of the ROM; some were taken by Jocelyn Gill of the CNC, except a few as noted here.

John Acorn 328

Tom Allen 102d-l, 105a-r, 121-r, 155a-r, 165-r, 201a-r, 251b, 253b, 265b-r, 267a-r, 295-r, 313-r, 317b-l, 317b-r, 323b, 325b-r, 331b, 342d-c, 342d-r, 343b-l, 349b, 351b, 363a-r, 365a-r, 367a-r, 375a-r, 377b, 381b-r, 383-r, 385a-r, 395-r, 401b-l, 403a-r, 405a-r, 409a-r, 413a-r, 415a-r, 419a-r, 421a-r, 423b-r, 425c, 427b-r, 429a-r, 431b, 435a-r, 439a-r, 441b, 445b

Karen L. Anderson 20a, 80, 135b-l, 325a-l

T.A. Armstrong - ROM copyright 307b

Wasyl Bakowsky 33b

Robert Behrstock 129b

Brian Boyle 17, 105b, 107b, 109b, 117-l, 119, 123-l, 127b-l, 127b-r, 321a-r, 327a, 329a-r, 331a, 333a

David Bree 294

Jim Brock 102d-r, 131b, 135b-r, 181b, 187-r, 195-r, 203b, 223a-r, 256, 257b, 291-r, 452a, 453a

Chris Bruce 293b, 410

Jerry F. Butler 199a-r

Canadian National Collection of Insects, Arachnids and Nematodes 151b-l, 167b-l, 173a-r, 183-r, 217a-r, 231c-l, 232d-c, 263-r, 269b-r, 273b-r, 283b, 289b-r, 293b-l, 301a-r, 329a-l, 333b, 342c-r, 359b, 361a-r, 389a-r, 437a-r, 443b-r

Rick Cavasin 23a, 24a, 26a-r, 26b-r, 28b-l, 28b-r, 85b, 90, 93-r, 95a-l, 104,

115b, 133-l, 134, 153a, 155b, 158, 159b, 161a-l, 174, 177a, 180, 182, 183-l, 184, 188, 190, 194, 209a-l, 209a-r, 209b-l, 212, 214, 215a-r, 249a-l, 262, 263a-l, 264, 265b-l, 269a-l, 270, 279-l, 289b-l, 299a-r, 300, 304, 305a, 306, 308, 309b-l, 312, 314, 316, 318, 319, 344, 354, 357a-l, 357b, 358, 359a, 363a-l, 364, 366, 367a-l, 367b, 373b, 374, 375a-l, 375b-l, 380, 381a-l, 394, 395-l, 397-l, 401a-l, 401b-r, 403b, 404, 405b, 407a-l, 407a-r, 415b, 418, 419a-l, 421a-l, 421b, 423a-l, 423a-r, 423b-l, 425a-r, 425b-l, 428, 429a-l, 429b, 431a-l, 431a-r, 434, 435a-l, 436, 439a-l, 441a-l, 442, 444

W.J. Crins 30

Nicky Davis 103a-r, 117-r, 123-r, 143-r, 189-r, 207a-r, 221b, 232d-l, 261-r, 335-r, 343a-l, 387-r

O. E. Devitt- ROM copyright 301b

Jason Dombroskie 161b-r

Chris Earley 342c-l

Chao Fang 26c-l, 82a-l, 84, 85-r, 150b-c, 150c-l, 151a-r, 205a-r, 211a-r, 230d-c, 231c-r, 233a-l, 245a-l, 279-r, 309a-r, 352, 382, 411a-l

John Fowler 21a, 150a-l, 150a-c

Jocelyn Gill 89-l, 199-l, 201b, 211b-r

Jeffrey Glassberg 97b, 111b, 116, 141a-r, 142, 145b, 156, 164, 165a-l, 165b, 171b, 186, 207b-l, 243, 258, 368, 369, 377a-r, 386, 387-l, 399b, 416, 417a-r, 417b, 427a-r, 438, 446a, 446b, 447a, 447b, 448a, 448b, 449b, 451a, 451b, 453b

Antonia Guidotti 27b-r, 46, 51, 59, 205a-l, 322

Peter W. Hall 16a-r, 19c, 21d, 26b-l, 26c-r, 26d-l, 27b-l, 27c-l, 27d-r, 28a-l, 32a, 32b, 34a, 35b, 35c, 41, 43, 44, 47, 48, 49, 50, 91b, 91-r, 93-l, 95a-r, 96, 112, 113a-l, 121a-l, 132, 137b, 167a, 171a, 173a-l, 181a, 185b, 187-l, 191b, 192, 205b, 219a-l, 219a-r, 219b-r, 224, 231b-r, 235-l, 236, 237a-r, 238,

Front Cover: Milbert's Tortoiseshell
by Glenn Richardson.

Back Cover (clockwise from top left):
Pink-edged Sulphur, Phil Schappert;
Eastern Tiger Swallowtail, Peter
Hall; Early Hairstreak, Maxim
Larrivée; Question Mark, Glenn
Richardson; Delaware Skipper, Bob
Yukich; Bog Fritillaries mating, Bob
Yukich; Spicebush Swallowtail cater-
pillar, Glenn Richardson; Baltimore
Checkerspot chrysalid, Brenda Van
Ryswyk.

ACKNOWLEDGEMENTS

We thank the following people who shared their expertise on the biology, distribution and status of Ontario's butterflies: David Allison, Ken Allison, Bob Bracken, Chris Bruce, Sue Bryan, Peter Burke, Paul Catling, Rick Cavasin, Bob Curry, Don Davis, David Edwards, David Elder, Nick Escott, John Hall, Louis Handfield, Christine Hanrahan, Linda Jeays, James Kamstra, Norbert Kondla, Don Lafontaine, Bill Lamond, Maxim Larrivée, Ross Layberry, Diane Lepage, Christine Lewis, Jessica Linton, Gillian Mastromatteo, Michael Olsen, Ed Poropat, Paul Pratt, Glenn Richardson, Bruce Ripley, Michael Runtz, Phil Schappert, Chris Schmidt, Jeff Skevington, Don Sutherland, Brenda van Ryswyk, Alan Wormington, Bob and Karen Yukich.

Taxonomic expertise on butterflies was provided by Jeffrey Glassberg, Don Lafontaine, Maxim Larrivée, Paul Opler, Jon Pelham, Bob Pyle and Chris Schmidt.

This guide would not have been possible without the outstanding photographs contributed by many individuals (see page 484).

We are indebted to Michelle Staples and Maxim Larrivée for their efforts in the production of the predictive distribution maps and the Toronto Entomologists' Association for providing access to records contained in the *Ontario Butterfly Atlas* for use in generating the phenograms.

Information and advice on "Where to Observe Butterflies" was provided by: Wasyl Bakowsky, Michael Butler, Rick Cavasin, Christine Drake, David Elder, Christine Hanrahan, Ross Layberry, Paul Pratt, and Alan Wormington.

Technical assistance was provided by Arthur Smith of the ROM library. Brian Boyle, ROM photographer, and Jocelyn Gill, CNC, photographed specimens for the comparative plates

Don Sutherland and Jeffrey Glassberg reviewed the original manuscript and provided many suggestions for improvements.

We thank Deb Metsger and Tim Dickinson of the ROM's Department of Natural History (Botany), and Michael Oldham of the Natural Heritage Information Centre, Ontario Ministry of Natural Resources for reviewing the common and scientific names of plants and for their assistance in the section on plants for use in butterfly gardens.

Our editor, James Burns, is thanked for his keen eye for detail and for his many suggestions that greatly increased the readability of the text.

We thank Google for the use of their maps.

Many thanks to our production team, Sheeza Sarfraz, Tara Winterhalt and Claire Louise Milne for managing the production and layout of the guide, especially to Tara for all of her patience and tireless creativity during our many edits and requests for additional work.

We thank the Louise Hawley Stone Charitable Trust for its generous support of this publication and Mark Engstrom, ROM Vice-President of Collections and Research, for his encouragement and support.

In addition, Peter thanks his patient wife, Judy; Colin thanks his family, Marianne, Shan and Klara, for their support, patience and encouragement during the life of this project; Antonia thanks her husband Chris and friends and colleagues for their patience and support; and Brad thanks his friends and family, especially Heather, for her on-going support.

ABOUT THE AUTHORS

Peter W. Hall retired in 2008 as Senior Advisor Biodiversity with the Canadian National Collection of Insects, Arachnids and Nematodes in Ottawa and was then made an Honorary Research Associate, curating the extensive butterfly collection. During his 32-year career he worked in a variety of executive positions with the Canadian government and national and international biodiversity and conservation organizations (including three years with the United Nations, at Cambridge, U.K.) in the fields of management, communications and research. He is a specialist in butterflies and their conservation, and his publications include co-authoring *The Butterflies of Canada* (1998, University of Toronto Press) and author of *Sentinels on the Wing: the Status and Conservation of Butterflies in Canada* (2009, NatureServe Canada).

Colin Jones is a zoologist at the Natural Heritage Information Centre, Ontario Ministry of Natural Resources where the majority of his work concentrates on insects (including butterflies) and birds, especially those that are rare. He is a member of the Arthropod Species Specialist Committee of the Committee on the Status of Endangered Wildlife in Canada (COSEWIC). He is the co-editor and compiler of *Ontario Lepidoptera* – the Toronto Entomologists' Association's yearly summary of Ontario's butterflies and moths, and is co-coordinator of the *Ontario Butterfly Atlas*. He also has a great interest in dragonflies and damselflies and is co-author of the *Field Guide to the Dragonflies and Damselflies of Algonquin Provincial Park and the Surrounding Area,* and the coordinator of the *Ontario Odonata Atlas.*

Antonia Guidotti has been an entomology technician in the Department of Natural History at the Royal Ontario Museum since 2000. Her MSc in Zoology from the University of Toronto examined a family of little-known parasitic wasps (Rhopalosomatidae). She was a contributing author to the *Butterflies of Toronto: A Guide to Their Remarkable World* (2011), part of the City of Toronto Biodiversity Series. She has been the Program Coordinator for the Toronto Entomologists' Association since 2011 and is presently a director on the Board of the Entomological Society of Ontario.

Brad Hubley is the entomology collection manager in the Department of Natural History at the Royal Ontario Museum. His more than 25 years of experience have included participation in numerous arthropod biodiversity surveys around the globe from Canada's Arctic to tropical forests in Central and South America and southeast Asia. An avid SCUBA diver, he has also participated in surveys of marine fishes inhabiting coral reefs in Vietnam and Palau. He was a member of the *Life in Crisis: Schad Gallery of Biodiversity* team and continues to participate in a variety of public programs for the ROM including the writing of popular publications such as *Spiders of Toronto: A Guide to Their Remarkable World* (2012), part of the City of Toronto Biodiversity Series.